THE BAD EARTH

THE BAD EARTH

ENVIRONMENTAL DEGRADATION IN CHINA

VACLAV SMIL

104443

M.E. SHARPE, INC. Armonk, New York
ZED PRESS London

Copyright © 1984 by M. E. Sharpe, Inc.
80 Business Park Drive, Armonk, New York 10504

First published in Great Britain in 1984 by
Zed Press, 57 Caledonian Road, London N1 9DN

Library of Congress Cataloging in Publication Data

Smil, Vaclav.
     The bad earth.
     Includes bibliographical references and index.
     1. Man—Influence on nature—China. 2. Human ecology—China.
3. Environmental policy—China. 4. China—Economic conditions—
1949-   . I. Title.
GF656.S65   1983   363.7'00951   83-14821
ISBN 0-87332-230-4
ISBN 0-87332-253-3 (pbk.)

British Library Cataloguing in Publication Data

Smil, Vaclav
     The bad earth.
     1. Environmental policy—China   2. Human ecology—China
     I. Title
     333.7'2'0951   HC428.5

ISBN 0-86232-188-3
ISBN 0-86232-189-1 Pbk

Printed in the United States of America

To the memory of my father

A corrective spirit includes stern destruction . . .

Du Fu (AD 712-770)
"Journey North"

CONTENTS

PREFACE

During the early and mid-1970s, newspaper, magazine and television reporting, numerous China travelogs and, unfortunately, not a few papers in scholarly journals created a twofold impression of the Chinese environment in Western minds (Smil 1980a). The one was of pre-1949 China—dirty and desolate, with barren hills and spreading deforestation, poor farming practices, low crop yields, and widespread soil erosion; with congested, ugly cities and primitive, polluting industries. The other was a Maoist miracle—clean and cheerful, with green hills and massive afforestation, ever-improving farming techniques and rising yields, soil erosion well under control, cities lightened by broad, tree-lined boulevards, and industries carefully preserving pure air and water.

There was more to the marvel: pests controlled by biological methods rather than by harmful synthetic chemicals, greatly expanded aquaculture, assorted industrial wastes thoroughly recycled, and much advanced planning devoted to the prevention of pollution. And, of course, no flies and a broad smile on everybody's face. Chinese policies, we were assured, "seem to have been successful in protecting and even improving the natural environment" (Kapp 1975). These laudatory appraisals have been part of an embarrassingly misinformed yet highly influential North American rediscovery of China exemplified in print by such tales as John K. Galbraith's *China Passage* (1973), Shirley MacLaine's *You Can Get There from Here* (1975), and M. E. and A. Ensmingers' *China—The Impossible Dream* (1973).

As often happens with Communist-run societies, foreign enthusiasts, admirers, fellow-travelers, and naïve visitors were let down by those whom they so assiduously adulated. For a variety of reasons, the old-new Beijing leaders have decided to unveil unprecedented doses of truth about the country's state of affairs, and among other surprises and revelations, the resulting image of China's environment is very disquieting. Without any doubt, the country's environmental degradation and pollution are very serious. In deforestation, soil erosion, and losses of arable land the country's poor record rivals that of the worst afflicted nations in the world, and China's urban environments and industrial pollution are at least as offensive as in any rapidly modernizing country. Critical shortages of water, its high pollution with heavy metals, the disappearance of protected as well as common animals, carcinogens in the air at levels far exceeding acceptable standards, excessive urban noise, advancing desertification—all these, and other, environmental ills can be found in China.

This book tries to document this decline, to convey one essential message: China's environment, natural or man-made, is in poor shape and still deteriorating. These often startling realities are reviewed with information taken solely from recent Chinese sources. Since 1978 even the official English-language propaganda has been punctuated by many critical items and articles, but it is principally in the domestic Chinese sources—in scores of articles in newspapers and in new scientific journals, in central and provincial broadcasts and news reports—where numerous descriptions of neglect, malice, failure, and abandon have emerged, the reality spilling out after long years of tragic suppression of even mild candor.

Without this new Chinese information, so staggering in its cumulative impact, this book could not have been written. What follows then, to a large extent, is a new Chinese look at China's environment— interspersed, of course, with my comments and observations which do not lack a personal flavor. The facts are the most reliable ones I could assemble, evaluate, and pass on. The opinions are not entered for stylistic effect: they are carefully considered judgments, an attempt to interpret Chinese realities, motivations, and potentials; should they appear sometimes too rough, may I be allowed to hide behind Lao Zi's words: "Better to rumble like rocks, than to tinkle like jade"?

V.S.

Winnipeg
February 1983

ACKNOWLEDGMENTS

Douglas Merwin of M. E. Sharpe suggested that I write this book after reading one of my papers dealing with China's environmental degradation in the early fall of 1980. I welcomed this opportunity but had to postpone the work until I had finished a just started book on biomass energy. However, in the spring of 1981 Robert J. Goodland of the Office of Environmental Affairs of the World Bank persuaded me to take some time off from the biomass book to prepare a report on China's environment for the Bank. I did so in the summer of 1981, and the report became the core of this book. Douglas Merwin and Robert J. Goodland are thus indisputable godfathers of this book. And I owe special thanks to Wolfgang Kinzelbach of the Institute für Wasserbau at the University of Stuttgart who generously shared with me extensive information (including internal papers otherwise unavailable outside of China) gathered during his nearly two-year stay in Beijing, and whose observations were very useful in confirming many of my conclusions.

I am also glad to acknowledge the permissions of the editors of *Agro-Ecosystems*, *Asian Survey*, *Bulletin of the Atomic Scientists*, *Current History*, *Environmental Management*, and *The Geographical Review* to use parts of my articles previously published in their journals (see references).

Photographs, maps, and graphs were meticulously prepared by E. Pachanuk and M. Halmarson; the manuscript, made difficult by hundreds of Chinese names, was ably typed and retyped by J. Koresvelt and F. Lewis.

Only after the book was finished did I get my first opportunity for an extensive journey in China as an exchange scholar under the new Social Sciences Research Council of Canada-Chinese Academy of Social Sciences bilateral agreement. Although there were no surprises or revelations during my stay, the trip was still a useful confirmation of this book's content: my thanks thus go to the two sponsoring institutions.

Eva and David are by now well used to my never-ending writing of books—but this in no way diminishes my gratitude to them for maintaining the milieu which makes my efforts possible.

ACRONYMS AND EDITORIAL NOTES

Chinese language publications

Acronym	Pinyin title	English translation
BJRB	Beijing ribao	Beijing Daily
DLJK	Dili jikan	Geographical Collection
DLZS	Dili zhishi	Geographical Knowledge
DZRB	Dazhong ribao	Mass Daily
GDNYKX	Guangdong nongye kexue	Guangdong Agricultural Sciences
GMRB	Guangming ribao	Guangming Daily
GRRB	Gongren ribao	Worker's Daily
HDSFDXXB	Huadong shifan daxue xuebao	Journal of East China Teachers University
HJ	Huanjing	Environment
HJBH	Huanjing baohu	Environmental Protection
HJKX	Huanjing kexue	Environmental Science
HQ	Hongqi	Red Flag
JFRB	Jiefang ribao	Liberation Daily
JHJJ	Jihua jingji	Planned Economy
JJGL	Jingji guanli	Economic Management
JJYJ	Jingji yanjiu	Economic Studies
NCGZTX	Nongcun gongzuo tongxun	Rural Work Newsletter
NCKX	Nongcun kexue	Rural Sciences
NFRB	Nanfang ribao	Southern Daily
NYJJWT	Nongye jingji wenti	Agricultural Economic Issues
RMRB	Renmin ribao	People's Daily
SCRB	Sichuan ribao	Sichuan Daily
TJRB	Tianjin ribao	Tianjin Daily
TRXB	Turang xuebao	Acta Pedologica Sinica

Acronym	Pinyin title	English translation
WHB	Wenhui bao	Wenhui News
XDH	Xiandaihua	Modernization
XNY	Xin neng yuan	New Energy Sources
ZGLY	Zhongguo linye	China's Forestry
ZGNYKX	Zhongguo nongye kexue	Scientia Agricultura Sinica
ZJRB	Zhejiang ribao	Zhejiang Daily
ZRBZFTX	Ziran bianzhengfa tongxun	Journal of Dialectics of Nature
ZWBH	Zhiwu baohu	Plant Protection

English-language publications

Acronym	Title
BR	Beijing Review (formerly Peking Review)
CR	China Reconstructs
JPRS	Joint Publications Research Service
NCNA	New China News Agency
SPRCP	Survey of People's Republic of China Press
SWB	BBC Summary of World Broadcasts, Far East, Weekly Economic Supplement

---

Editorial notes

• All Chinese place-names in this book are Romanized in *pinyin* according to *Zhongguo renmin gongheguo fen sheng dituji* (Hanyu pinyinban)(Atlas of the PRC [Pinyin edition]). Beijing: Ditu chubanshe (Cartographic Publishing House), 1977.

• Agency releases are labeled NCNA when in English and Xinhua when in Chinese. This is a revealing clue to the distinction made in China between news for domestic and foreign consumption.

• All the measurements in this book are in metric units; in a few instances where the traditional Chinese measure is given it is immediately followed by its metric equivalent.

THE BAD EARTH

1

CHINA'S ENVIRONMENT

Yi set the mountains and valleys alight and
burnt them, and the birds and beasts went into hiding. Yu dredged the Nine Rivers, cleared the
courses of the Chi and the T'ao to channel the water into the Sea, deepened the beds of the Ju
and the Han, and raised the dykes of the Huai and
the Ssu to empty into the River. Only then
were the people of the Central Kingdoms able to
find food for themselves.

Meng Ke, Book III
(in D. C. Lau translation)

Harmonious the natural order
Fruitful and flourishing the level land.
Plants and trees are covered with blossoms.
A gentle breeze blows freshly and softly.

Tao Qian, "An Exhortation to Farmers"
(in J. R. Hightower translation)

All settings are unique but China is surely the most unusual country of
all: a land spanning tropical coral reefs and snowy boreal forests as well
as the world's tallest mountains and most densely settled river lowlands, a country where one can find wild elephants hidden in
monsoonal thickets as well as camel caravans plodding through frigid
deserts, a territory open to the influences of the world's most vigorous
pressure cells. And this land has embraced the planet's longest continuous civilization and harbors nearly a quarter of mankind, its ways and
achievements imprinted in countless details by the environment,
which, in turn, has been so greatly influenced by the long human
habitation, a civilization that has achieved so much—and yet also failed
so astonishingly.

The understanding of Chinese affairs is always enhanced by the
knowledge of the country's intricate and intriguing civilization but, as
historians, linguists, and sociologists have been by far the most frequent Western students of China, the cultural approach, I believe, has
been considerably overplayed. Understanding the Chinese environ-

ment—I use the term in its broadest sense including the physical setting as well as the essential extractive activities such as farming and the harnessing of energy—means appreciating a key determinant of the nation's fortunes. Compared with masses of social scientists, however, there are too few Westerners well familiar with the country's physical endowment and limitations. This, inevitably, has led to a disproportionate output of culturally, as opposed to environmentally, oriented scholarly works as well as to some embarrassingly ignorant writings on the physical nature of China; and the degree of Western misinformation on the country's environment, natural resources, farming, food, and energy remains staggering, with a flood of "eyewitness" accounts of the 1970s only making the situation worse.

This book was not written to offer a systematic detailed appraisal of various aspects of the Chinese environment: its aim is to focus on the many degradative trends to which this environment has been recently subjected. Obviously, this cannot be done without introducing many particulars concerning the distribution, quantity, quality and some peculiarities of environments, ecosystems, resources and phenomena that have suffered damage, decline, or deterioration, and such information appears, at appropriate places, in this book.

In the rest of this chapter I offer merely a brief sketch outlining the most basic features of China's physical environment, the key constraints and limitations of its economic and social development. For those without ready access to detailed appraisals of China's physique, Appendix A will serve as a guide.

1.1 The natural setting

If one subscribes to the theory of plate tectonics—and most geologists do these days—China's surface offers one of the most perfect illustrations of the processes of crustal upheavals. The collision of the Indian subcontinent with Eurasia formed the world's highest plateau in Xizang (Tibet) and created a rather steep west-east gradient between the high mountain ranges of Xizang, Qinghai, and Sichuan and China's seacoast in a belt ranging from 20 to 40°N. Her tectonic history had thus largely limited China's prime cultivable lands to the plateaus, river basins, and coastal lowlands east of 100°E, the only major exception being the sheltered, fertile Sichuan basin.

Here is the country's first essential environmental limitation: no other large populous nation has so much of its territory in high mountains (Appendix A.4). No less than 58 percent of China's area is covered by either mountains or high plains and plateaus more than 1,000 m above sea level, and the surfaces higher than 2,000 m cover 33 percent (Yu Guangyuan 1981). In comparison, mountains cover 10 percent of the Soviet Union and about 15 percent of the United States. Obviously, not all mountains and hilly regions (the latter cover about 12 percent of China) are unsuitable for some form of farming; many southern locations have outstanding conditions for growing subtropical and tropical crops, and extensive inland mountain grasslands have traditionally supported large animal herds. Still, the limitations imposed by an unusually large share of elevated land are undeniable: generally more difficult cultivation, restrictions on cereal cropping, greater susceptibility of soils to erosion after deforestation, difficult transportation.

The second critical environmental constraint arises from the combination of the country's large-scale terrain features and its position at the eastern fringe of Eurasia: China is open to the cold, dry outflows of the Siberian anticyclone in the winter and to the monsoonal flows, including some violent typhoons, in the summer. Consequently, the country does not go through a single year without some serious droughts or floods, and insofar as the large continental or hemispheric pressure cells and air flows are far beyond human intervention, China's situation will be, in this respect, always precarious.

The irregularity of precipitation patterns is, of course, most troublesome in the densely populated plains of the eastern third of China. Mean annual rainfall is greatest in the southeast and decreases gradually toward the northwest: coastal Fujian has on the average in excess of 2,000 mm of rain a year, the 1,000 mm isohyet runs approximately from the mouth of the Chang Jiang (Yangtze River) to central Sichuan, Beijing has just over 600 mm, and Urumqi in Xinjiang gets less than 300 mm (Appendix A.7). There are at least 100 days with precipitation a year everywhere in the Jiangnan (area south of the Chang Jiang) but only about 50 in the Huang He (Yellow River) basin.

In both the south and the north most rainfall is associated with the moist monsoonal southeasterlies—as much as 90 percent of the annual precipitation may fall between May and September—but when these arrive early and move the intensive rain belt northward faster than usual, the normally wet Jiangnan may suffer a prolonged drought; in contrast, when a cold continental air mass blocks the southeast monsoon from penetrating farther inland, the Chang Jiang valley may be flooded, while parts of the north may remain rainless for the entire summer. The recurring cycles of floods and droughts thus affect the entire densely populated eastern part of China, and especially the basins of the Hai, Huang, and Huai rivers.

In the more than two-and-a-half millenia of recorded Chinese affairs the Huang He broke the dikes in its lower reaches twice every three years and experienced a major change of course every century. The Huai He (Huai River) basin in the heart of densely populated China suffered more than 900 droughts and 900 floods between 246 BC and 1948. The Hai He (Hai River) basin had 387 disastrous floods and 407 drought years between 1368 and 1948.

The scarcity of cultivable land and the spatially and temporally unequal distribution of water have resulted in much manipulation of the environment over the long course of Chinese history: multicropping, intercropping, terracing, field leveling, intricate canal and reservoir irrigation schemes. Today, China's eastern third is a landscape molded as much by man as by nature (Appendices A.5, A.6). What attitudes can one discern in this long interrelationship?

1.2 Attitudes

A reverence for nature runs unmistakably through the long span of Chinese history. The poet, always ready to pour full goblets of wine and "drink three hundred cups in a round," found the mountains his most faithful companion; emperors, between wars and court intrigues, painted finches in bamboo groves and ascended sacred mountains; Buddhist monks sought their *dhyana* "midst fir and beech"; craftsmen located their buildings to "harmonize with the local currents of the cosmic breath"; painters were put through the rigors of mastering smooth, natural, tapering bamboo leaves and plum branches; and who wouldn't admire the symphony of plants, rocks, and water in countless gardens (Smil 1980b).

Attitudes, poetry, paintings, habits, common sayings, and regulations abound with images of nature and a view of man as a part of a greater order of things. Old trees are prized for their antiquity and dignity: ancient pines, frost-defying plum blossoms, elegant bamboo. Flowers are loved and admired: magnolias, lotus, chrysanthemums, peonies. There are birds of exquisite plumage—mountain pheasants, finches, ducks, magpies; animals ordinary—horses and oxen—and extraordinary—dragons and unicorns. There is a universe of peaks and

Figure 1. Completely deforested landscapes—such as these hills on the northern slopes of Jundu Shan some 50 km north of the capital—have been a common sight in North China for centuries.

clouds, snow and wind, waterfalls and ponds, reeds and shores, hills and dense forests. The titles of old paintings envelope the mind in the magnificence of nature and induce reverence: Light Snow on the Mountain Pass; Brocaded Sea of Peach-Blossom Waves; Summer Retreat in the Eastern Grove; Ode on the Red Cliff; Listening to the Sounds of Spring Under Bamboo; Peaks Emerging from Spring Clouds.

To stop here, however, as many an uncritical admirer might, would be telling only the more appealing half of the story. There was also a clearly discernible current of destruction and subjugation: the burning of forests just to drive away dangerous animals; massive, total, and truly ruthless deforestation (Figure 1) to create new fields, to get fuel and charcoal, and to obtain timber for fabulous palaces and ordinary houses, wood for cremation of the dead and (to no small effect) for making ink from the soot of burnt pines (one of history's many ironies: glorious accounts of civilization underwritten by the destruction of its natural foundations); the erection of sprawling rectilinear cities (fires would rage for days to consume the vast areas of wooden buildings) eliminating any trace of nature, save for some artificial gardens.

This traditional discrepancy between the environmental ideal and reality, the clash of attitude and actual behavior so well elucidated by Tuan (1968), could not cease on that October day in 1949 when Mao Zedong spoke from the Tian'anmen proclaiming the founding of a new China. The environmental record of this new China thus carries clear parallels with the past as well as, inevitably, marks of the ruling ideology and advancing modernization. To describe it unequivocally is impossible: what a mixture of some excellent intentions and notable achievements with much casual neglect, astonishing irresponsibility, and staggering outright destruction! If a simplifying verdict were still sought, I would summarize that record, without being alarmist, as genuinely disquieting. The following chapters will substantiate this assessment by reviewing all the major degradative trends of recent decades. In addition, the most recent awareness of the problems and important measures to reverse the degradative trends will be described, and future complications, opportunities, and limits will be analyzed.

2

LAND

If there's a mountain, we'll cover it with wheat.
If there's water to be found, we'll use it all to plant rice.
. . . .
We exhaust our energies in such undertaking,
All in the hope of enjoying a little peace.

Lu Yu, "The Farmer's Lament"
(in L. S. Robinson translation)

There was a time when the trees were luxuriant on the
Ox Mountain. As it is on the outskirts of a great
metropolis, the trees are constantly lopped by axes.
Is it any wonder that they are no longer fine?

Meng Ke, Book VI
(in D. C. Lau translation)

The millennia-old course of environmental degradation—most manifestly represented by large-scale land cover and land use changes caused by deforestation, erosion, desertification, and losses of cropland—not only was not reversed by the Communist regime but all of these destructive trends have actually intensified since 1949. In some instances this has been the result of deliberate, and irrational, policies promoted by the state, such as the massive conversion of forests, grasslands, and lakes into grainfields; in others it has come about as a combination of careless resource expolitation by the state and the desperate actions of poor peasants: much deforestation is in this category.

And although any ranking is not only difficult but perhaps even meaningless, deforestation would appear to be the country's most critical environmental problem. Chinese writings, in the not so distant past so complacently citing huge newly afforested areas, have since 1978 revealed a wealth of truly stunning information about the problem, and their portrayal of the current situation and likely prospects adds up to, it can be stated without exaggeration, a grave environmental crisis of global importance.

2.1 Deforestation

Since the mid-1970s a great deal of belated attention, both in scientific and popular writings, has been focused on the growing extent and rapidity of deforestation throughout most of the poor world (see, for example, Eckholm 1976 and Meyers 1980). Unlike the rich countries of Europe and North America where the forests areas have either stabilized or actually increased during the past three decades, most of the Asian, African, and Latin American countries have experienced dangerously advancing deforestation. The continuing disappearance of tropical moist forests, the greatest repository of living mass on this planet, has been especially troubling (Myers 1980).

While numerous nationwide, regional, and local estimates and, less frequently, actual statistics on the decline of forestlands have been available for dozens of poor countries on the three continents, and while Brazilian and Indian deforestation have become almost textbook examples of environmental deterioration, there were no comparable Chinese figures. Indeed, outside China there was a widespread belief that the country was an encouraging exception to the dismal rule (South Korea being the other success story). These impressions were strengthened by the incessant roll of afforestation reports, put out by the Chinese media in general and Xinhua (New China News Agency) in particular, and by the enthusiastic descriptions of advances in tree planting offered by many (not particularly observant and touchingly unsuspicious) Western visitors to China in the early 1970s (Westoby 1979 is a good example).

John K. Galbraith summed it up with a grossly erroneous generalization: "The hills of China, which I had always heard of as being bare, are no longer so" (Galbraith 1973). Unfortunately inaccurate as this statement is, the fact that the Chinese have been engaged in massive afforestation campaigns ever since 1949 seems equally undeniable. Therefore some discussion is called for to show that, contrary to the claims, the extent of productive natural forests has actually declined during the past three decades.

2.1.1 China's forest resources

To begin with, official Chinese figures, old and new, are contradictory and, as in the case with most other area and volume values in global forestry, not particularly reliable. During the 1950s the published estimates of the area covered by forests ranged between 5 to 10 percent of China's territory (Richardson 1966). In recent Chinese publications shares of forest cover in 1949 are given as low as 5 percent (*BR*, March 2, 1979, p. 4) and as high as 8.6 percent (for example Yue Ping 1980), a considerable discrepancy. The latest official figure, first published in 1979 (and repeated since), is 12.7 percent, or 122 million ha, and when it was first published it was compared with the 8 percent (about 77 million ha) share in 1949 (Anonymous 1979a).

But the new total does not agree with another official figure, which states that between 1949 and 1979, 28 million ha were newly afforested (Beijing home broadcast, January 14, 1980, *SWB* 1067); the 1979 total then should be only 105 million ha or, starting with the 8.6 percent share, no more than 110.6 million ha—assuming, of course, that no deforestation took place (of course, starting with the 5 percent coverage figure for 1949 would bring the total to just 76 million ha). The discrepancies do not end here. The new figure of 12.7 percent is claimed to be the result of a "comprehensive check of forestry resources" made originally nationwide between 1974 and 1976 and updated continuously since 1978, and it refers to "fully stocked" productive forests with canopies covering at least 30 percent of the ground (Lin Zi 1980; Hsiung and Johnston 1981).

In 1963, however, officials of the Ministry of Forestry admitted to Richardson (1966) that "nearly 50 percent" of the then estimated 96 million ha was a secondary forest following partial or complete exploitation and hence of low productivity: how those nearly 50 million ha became "fully stocked" just a decade or so later is left unexplained! The latest afforestation claim itself is very dubious: previously the almost identical total of 27 million ha of afforested land was claimed just for the years 1949-1959 (CIA 1976). Moreover, Zhang Anghe and colleagues (1981) state that the wood reserves in the surviving afforested areas are less than 200 million m³, or no more than 2 percent of the national total—although these new plantings account for 23 percent of officially "fully stocked" forests!

Not surprisingly, then, the official nationwide total of forest reserves—9.5 billion m³—reconfirms that Chinese forests are not "fully stocked": it translates to about 78 m³/ha, while, for example, the Soviet average is 109, and the U.S. mean is 106 m³/ha, a 35-40 percent difference! A similar situation exists in terms of average annual increments and harvests: in the Northeast, China's most productive forest area, the growth amounts to only 1.5 m³ per ha, and timber output is just 0.7 m³ per ha, compared with Scandinavian values of, respectively, 3 and 2 m³ per ha (Zhang Anghe and others 1981). And the total annual increment of 220 million m³ is barely equal to the officially acknowledged cuttings; the real disappearance is, of course, considerably higher.

In a way, all of these discrepancies and uncertainties, though very large, are irrelevant. China may now have some kind of tree cover over nearly 13 percent of its territory, but a good part of it will be less dense (after all, canopy densities for large areas cannot be reliably determined without expensive aerial surveys) and much less productive than the "fully stocked" label implies. Subtracting the poorly stocked secondary growth (at least 46 million ha), the newly planted areas (28 million ha), and the climax forests destroyed during the past three decades (conservatively estimated at about 5 million ha; for details see the next section) from the official 1979 figure leaves about 43 million ha of good, productive natural stands, or about 35 percent of the claimed total. Significantly enough, at the 1979 National Symposium on Forestry Economics it was stated that "only one-third" of China's forests is suitable for commercial logging (Anonymous 1979a).

But even if all the claimed area were a fine productive growth, China's share of forested land, absolute and per capita (0.12 ha), would be very low, placing the country, respectively, 120th and 121st among 160 nations. Among large populous nations, forests occupy about 18 percent of total land area in India, 50 percent in Indonesia, 30 percent in Nigeria, and 40 percent in Brazil; respective per capita figures for these nations are roughly 0.1, 1.0, 0.5, and 4.0 ha (FAO 1980). In terms of commercial wood resources, China is, with about 9 m^3 per capita, 57th among the 75 nations for which this measure is available, and the country's annual wood production translates into a minuscule 0.05 m^3 per capita. The United States, with a nearly identical land mass, has 32 percent under forests (1.5 ha per capita, or 12.5 times that in China), and the U.S. per capita use of wood products is more than 40 times the Chinese figure. Clearly, China's poor forest resources put the country at a disadvantage in both environmental and economic terms, and the difficulty is compounded by the extremely uneven distribution of forested land.

The main forested region in China, containing some 60 percent of all timber resources, is in the Northeast: the Da Hinggan and Xiao Hinggan mountains in Nei Monggol; the provinces of Liaoning, Jilin, and Heilongjiang; and the Changbai Shan near the Korean border in Jilin. Heilongjiang alone, with its 16.66 million ha of productive forests (38.5 percent of the province's land), has 13.7 percent of the national total, but it produces nearly half of China's commercial timber

(NCNA, November 20, 1980, *SWB* 1121). These boreal (northern coniferous) forests closely resemble their Siberian, European, and North American counterparts, being composed mainly of slow-growing pines (*Pinus*), larches (*Larix*), spruces (*Picea*), and firs (*Abies*). These trees may attain grand sizes, making them ideally suitable for railway ties and large construction timber, but their felling age is 40-50 years, even 100 years.

The forests of western Sichuan (in the Daxue Shan and the Shaluli Shan) and western Yunnan (especially near the Burmese and Laotian borders) are China's second largest store of forest biomass. A rich variety of broad-leaved evergreens predominate in the natural stands, and their felling age is usually less than 30 years. China's third largest area of natural forest is in southeastern Xizang, centered in Bomi and Baxoi counties. In this region there are nearly 100 different tree species, including the tropical Dipterocarpaceae in the humid, low-lying Yarlung Zangbo valley.

All three of these heavily wooded regions, containing three-quarters of China's forest resources, are far removed from the densely populated farming and industrialized areas of the North, the Center, and the East, which have been virtually stripped of any important productive forests; North China and the intensively cultivated central plains, with some 320 million people (about a third of China's total), have only 13 million ha of forests (mostly in smaller disjointed patches), or a mere 0.04 ha and one m³ per capita (Lin Zi 1980). And, naturally, forests are also extremely scarce in China's arid Northwest, which embraces 37 percent of the country's territory but contains only 3.2 percent of its forest lands.

As the Xizang timber is not yet commercially exploited and the Sichuan-Yunnan resources serve mostly just regional needs, it is necessary to continue large-scale transfers of logs and sawn wood from the Northeast, which constitutes, together with coal transport, the major burden on the overextended North-South railway links. To achieve a better distribution of forest resources and also to improve the country's environment, the Chinese have been engaged for decades in truly massive afforestation campaigns, and if all the staggering claims issued since the early 1950s were taken seriously, the country would not be in the unenviable position it finds itself in today.

There are enough Chinese admissions (and outside observations), however, to conclude that *most* of the claimed afforestation totals reflect abstract targets, passed downward through the bureaucratic maze,

Figure 2. Some 50 planting wells prepared in the rocky soil of Jundu Shan can be counted in this picture—but only a handful of the planted trees took root, an all too frequent result of China's afforestation campaigns.

whose fulfillment is reported upward in due time by the lower-level officials to be collated into impressive totals regardless of how well, if at all, the work has been done. Xu Dixin writes in *Hongqi* about many places that "reported to higher authorities every year the area and the number of trees and, having done this, considered that their task was completed. Few people care about the management and survival rate of the trees" (Xu 1981).

Shoddy planting and the absence of follow-up have been the undoing of China's afforestation campaigns (Figure 2). Undeniably, large numbers of trees have been planted in China since 1949, but Wang Jingcai, an associate professor of forestry at Northwest Agricultural College, quotes a revealing folk saying to explain why some areas have been planting trees everywhere and still have no forests: "Trees everywhere in spring, just half left by summer; no care taken in the fall, all trees gone by winter" (Wang Jingcai 1978).

Survival rates of new plantings have been appallingly low, often much below 10 percent, for several reasons. Careless planting (bare-root saplings put into rocky or sandy soil), no or inadequate follow-up care (no weeding, watering, protective fencing), and lack of scientific approaches to afforestation (choice of species inappropriate for the location or for the soil) have been the key causes. The best available nationwide appraisal of this persistent and extensive waste of resources can be found in a paper by the Policy Research Office of the Ministry of Forestry (1981), which states that of all China's plantings since 1949 "no more than one-third managed to survive." And not a few surviving trees have been recklessly destroyed long before maturity in the search for scarce fuel (see section 6.1.3).

But even those critical observers who distrusted the staggering official afforestation claims of the past and who were aware that as in any other poor, populous country appreciable deforestation had been taking place in China during the past three decades were surprised by the magnitude and ubiquity of deforestation reports that have come out of the country since the late 1970s.

2.1.2 Deforestation

Recently published accounts of deforestation portray a destruction comparable with the disappearance rates in other of the worst affected forests of the poor world, such as the tropical biomes in Southeast Asia, Central America, and parts of Africa (Myers 1980). Before I summarize the most appalling examples from the Chinese sources since 1979, let me make a few comments about the general causes of the problem.

To begin with, the growing timber demands of a rapidly industrializing society put a damaging stress on China's best commercial forest resources. Official figures for the years 1950-57 show that 1.332 million ha of productive forests were clear-cut, but only 241,977 ha (or 18.2 percent) were regenerated (Ministry of Forestry 1958). Severe damage was done to all kinds of forests throughout China owing to the large-scale iron-making campaign started in 1958 as a key ingredient of that Maoist economic delusion called "The Great Leap Forward." Much of the accessible timber around tens of thousands of villages and towns was cut to provide charcoal for the primitive"backyard" furnaces producing useless pig iron.

For several years after the inevitable collapse of the "Great Leap," pressure on the forests eased; high lumber production targets were scaled down as a part of general economic readjustment, more attention was given to reforestation, and the demand for charcoal for the remaining small-scale pig iron furnaces dropped sharply. But after only a brief respite came a decade of lunatic policies labeled so inappropriately the

"Cultural Revolution." The general lawlessness of its first few years, spilling into localized civil war and prolonged absences of any authority protecting the common good, left a tragic legacy that, combined with repeated policy reversals (during and after the period), punishments for taking initiative, and widespread rural poverty, has been obvious grounds for the destruction of any natural resource for a short-term gain.

Illegal felling of forest trees, always a problem in wood-short China, became truly rampant, and the worsening rural energy supply (see section 6.1.3) intensified the damage. Trees were also cut, and often sold illegally, for otherwise unobtainable construction lumber or raw material for various manufacturers. Villages in the plains would make such deals with loggers in nearby forested mountain areas on a not inconsiderable scale. By far the most important reason for accelerated deforestation in the late 1960s and during most of the 1970s, however, was another disastrous Maoist policy, "taking grain as the key link." As understandable as the concern is in the world's most populous nation with very limited area of farmland and barely adequate nutrition, the expansion of cereal production could not be achieved in a more damaging, environmentally *and* economically, and less sustainable manner than by cutting down the forests and planting grain in their place. The Policy Research Office of the Ministry of Forestry (1981) states that the reclamation of forests for grainfields and fires have destroyed at least 6.7 million ha since 1949.

In most places the inevitable vicious circle set in soon after slopes were deforested to make way for grainfields: after a few years, as the accumulated organic matter was sharply reduced and the thin soil rapidly eroded, yields on the newly reclaimed land plummeted and more land was deforested just to maintain the harvests. The abandoned, barren land then succumbed to erosion, often with the irreparable result of all soil being removed to the bedrock. Conversion to grainfields, state-run commercial logging, and illegal private cutting, mainly for fuel, have thus been responsible for the disappearance of China's forests.

As noted earlier, most of China's productive boreal forests are in the northernmost province of Heilongjiang, which supplies nearly 50 percent of the country's timber. Between 1949 and 1978 wood removal in Heilongjiang's forests totaled over 1.1 billion m³, while the new growth amounted to only 600 million m³; in the Da Hinggan mountains, the heart of the province's logging area, nearly 200,000 ha were cut without any reforestation during the years 1964-1978 (Heilongjiang provincial broadcast, March 22, 1979, *SWB* 1028). In the Yichun area of the province the number of trees felled annually is 2.5 times that of the newly planted ones, and the forests have receded by 100,000 ha in the past two decades (NCNA, October 8, 1979, *SWB* 1059). A recent survey shows that the province's forests are declining by 1.7 percent annually (Heilongjiang provincial broadcast, November 27, 1980, *SWB* 1121), and a reforestation survey completed in late 1980 shows that since 1949 the province has cut 2.418 million ha of forest and afforested only 2.073 million ha, a difference of 345,000 ha (Xinhua, February 27, 1981, *SWB* 1133).

Elsewhere in the Northeast, "regeneration is falling behind lumbering" in Nei Monggol's eastern forest areas (Nei Monggol regional broadcast, March 25, 1981, *SWB* 1133), and in Jilin "forest resources have gradually diminished during the past few years" because the reforestation rate of cut areas has been a mere 12.7 percent, and also owing to the large number of fires that could not be fought because there is "always a lack of professional firemen and funds" (Xinhua, November 26, 1978, *JPRS* 72421; Figure 3).

The destruction of the few surviving forests continues in the arid North where, simultaneously, an immense planting project (the "Green Great Wall," see section 2.1.4) is under way to reverse the massive erosion and desertification (see sections 2.2 and 2.3). Devastated forests in some provinces and autonomous regions in that area are twice the size of afforested land (Xinhua, June 10, 1979, *JPRS* 73796), and in some counties nine times; where millions of trees are to be planted before 1985 as a "strategic measure" to control erosion and desertification, animal or tractor-drawn carts can be seen on the roads, loaded with indiscriminately and illegally cut trunks, branches, and roots (Jiang 1979), and on the already heavily eroded Loess Plateau and in the Wei He (Wei River) valley unscrupulous lumbering has not only not ceased, but is actually increasing in some places.

The situation is hardly different in the densely settled farming provinces on the North China Plain were forests survive only on remote mountain slopes. In Anhui, timber consumption exceeds the natural growth of 400,000 m³, forest resources in many localities have been totally exhausted, "while an insufficient number of trees has been planted in time to replace them" (Anhui provincial broadcast, March 12, 1981, *SWB* 1133). In Hebei, one half of the mountain slopes (about 33,000 ha) are now barren, and as recently as 1980 a provincial broad-

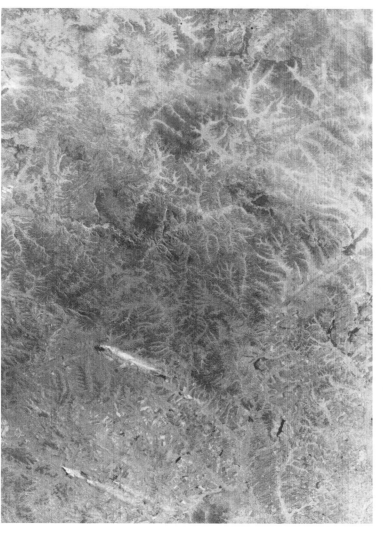

Figure 3. This LANDSAT image scanned on September 15, 1976, shows a part of the Xiao Hinggan Ling in northern Heilongjiang (near the Soviet boundary, in the basin of the Keluo He) with two large and five smaller forest fires burning, one of the contributing factors to forest losses in the North.

cast stated that "unscrupulous lumbering is rampant in quite a number of areas, and the destruction of forests to open up more land is still very serious" (Hebei provincial broadcast, March 6, 1980, *SWB* 1090).

Perhaps the most disquieting reports on deforestation come from the Chang Jiang basin, and notably from Sichuan (Figure 4), where the decline did not start until the late 1960s but has since accelerated rapidly. What must be termed planned destruction has been one of the leading causes of Sichuan deforestation: in 104 state forest areas of the province 760,000 m³ of timber could be cut annually in a sustainable manner—but every year the quotas fixed by the state departments have been reaching as much as 2 million m³, occasionally even higher (Xu Dixin 1981).

Logging, clearing of forests for cultivation, expansion of pastures, and forest fires have so seriously upset the ecosystem balance in mountainous Aba, Garzê, and Liangshan prefectures that even the premier of the country has been speaking of the problem since 1980, and some environmentalists fear that the Chang Jiang, whose tributaries drain the prefectures, is in danger of becoming a second Huang He (see section 2.2.4). In total, Sichuan's forests have been reduced by about 30 percent since the 1950s (from 19 to 13.3 percent of the province's territory), but in Aba Prefecture the loss has been a staggering 68 percent; of the province's 139 counties only 12 now have forest covering more than 30 percent of the land, 22 have between 20 and 30 percent, but 91 have less than 10 percent, and 14 counties have below one percent (Wang and Chen 1981)—a very serious handicap for the country's most populous province with 100 million people!

Yunnan still ranks fourth in China with its total timber resources, but in relative terms the province's deforestation has been even more extensive than in Sichuan, and its loss of forest land appears to be by far the worst in China: about 55 percent of Yunnan's territory was covered by forests in the early 1950s, but by 1975 the share dropped to 30 percent; and the annual wood consumption rate of 26 million m³ is double the growth rate (Xinhua, August 20, 1980, *JPRS* 76376). Yunnan's southernmost region—Xishuangbanna on the Thai border, formerly the country's richest intact tropical moist forest—is being devastated: illegal logging, forest fires, and shifting cultivation have been destroying 3,300 ha a year. Although the area is a protected national reservation, more than 7,000 people have migrated in, establishing 40 villages and cutting the trees for buildings and firewood (Yang 1980).

Figure 4. How deforestation begins: fields starting to climb into the hills near Qingcheng Shan (Guan County), about 80 km north-west of Chengdu in Sichuan. Note that some of the crops are grown in rows along the slope, further increasing the potential for rain erosion.

China's other large area of tropical moist forest, Hainan Island (Guangdong Province) in the South China Sea, has suffered even greater ravages. In 1949, 25.7 percent of the island's area (863,000 ha) was covered by tropical forests; today only 7.2 percent (242,000 ha) is left, with timber resources down from 64 million m³ in 1949 to 29 million m³ in 1980 (Zhang Tianxiong 1980; Figure 5). Elsewhere in Guangdong, Lin Xi (1979) reports on the destruction in the north of the province, where most of the standing trees are less than 10 years old, more is logged than planted, and stealing even from the national forests is flagrant. New plantings along the roads fare no better: a peasant complains in a letter to a Guangdong newspaper that one-third of his county's roadside trees were destroyed by breaking off branches, peeling off bark, and digging up roots (Guangdong provincial broadcast, January 28, 1978, *JPRS* 70685). The Policy Research Office of the Ministry of Forestry (1981) estimates that in just 3 years between 1978 and 1980 nearly 470,000 ha of forest containing more than 9 million m³ of wood were destroyed in the province.

In Zhejiang, forest reserves declined rapidly from 29 million m³ in 1973 to 18 million m³ in 1977; at this rate all forests would be cut in about 7 years (Xu and Qi 1981). China's richest subtropical evergreen forest used to be in the moist maritime province of Fujian: in 1949 timber reserves totaled 178 million m³—now they stand at 89 million m³ (Anonymous 1980a). Forest fires are destroying millions of trees every year: more than 54 million in 1977, more than 30 million in 1979. The province's annual harvesting plans call for cutting 3 million m³, but actually removals are over 20 million m³, and in the second half of the 1970s Fujian was losing almost 270,000 ha of forest every year, a rate at which all mature and maturing forests would be destroyed in just 8 years (Policy Research Office of the Ministry of Forestry 1981; Zhang, Xiao, and Xu 1980).

A flood of deforestation reports from virtually all other parts of the country has been featured in Chinese newspapers and journals. Even the minuscule remaining forests and groves of tree crops (tung oil, mulberries, bamboo, oranges) have not been spared; they were cut down, the land sown to grain crops, and the yield from these officially nonexistent fields added to the output from long-established fields to boost artificially their yield and overfulfill the planned targets. This so-called "helping field" phenomenon was still widespread in 1979 (Xing 1979), although a greater ecological lunacy is hard to imagine.

Thus China's forests—from the boreal stands of firs and pines in

Figure 5. LANDSAT image (acquired on December 27, 1973) of the northern part of Hainan Island, Qiongzhou Strait, and the southernmost tip of Leizhou Peninsula. Three decades ago the island's surface would have been overwhelmingly covered by black or a very dark gray color signifying extensive natural tropical rain forests; today only patches remain, as fields, denuded slopes, and poor secondary growth on deforested sites (all light shades) have taken over.

Heilongjiang to the mangroves of Hainan, from the mixed subtropical forests of Sichuan to the bamboo groves of Zhejiang—are rapidly receding. Adding up just the cited provincial deforestation totals— 345,000 ha for Heilongjiang (1949-1980), 3.24 million ha for Sichuan (1949-1980), a staggering 10.83 million ha for Yunnan (1949-1980), 470,000 ha for Guangdong (1978-1980), and 1.3 million ha for Fujian (1976-1980)—produces a sum of over 16 million ha. Because this partial nationwide loss figure includes the values for the whole three decades in the three most forested provinces—Heilongjiang, Sichuan, and Yunnan—as well as most of Fujian's loss, the all-China aggregate for the years 1949-1980 would likely be no more than 20 percent higher, or some 20 million ha. Assuming that the 1949 total was 83 million ha (8.6 percent), the country's loss in just three decades amounts to no less than 24 percent, much of it involving the destruction of rich natural climax forests, a loss which cannot possibly be made up by extensive but inadequate and largely monocultural plantings.

China's forestry, farming, and environmental scientists clearly realize the crippling dangers inherent in the continuation of this destructive trend, and they have been able to impress their arguments on economists and politicians. The top central leadership, political and managerial, and the country's scientific elite are now fully aware of the scope of the past damage and of the urgent need to stop further extensive destruction. The premier of the country pleads for greater understanding and more attention to the problem, the official Communist Party daily, *Renmin ribao*, runs frequent first page appeals to save "the vital resources of the nation," and a new forestry law went into effect in 1979—but the situation continues to deteriorate.

The causes are various and intractable. The forestry law is a simply unenforceable legalistic document. Its provisions are strict: the illegal felling of trees in state forests is absolutely forbidden, and the guilty party not only has to pay high fines but also has to plant three new trees in place of the destroyed one and is held responsible for the saplings' survival. The regulations also forbid any forest clearing to reclaim farmland and hold the leading forestry officials responsible for losses caused by large forest fires.

The reality is quite different. The Policy Research Office of the Ministry of Forestry (1981) asserts that since the latter half of 1979 forest destruction on a national scale has actually spread, with "hordes of people" illegally cutting and buying wood. The already mentioned legacy of lawlessness, the absence of personal responsibility in a system of collective leadership, unrealistic economic goals, the desperation of poor peasants, and now the understandable wish to live better while the circumstances allow are the deeply intractable causes of deforestation—and of other environmental and societal *mals* of today's China. A recent description of the situation in Fujian, published in *Renmin ribao*, is a remarkable example worth recounting in detail (Anonymous 1980a):

All levels of the leadership, preoccupied in the past with implementing the policy of "taking grain as the key link" (i.e., cutting the forests to plant the cereals) now have as their only concern "seizing money before their eyes" (a not so surprising personal interpretation of the current "Four Modernizations" policy which is to make the country rich). As long as everybody's income rises during a cadre's tenure all is now well, and therefore some responsible persons "even lead the masses in large-scale cutting"—surely an ominous portent for the future!

The management of forests is chaotic, with overlapping, competing, uncoordinated bureaucracies trying blindly to fulfill assorted plans or to make quiet money: "One hoe making forests, but several axes cutting them down" goes a new Chinese saying. Past destructive practices continue: forest fires, often intentionally started (!), illegal purchases of lumber by mining enterprises and army units, widespread (of course, also mostly illegal) use of wood as industrial fuel. Two examples from Fujian are again most illustrative: exporting out of the province more than 650,000 m³ of timber outside the state plan in just one three-month period, and burning an equivalent of 230,000 m³ of lumber in only one county with 103 industrial plants and 55,000 inhabitants.

Especially popular throughout Fujian now is the conversion of large lumber pieces into small manufactured items that fetch higher prices (three- or four-fold the price of the original wood). Needless to say, the waste of wood in the process is phenomenal, but some counties have literally hundreds of small processing enterprises engaged in this practice. A decree to stop this waste was issued in June 1978, but it was still being completely ignored as of spring 1980. And the news of indiscriminate cutting of trees in Wuyishan, China's major natural natural preserve (where "no one obeys . . . the forestry ordinance" and the "illegally cut timber is stacked all over the place so that vehicles cannot get through, but no one does anything about it") rounds out a picture that tells more about real concerns and public order in China than all the silky travelogs brought back by the friendship delegations of the past decade.

The destruction of the most productive climax ecosystems on such a scale, moreover, in a nation whose phytomass resources had been in decline for centuries yet whose population has nearly doubled in just 25 years and whose aspirations to modernize are all but modest, has had predictable direct economic and environmental consequences, the latter bringing, with a delay of just few years or a few decades, additional and stronger economic and social impacts.

2.1.3 Consequences

The direct economic effects of the destruction and misuse of China's forests are everywhere to be seen: pervasive shortages of roundwood, sawn wood, and paper. Coal remains China's principal source of primary energy, and further expansion of its mining is imperative for China's economic survival. Each 1,000 tons of coal extracted in underground mines (and, unlike the United States and the Soviet Union, China has almost no surface coal mining industry) requires 13-25 m^3 of softwood pitprops. Each km of railway track requires 200-300 m^3 of roundwood to manufacture the ties, which last at best 7 years in the North, much fewer in the South; and the needs for new track are enormous in a nation with mere 50,000 km of railways (the United States, with a virtually identical amount of territory had that much more than 100 years ago). And for each 1,000 m^2 of new floor space, 50-70 m^3 of timber is consumed (Yue Ping 1980).

Even with considerable recycling, each ton of typical paper products requires about 1.5 tons of new wood, while new paper consumes 3.5-5.5 m^3 per ton. And because China's population will increase by a quarter billion during the next generation, schoolbook needs alone will be staggering; the spread of the massive amounts of technical information without which China's modernization is unthinkable cannot be accomplished without paper in a nation where most people do not have electricity. The timber requirements of the Chinese construction industry have been going up exponentially by 6 percent a year for the past decade, but housing conditions in cities remain unspeakably poor, with an average of 3.6 m^2 of floor space per person (Xinhua, June 1, 1980, *SWB* 1087).

Pent-up demand for just replacing the rundown housing in the villages is even greater, creating enormous potential needs for wood. And as the unprecedented wave of marriages, the legacy of no population controls in the 1960s, rises in the coming years, the young couples will want a roomful of furniture, a sign of prosperity difficult to achieve for tens of millions of newlyweds. And the shortages of fuel wood are already cripplingly acute in a large part of China's countryside (see section 6.1.3).

The current situation is serious. Mine pitprop shortages are chronic, delaying coal extraction; railway ties have to be made of concrete, consuming scarce fossil fuels in the process; and the same is true for transmission poles needed in huge numbers to electrify the countryside; people line up for an overnight wait to buy a single piece of plywood; more than a million sewing machines stand unfinished in Shanghai waiting for little wooden boards; urban newlyweds have to wait another year to get a couple of pieces of simple furniture (examples are from Xinhua, October 10, 1979, SWB 1054). And today's shortages are bound to increase in the future, affecting nearly every aspect of the modernizing economy and the people's aspirations for a life a bit more affluent.

As serious and retarding as these wood shortages are, the problem hardly bears a comparison with the deep environmental effects of China's deforestation: indeed, few of the difficulties facing the nation are as grave in their impact on the society's well-being as the degradative processes set in motion by the destruction of forests. No other ecosystem offers as many irreplaceable services as natural climax forests. Before citing a variety of specific Chinese examples detailing the loss of these benefits, I will briefly review their general nature.

The influences and benefits of forests encompass a wide range of climatic, soil, water flow, and biotic phenomena, and these have been extensively studied in many locations around the world (Kittredge 1948; FAO 1962; Heinsdijk 1975). Climatic effects include moderation of temperature (lowering of the maxima and raising of the minima)—an influence similar to that of large bodies of water and most valuable for crop farming in nearby areas; dissipation of wind and reduction of wind speeds for a distance of more than 40 times the tree height and hence a high effectiveness in combating wind erosion; and high potential evapotranspiration (although rarely any meaningful increase in precipitation).

The most beneficial influence on soils is the outstanding protection trees offer against water erosion. Owing to the interception of rain in the canopies and to the presence of organic matter (litter) on the soil, differences of an order of magnitude between forested and barren surfaces are not uncommon. The rich organic layer on the forest floor also reduces the runoff through increased infiltration and retention.

These abilities are critical for removing water more rapidly from the surface between storms and thus decreasing both the frequency of flooding and its peak flows; in turn this, again, reduces soil erosion and the resulting stream and reservoir silting. And, obviously, the decomposing litter adds significantly to the soil's fertility. Ecosystemically, forests are the richest assemblies of plants and heterotrophs, the irreplaceable repositories of genetic diversity and variability.

The importance of all these always invaluable services is heightened in the world's most populous nation, whose fields are open to strong seasonal winds, whose fluctuating water supply is a key determinant of the harvest, and whose soil erosion problems have been traditionally severe. Accelerated erosion is, undoubtedly, the most widespread and most dangerous consequence of China's rapid deforestation, and as such it will be treated separately in some detail (see section 2.2), as will desertification (2.3). Below are just a few illustrations of some large-scale and some local effects of deforestation.

That the aggregate water retention capacity of forests is very large can be easily illustrated by this simple calculation. Assuming that each ha of forest retains 300 m³ of water, the afforestation of all barren hills and mountains in the Chang Jiang basin would result in an effective storage of 20-30 billion m³ of water, twice the capacity of Danjiangkou, China's largest reservoir on the Han Shui (Han River) (Wang and Chen 1981). The removal of tree cover from extensive areas, such as the reductions on the order of 30 or 50 percent in some large southern provinces during just two or three decades, therefore leads inevitably to a markedly decreased water retention capacity and hence to the greater frequency and deeper impact of natural disasters. Chinese scientists believe that the link is unmistakable.

During the years 1950-58, 20 million ha of cropland was annually affected by natural disasters (mainly prolonged droughts or extensive flooding), while between 1972 and 1977 the annual average rose to more than 35 million ha, or a third of all farmland (Yi Zhi 1980). The same source states that in wet South China where two out of three days used to be rainy, now two out of three years are excessively dry. In Heilongjiang, formerly China's most forested province, overcutting and grassland destruction have brought previously unknown serious droughts and duststorms. On the opposite end of the country, in subtropical Yunnan, long-range climatic records show a severe drought once in every 9.6 years between 1470 and 1950—yet since the establishment of the People's Republic of China (PRC) in 1949 until 1978, extreme spring and spring-summer drought occurred every 3.2 years, and the frequency of floods also tripled (Wang and Zhou 1981).

One of China's worst floods in decades was certainly aggravated by widespread deforestation: the Chang Jiang floods in the summer of 1981—an extraordinarily large one in mid-July, the worst inundation since 1877, a smaller one in mid-August—directly affected 135 countries and cities with 11.8 million people, inundating 1.6 million rooms, 2,600 factories, and 830,000 ha of mostly level, fertile farmland (destroying or badly damaging potential harvests of some 1.5 million tons of grain) and damaging 38,000 water conservancy works; direct monetary losses were put at ¥2.5 billion (Du 1981). This crippling experience led both the central and provincial leadership to search for contributing causes, and a consensus on "painful lessons" quickly emerged: besides uncontrollable natural factors, the loss of 30 percent of the province's forested area, blind conversion of slopeland to grainfields, and improper construction of water conservancy projects were clearly to blame (Anonymous 1981a).

On Hainan Island, the massive destruction of forests has been accompanied by a greater frequency of floods, droughts, and blowing sand and the near extinction of several wildlife species (see section 5.1). When the villages in the hilly and mountainous regions immediately west of Beijing were required to become self-sufficient in grain they predictably cleared many slopes for grainfields, causing not only serious water losses and soil erosion but also becoming a source of repeated duststorms blanketing the capital (see section 2.3).

On a smaller scale, the experience of the Dayao Shan forest area (Liuzhou Prefecture, Guangxi) is notable. Two decades of rapid deforestation destroyed 21,300 ha of trees, and an additional 13,300 ha succumbed to uncontrolled fires. Because this forest region is the source of 25 rivers whose waters irrigate nearly 60,000 ha in eight neighboring counties, water shortages and droughts induced by this destruction have been crippling. A 1977 survey found the regular flow of 22 out of the 25 rivers reduced by one-third compared with the years before 1958. And the destruction continues even after the focusing of widespread attention on the problem: peasants in mountain villages, who are urged to protect the forests, have a low grain ration (just 210 kg compared with over 300 kg in the surrounding farming regions), and because they "are not given enough food to eat, what can they do if they do not choose to reclaim some forest land to grow grain crops?" (Xinhua, October 22, 1980, SWB 1110).

The experience of Qingzhen County on the Guizhou plateau is similar (Wang Ganmei 1981). In 1949 the county had a 30 percent forest cover; by 1975 this was reduced to a mere 4.7 percent. The impacts: 54 percent of the nonirrigated farmland now suffers serious erosion; the average annual rainfall has dropped by 120-155 mm, and prolonged droughts (up to 74 rainless days) have become more common; despite large increases of cultivated areas there has been hardly any growth in grain output, and the degeneration of grasslands reduced sheep and goat counts by nearly 90 percent between 1957 and 1978. Now the reversion to forests has been begun, and by the year 2000 the county should again have a 30 percent tree cover. What an unnecessarily destructive cycle—and over the past three decades how many localities have developed along the same sad path!

2.1.4 Solutions

The conclusion is unequivocal: if the Chinese are not able to reverse the current deforestation trend very soon, they will face within a genera tion major environmental disasters deeply affecting the very capacity for decent human existence in the worst-off regions and undermining the modernization of the whole nation. What are the measures that must be taken to lead toward recovery? There are many, some traditional, some innovative—all promoted relentlessly and with the utmost commitment. No frenzied mass campaigns similar to the delusive outbursts of the past will do, but participation in the necessarily long-range efforts will have to be massive.

Strange as it might seem in a country with such a relatively minuscule per capita consumption of wood (and despite the chronic shortages!), there is a considerable potential to conserve wood in many ways and hence to relieve some of the overcutting. The Ministry of Forestry estimates that throughout China over 12 million m³ of timber and processed timber remnants are either rotting in the forests or are eventually collected for firewood instead of being turned into useful products (Xinhua, October 10, 1979, SWB 1054). In 1978 a mere 9 percent of timber remnants was used by the artificial board industry or in papermaking, a sharp contrast with the situation in the relatively so much richer in wood United States, where the current rate of wood residue utilization is around 75 percent and rising.

Nationwide sawmill refuse in China is 37 percent of the total timber output (i.e., nearly 20 million m³ a year), but the particle board industry, the best user for this prodigious waste, is so mismanaged (up to 10 different organizations and government departments run a single factory!), outdated, and lacking in investment (less than 8 percent of all investment in forestry has been earmarked in recent years for the industry) that it cannot absorb this precious raw material.

The papermaking industry is no less wasteful. In Fujian all but 3 of the 60 paper mills in the province are using wood as the process fuel, and while the timber consumption for woodpulp came to 400,000 m^3 in 1978, the wood burned by the inefficient mills totaled 4 million m^3, an amount sufficient to turn out an extra 1 million tons of paper annually (Xinhua, June 9, 1979, *SWB* 1037). Paper recycling, another obvious conservation measure, appears to be already fairly extensive in China— although it probably doesn't match Japan's nearly 90 percent rate.

Obviously, even the most practicable conservation measures could not stop the deterioration of Chinese forests: higher investment in forestry, much better management of young and middle-aged forests, aggressive replanting of all commercially cut areas, extensive afforestation of barren wastelands, and effective measures against any further conversions of forests into grainfields and against illegal tree cutting are essential to any successful long-range policy. On all of these counts—save the conversion to grainfields, which was long officially sanctioned and promoted—one finds that the past attitudes, decrees, proclamations, laws, and orders issued by the central and provincial governments have been mostly correct, strict, and farsighted—but the actual results have been at best disappointing (e.g., only one-third of all the prodigious afforestation efforts have taken root, there are chronic shortages of fire-fighting equipment), and more often outright appall-ing (recall the "responsible officials" leading the masses in deforesta-tion drives and the state and army units black-marketing wood).

Official government policy since the founding of the PRC has been that regeneration must follow commercial harvesting to provide for sustained yields, and generally the Ministry of Forestry appears to have favored the forest management, rather than the purely forest utiliza-tion, approach. As mentioned earlier, the illegal felling of trees in state or local forests has been strictly forbidden by repeated regulations starting in the 1950s, and in 1979 the State Council issued a new law that not only requires fines and the planting of three trees in place of the one destroyed but also demands the guarantee of the new saplings' survival (Xinhua, January 26, 1979, *SWB* 1024).

These new regulations also absolutely forbid any forest clearing to reclaim new farmland and call for punishment of leading forestry officials responsible for huge losses caused by major forest fires. A new urgent circular was published on December 5, 1980 (Appendix B), placing distribution of all timber products in forest zones under the unified management of the forest departments, forbidding all other organizations and individuals to fell or to purchase any trees, closing all free markets for lumber and wood products, and forbidding the railways to ship any wood without a forestry administration certificate (NCNA, December 6, 1980, *SWB* 113).

Past laws have been nearly as strict, yet the rates of deforestation were hardly affected by their issuance. As long as the need for lumber or fuel wood remains acute, as long as quick cash can be made on the sale of wood and wood products, false permits and certificates will be issued, payoffs will be accepted, and the black market will continue to thrive, as past Chinese experience shows all too clearly.

I would suggest that rather than in these punitive and proscriptive measures, necessary as they may be, hope lies elsewhere. Much has been written in the modern sinological literature about the social pressure traditionally operating in Chinese society; when this is reinforced by the coercive nature of the ruling totalitarian regime, one might expect some impressive achievements in the quest for the common good. Not a few Western admirers of Maoist truths subscribed to such ideas, but as the rich, and often tragic, reality of three decades has shown, there is a limit, and a rather low one, to the effectiveness, quality, sustainability, and real success of all such efforts.

Since 1978 there have been many changes clearly indicating that the Chinese understand this and are willing to change some of their longstanding ways of managing basic affairs. Herein lies the hope, because people cannot be forced to grow trees. Foresters promoting new planting schemes all around the poor world have learned this lesson very well indeed (Arnold 1979). The high failure rate of Chinese plantings clearly demonstrates that assuring the saplings' survival is the key to success—and clearly the best way to sustain interest in the tiresome but necessary weeding, watering, thinning, and soil cultivation, as well as the subsequent protection of an established tree before maturity, is to let the people who planted the trees own them.

For long years, of course, this has been one of the clear signs of destructive bourgeois mentality, an unhealthy longing for despised private ownership. This ideological obduracy would be, *by itself*, almost comic, if it had not brought so much suffering. The best example I know of this is from Shaanxi's Yan'an-Yulin region, a dry and severely eroded loess area (see section 2.2.1) drastically short of fuel wood, where the private planting of trees was repeatedly prohibited, most recently by a provincial administration order in October 1979, as a clear sign of "promoting capitalism" (Jiang 1979). Yan'an, of course, was Mao's headquarters during the Sino-Japanese War, and three decades later this was the Maoist reward to the wartime revolutionary base: the peasants forced to burn dried animal dung or to dig grass roots so that a backyard willow would not turn them into Wall Street monsters.

The reversal of this irrational policy came, finally, in the spring of 1980, when a joint Chinese Communist Party (CCP) Central Committee-State Council directive issued on March 5 stated, among other things, that all the trees planted by the villagers in a communal effort belong to them rather than to the state, and that the trees the peasants are encouraged to plant in any suitable place, either on their private plots or on land specially allocated to them, will belong to their families. The critical rider: this policy is to remain unchanged for a long time, presumably for decades.

After this directive was issued, one province after another adopted new regulations promoting private woodlots. In Heilongjiang, China's foremost wood producing province, where 2 million out of 3.65 million peasant households are now short of fuel, the new policy is summarized by the slogan "Whoever afforests the land owns the trees." Forestry licenses will be issued to those families whose plantings have a survival rate of 80 percent; households that fail to meet this target will have to try again to get the license. Each household can get 3 *mu* (0.2 ha), or more if available, of land once it earns the license that guarantees, based on the new measure, the ownership of trees (Heilongjiang provincial broadcast, October 13, 1980, *JPRS* 76079). The authorities expect that 666,000 ha of new woodlots will be producing in three to five years.

On the opposite extreme of the country in Guizhou, the allocation of hilly land to peasants for fuel wood, timber, or oil-tree lots is similar: between one-fifth and one-third of a ha will be granted to each household in the form of a long-term utilization license enabling the peasants to use or to sell the wood as they wish. This measure is expected to increase the share of the province's treed area from 14 to 20 percent in just four to five years (NCNA, June 21, 1980, *SWB* 1089).

The combined contribution of private woodlots can be enormous. Assuming that two-thirds of China's 170 million peasant households would set up woodlots averaging 3 *mu* (this appears to be the typical size, with the extremes ranging from one to 10 *mu*), the aggregate area would cover nearly 23 million ha—the equivalent of about four-fifths of the total land afforested in successive waves of mass-planting campaigns during three decades since 1949! Yet these plantings could take root and be growing in a matter of just a few years with, as a vice-chairman of the State Agricultural Commission stresses, excellent quality and a high survival rate owing to assiduous care, and without any state investment (Zhang Pinghua 1981).

Private woodlots are undoubtedly the best step toward rapid afforestation of hills, mountains, and wastelands adjacent to settlements; they would be a major contribution to a sustainable household energy supply and relieve the pressure on illegal cutting. But they must be augmented by state and collective afforestation on larger scales in principal forest regions as well as by effective measures and incentives against conversion to farmland.

Large-scale afforestation continues to be promoted in a variety of ways. There are extensive plans for reforestation in Heilongjiang; a short-term plan to plant some 700,000 ha of fast-growing, high-yielding trees in the Jiangnan to obtain useful timber in 10-15 years; a grand scheme for a system of shelterbelts in the three northern arid areas (see section 2.3); and a nationwide goal of planting nearly 67 million ha (one billion *mu*) by the year 2000, when China's afforested area should reach 20 percent of the country's territory, with 30 percent being the eventual long-term goal.

The most recent claims of work actually completed indicate a rate of progress more than sufficient to achieve the end-of-the-century goal, but as with so many current encouraging changes, a wait of several years, or even a decade, is necessary to perceive the real trend. While China's environment certainly needs the new huge forest cover planned for the year 2000, I have deep doubts about the effective fulfillment of such a task; half of the goal properly achieved would have to be considered an enormous success.

Whatever the actual extent of the afforestation effort, it will rely critically on two very different approaches: modern aerial seeding without which the revegetation of inaccessible mountain slopes would be extremely difficult, and mass-participation "voluntary" drives. Aerial seeding was an important part of earlier large-scale afforestation in 458 counties in 22 provinces: in the two decades before 1979, slightly over 11.3 million ha was seeded from the air with a claimed average survival rate of about 40 percent, accounting for about one-sixth of the total area afforested since 1949 (NCNA, March 12, 1980, *SWB* 1090). Most of the air-seeded areas are in warm and rainy southern provinces (above all Guangdong, Sichuan, Guizhou, and Guangxi), and of the 4.5 million ha surviving by 1980, grown forests accounted for one-third of the total (1.5 million ha), young trees for about two-fifths, and seedlings for the rest. The air-seeded area is expected to be around 6.7 million ha by 1985, and experiments are to extend the technique to northern China (NCNA, May 5, 1980, *SWB* 1083).

Aerial seeding may present considerable technical and environmental challenges, especially in the north, but to me the new "voluntary" tree-planting campaigns are a much more dubious undertaking. Initiated in 1981, they are anything but voluntary: everybody between eleven and sixty years for males and eleven and fifty-five years for females is to take part, and the trees so planted will be collectively owned (see Appendix C). March 12 of every year is the official day to begin the annual plantings, and on its eve in 1982, 10,000 people attended a rally at the Great Hall in Beijing; and the next day nearly all the top Chinese leaders, including Hu Yaobang, Deng Xiaoping and Zhao Ziyang, joined the masses in planting. All of this may be a valuable public relations exercise, but when the city dwellers leave the saplings on the suburban hills (each one is supposed to plant three to five of them) who will take care of them? Old habits die hard: the new private woodlot regulations are as sensible as this continuation of Maoist-type campaigns preceded by exhortation rallies is dubious. To ensure that forest lands will not again be converted to farm fields will require more than exhortations and regulations. Encouragingly, new provincial polices in Yunnan include not only the allocation of some state mountain forests to village and individual care and absolute prohibition of forest conversion to new farmland but also efforts to settle slash-and-burn farmers in permanent areas and, most importantly, the option to exchange forest, livestock, and local products for grain from the state supplies, the arrangement for sufficient grain for food-deficient areas having no products to exchange, and the forbiddence of the establishment of new fields (Xinhua, August 20, 1980, *SWB* 1108).

The Sichuan provincial government allocated 4 million yuan as rewards for communal efforts to protect the woodlands, especially in mountainous Garzê, Aba, and Liangshan prefectures, which contain four-fifths of Sichuan's forest land (Beijing home broadcast, October 20, 1980, *SWB* 1110). Also, the strict ban on the conversion of forest to farmland must be complemented by no less strict and effective measures to prevent further losses of arable land (see section 2.5); otherwise, the already difficult task of intensifying farm output will become impossible.

Deforestation surely causes more ecosystemic, economic, and everyday human problems than any other form of environmental degradation in China. The trends of the recent past have been outright frightening—yet the very gravity of the situation presents hope and opportunity. When a nationwide conference on forestry is told that "according to the estimate based on the actual annual rate of reduction, by the end of this century there will be no trees to harvest" (Anonymous 1979a), the assessment is undoubtedly accurate, but it is equally clear that such a reality is truly unthinkable and that the trend cannot be allowed to continue. By a combination of efforts, none of them easy or yielding rapid results, the trend has to be reversed if the very physical foundations of China are to be preserved. And as hundreds of millions of Chinese are poor peasants living on the vast river and coastal plains where there are no true forests and no space left by intensively cropped fields, canals, houses, and roads to establish them, the planting of trees on any available spot in the lowland farming regions—a prodigious agroforestry effort— will have to be a part of the solution.

2.1.5 Agroforestry

Strictly defined, agroforestry, or agrisilviculture, is the practice of growing crops and trees together— crops for food, feed, or cash income and trees for one or more of these reasons (i.e., trees themselves may be crops), for fuel wood, as well as for environmental (soil, water) benefit. Here I intend to use the term in the broad sense to embrace all practices of tree growing in predominantly farming and virtually deforested areas, that is, not only true intercropping but also all tree plantings in what the Chinese call the "four besides": beside water (streams, ponds), beside roads, beside fields, and beside houses.

But first I will devote a few paragraphs to agrisilvicultural practices as narrowly defined. These have many understandable appeals: ecosystemic, agronomic, silvicultural, economic, nutritional (Budowski 1978; Weaver 1979). Land competition is lessened or eliminated outright by the joint production, while the trees create a desirable microclimate and provide nutrients for the crops (through litter in all cases, more significantly through nitrogen fixation when leguminous species or nodulated trees are planted) as well as a continuous or cyclical harvest of food, fodder, fuel, timber, medicinal ingredients, and extractives. The integration of trees and pastures is also possible, an interesting way of controlling weeds, fertilizing grass, diversifying nutrition, and increasing land productivity.

The Chinese have traditionally been among the most proficient practitioners of agroforestry, and today they frequently interplant peanuts and corn and small grains with Chinese dates (*Ziziphus jujuba*) in the North, and the fast-growing *Cunninghamia lanceolata* and the oil-bearing tea oil tree (*Thea oleosa*) in a variety of agroforestry combinations in the South (FAO 1978). The potential for the substantial expansion of these worthwhile practices is very large, especially in the South and when *Thea oleosa* is involved. This small slow-growing tree appears to be an outstanding agrisilvicultural choice in warm (annual mean 15-22°C), moist (700-2,400 mm), and hilly (above 800 m above sea level) locations, precisely the conditions throughout most of the South.

In deep soils the smallish tree will grow for more than 100 years, and its seeds yield good edible oil (also easily storable); its long flowering period (five months) is excellent for beekeeping; its dense wood makes fine farming tools, and its pruning (necessary for maximum crown) provides some fuel wood. Intercropping with soybeans, peanuts, sweet potatoes, and in tea plantations is common, and the oil yields of well-managed stands are over 100 kg per ha, plus over 200 kg of oil cake, an excellent animal feed. And, of course, the tree's preference for hilly locations makes it an outstanding choice for reducing slope erosion.

But even the most extensive tree intercropping imaginable would give neither sufficient protection to rural China's deteriorating environment nor enough fuel wood to its households, especially throughout the country's densely populated farming plains. There the planting of suitable species in all available locations is imperative, and despite some impressive progress, much more can be done, as shown by the statistics for the large Jiangsu-Shandong-Henan plain (Hao 1981). The plain's farmland that is networked with trees now totals 4.8 million ha, but this still represents only about 43 percent of the total suitable for such interplanting. About 1.2 million ha of farmland is now intercropped with tung oil trees (*Aleurites fordii*), but there is the potential for at least double this amount.

Over 3 billion trees have been planted on the plain since 1949 in the "four besides," but because this land and other scattered uncultivated patches amount to only about 15 percent of the provinces' farmland (even in the Shanghai suburbs the share is 10 percent) and because 200 trees could be planted for each *mu* (that is, up to 3,000 per ha), there is the potential for nearly tripling the amount or, again, certainly for at least doubling it. The trees most suitable for these plantings are various fast-growing poplars (*Populus*), willows (*Salix*), foxgloves (*Paulownia*), *Sassafras*, and locusts (*Robinia pseudoacacia*). Small groves, rows, or belts of these trees have proved their environmental worth in China: measurements within sheltered areas show wind speeds reduced by 30-50 percent, humidity raised by 10-30 percent, and evaporation reduced by 14-40 percent compared with the open plains; these beneficial changes can help to raise grain yields by up to 25 percent (NCNA, October 9, 1980, *SWB* 1105).

In addition to the usual advantages of more fuel wood (especially with fast-growing coppicing species), the leaves of most of the trees just mentioned can be used as feed for hogs, sheep, and rabbits, an important consideration in intensively farmed regions where little or no land can be set aside for feed crops. Another desirable option is to grow oil-yielding, nut-bearing, or fruit trees. As already detailed, in the South it is tea oil trees, currently grown on about 2.7 million ha (Lin Zi 1980) and suitable for a severalfold expansion; in the North the tung oil tree is the species of choice, planted usually with a density of three or four per *mu*. Tung oil trees, whose valuable industrial oil is an ingredient in some 2,000 different products, are now also enjoying a renaissance in Sichuan and other southern provinces (Xie Zijun 1980). The olive tree (*Olea europaea*) has been spreading quite rapidly since its introduction in 1964.

Fruit trees favored in "four besides" plantings are apples (*Malus*), Chinese chestnuts (*Castanea mollissima*), walnuts (*Juglans mandshurica*), persimmons (*Diospyros kaki*), and Chinese dates (*Ziziphus jujuba*). The dates are especially popular, with dry yields of up to 250 kg per ha. In the South the preferred trees are lichees (*Litchi chinensis*). Fruit trees are particularly desirable for enlivening the overwhelmingly vegetarian diet (see section 6.1.1), and their direct financial benefit can be surprisingly large: a village in Qianxi County in eastern Hebei found that each yuan invested in chestnut-growing returned over 100 times more than the money earned from general field farming (Luo 1981). Chinese dates and lichees are also fine export items.

2.2 Erosion

Deforestation invariably accelerates erosion. While in heavily forested regions virtually no raindrops fall directly on the ground—and even if they did they would be intercepted by the accumulated layer of organic debris—it is the impact of the drops on bare devegetated soil (and not, as it might intuitively seem, the runoff velocity of water) that detaches the largest quantities of soil particles and causes the heaviest soil losses. The greatest water erosion results from intensive summer storms, while the most severe wind erosion problems arise in arid and semiarid regions often swept by strong seasonal winds. And if the soils subjected to such storms and winds are light and easily erodible, the stage is set for a virtually uncontrollable natural hazard.

Unfortunately, a combination of all three preconditions is present in a large area of Northwest China—on the Loess Plateau, which extends over more than half a million km², a region that has served as a classic paradigm of massive erosion in the world's geomorphological and pedological literature.

2.2.1 Loess erosion

The origins of this phenomenon are still debated, but it appears certain that the genesis of the problem goes back as far as 1.2 million years ago, when huge amounts of fine yellow particles, composed mainly of quartz, feldspar, and mica, were lifted by the northwesterly winds from the deserts of Mongolia and Xinjiang and deposited in the area bordered by the Lüliang Shan in the east, the Qin Ling divide in the south, the Ordos Desert in the north and northwest, and the mountain ranges of Qinghai in the west.

There are many other loess areas elsewhere in Asia and on other continents, but this is the world's largest aeolian accumulation of fine grained (0.05-0.005 mm in diameter) sand: the Loess Plateau (Huangtu Gaoyuan—Yellow Soil Plateau) covers some 530,000 km² in 200 counties in eastern Qinghai, south-central Gansu, southern Ningxia, central and northern Shaanxi, southwestern Nei Monggol, and western Shanxi. Other loess deposits in China are in Liaoning and Jilin in the Northeast and in Xinjiang on the fringes of huge intermountain basins, but the layers are not too extensive (they total only some 50,000 km²), and they are relatively thin (less than 50 m). In contrast, the heart of the Loess Plateau has deposits 100-200 m thick, and large parts between Baiyu Shan and Xifeng and east of Lanzhou are covered by deposits more than 200 m thick, in places as much as 300 m thick (Wang and Zhang 1980; Figure 6).

Surficial features of these thick loess deposits largely correspond to

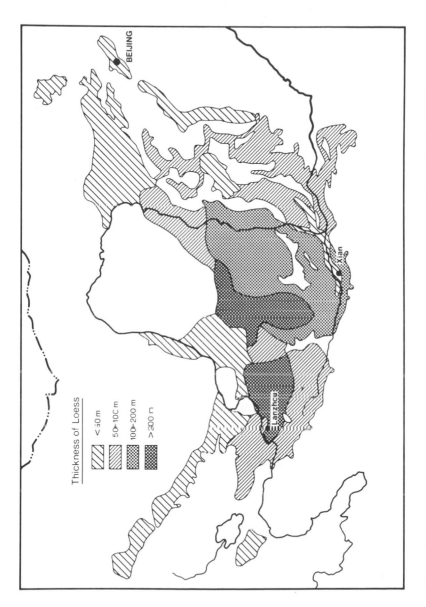

Figure 6. Loess areas in the Huang He basin according to Wang Yongyan and Zhang Zonghu (1980).

Thickness of Loess

< 30 m

50–100 m

100–200 m

> 200 m

BEIJING

Xian

Lanzhou

the underlying palaeotopography. Where there were ancient rolling hills there are now *liang* (elongated mounds) and *mao* (round mounds); where the flat bedrock was overlain there arose *yuan* (high table-like plains with abruptly descending edges); and on the terraces of different heights produced by faults, loess layers form flat *taiyuan*. Naturally, there are many transitional forms created by denudation. Characteristic erosional landforms, shaped largely by running water from summer thunderstorms, are countless loess gullies, gorges, walls, columns, caves, funnels, and grooves (Wang and Zhang 1980). The appearance of heavily eroded loess landscapes is wild and depressing: one is awed by the power of natural processes as well as by the magnitude of the task required to bring these forces under control (Figure 7).

Yet this region, now predominantly desolate and wasted, harbors in its southern part, in the valley of the lower Wei He (Wei River), the core of ancient Chinese civilization: Banpo Village, a neolithic settlement, is just a few km east of Xi'an on the Wei He, Xi'an being the 3,000-year-old city that served intermittently as the capital of 11 dynasties for 1,100 years; some 30 km east of the city were buried the sculpture legions of Qin Shi Huang (259-210 BC), the first great unifier of China; about 150 km north of the city, in Huangling County, is the tomb of the Yellow Emperor, the legendary founder of the Chinese nation.

This long and conspicuous history paved the way for the vast environmental destruction of the region because, previously covered by forests and fine grasslands, it was stripped of its vegetation to build cities and imperial palaces, to heat houses, to cultivate crops. For centuries the erosion has been advancing. The tragedy of the recent past is that this advance has been, in general and in spite of much local effort to control it, dangerously accelerated. Severe erosion now exists on some 430,000 km² of the plateau, or about four-fifths of its total (an area larger than Japan), and 280,000 km² are particularly seriously affected (NCNA, April 17, 1980, *SWB* 1080).

As long as vegetation, and above all trees, protects the ground from the direct impact of raindrops and from wind erosion, topsoil losses in the loess region are not unusually high. As soon as the protective plant cover is stripped away, however, the extremely porous and easily erodible loess layers are washed or blown away. Water erosion is by far the most crippling; although the region is relatively dry (average annual rainfall is just 200-400 mm while evaporation is up to 1,400 mm), over two-thirds of all precipitation comes down in heavy summer thunderstorms when the high kinetic energy of raindrops easily dislodges the loosely accumulated loess particles.

Figure 7. Heavy soil erosion in deep loess layers in Gansu eats away fields, forces roads to change course, and displaces peasants' houses cut into the earth (sunken rectangles in the foreground).

The annual losses of topsoil are now over 10,000 tons per km^2 in Yulin and Yan'an prefectures in Shaanxi and in Lüliang and Xinxian prefectures in Shanxi, and they average 4,000-5,000 tons per km^2 a year throughout most of the region, whose most eroded parts are now just a lifeless maze of deeply cut narrow and steep-sided gullies (Figure 8). The main reason for such staggering losses has been the widespread and indiscriminate application of the Maoist "grain-first" policy and the resultant conversion of remaining thin forests (a mere 3 percent of the plateau still has some forest cover) and good grasslands into fields.

The grandiose Huang He basin control plan published in 1955 envisaged a "comprehensive solution" of the erosion problem by large-scale afforestation, grassing, terracing, and dam building. Instead, the Chinese are now admitting that the ecosystemic destruction on the loess highlands has been especially severe during the past 30 years (NCNA, March 7, 1979, *SWB* 1026).

In their pioneering, unorthodox *Renmin ribao* article (which opened a lively debate on the future developmental strategies for the region) Tong and Bao (1978) gave some shocking examples of the conversions and their effect on the livelihood of the peasants. For example, in Guyuan County in Ningxia the average grain share per capita was 410 kg in 1949, enough to give an adequate if not rich nutritional supply, and in the mid-1960s peasants were able to sell over 4,300 tons of edible oil and more than 3,000 head of cattle to the state each year. Then came the destruction of previously lucrative cattle breeding (in 13 communes of the county all of the grassland was converted to grain-fields) and the cutting down of local forests (20 percent of the total area is now lost).

Cultivated land increased by about 82,000 ha, but after the first few years of good harvests the yields on the land unsuitable for cultivation plummeted to a mere 250 kg/ha. By 1977, per capita grain availability shrank to a mere 100 kg, a clear starvation level, only 400 tons of oil and 800 head of cattle were sold, and the cash income stood at a pitiful 19 yuan per capita. Similarly, in Maolin Village (Yan'an Prefecture, Shaanxi) each person could be provided with 700 kg of grain in 1943, a very comfortable supply; by 1977 the harvest was down to 250 kg per capita—and many localities have shared the same fate. Tong and Bao's (1978) startling conclusion: "What merits our attention is the fact that to this day the production levels and living standards of the masses in quite a number of places are still lower than during the early postliberation period or during the War of Resistance against Japan."

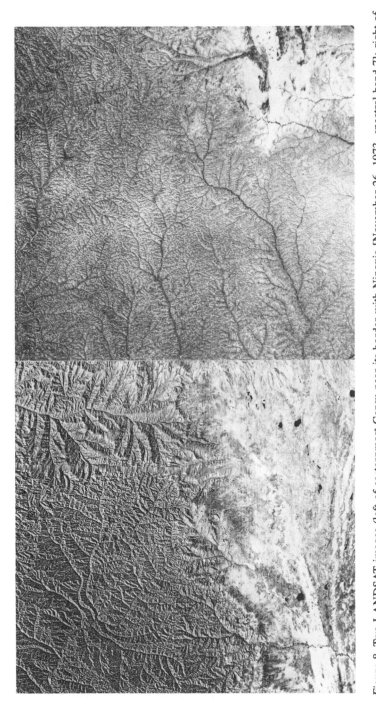

Figure 8. Two LANDSAT images (left of easternmost Gansu near its border with Ningxia [November 26, 1973, spectral band 7]; right of the Yan'an region in north central Shaanxi [August 19, 1978, spectral band 5]) show extremely heavy erosion in deep loess layers: the landscapes are just mazes of myriads of gullies and ridges; the terrain flattens only where the loess changes into semideserts and deserts. Both images were rotated 180° (i.e., north is at the top) to show the relief approximately (otherwise ridges and valleys would look reversed).

Few admissions among the recent Chinese revelations are so damning about the consequences of Maoist developmental policies.

Regionwide statistics show that the per ha grain yield is now only 1,275 kg (compared with the nationwide average of about 4,300 kg/ha), with a considerable portion of the land yielding only 225-375 kg per ha and, consequently, with food rations below subsistence levels—not even 150 kg per capita in 1977! The effects of the rapid erosion do not end with ruined fields and starvation harvests. Local precipitation is lowered as the ground moisture, and hence evaporation, declines, and unpredictable frosts become more common, making the selection of proper crop varieties for sustainable farming more difficult.

And eventually the tiny loess particles end up in the region's streams. The main rivers draining the Loess Plateau—the Wuding He, the Yan He, the Luo He, the Huan Jiang, the Jing He, and the Wei He—annually contribute hundreds of millions of tons of sand and silt to the Huang He, making it the siltiest river among the world's major streams; from the Wuding He basin alone 300 million tons enter the Huang He each year (Huang Yongshi 1981). Before the river enters the loess land it carries, on the average, just 2 kg of silt per m^3 of water; when it leaves the region, after its confluence with the Wei He near Laotongguan in Shaanxi, there are, on the average, about 35 kg of silt in every m^3, and the highest recorded content was 651 kg/m^3 (several Shaanxi rivers during peak stormflows carried slurries with more than 1.5 tons of silt per m^3!).

This process, elevating the Huang He's riverbed in its lower course and posing a permanent threat to the large populous areas of the North China Plain, has been greatly accelerated by the recent environmental destruction on the Loess Plateau. In the early 1950s the Huang He annually carried about 1.3 billion tons of silt through the Sanmenxia gorge (between Shanxi and Henan, just before the river enters the North China Plain). By the late 1970s this staggering mass rose to 1.6 billion tons, roughly a 25 percent increase in less than three decades (Tong and Bao 1978). This accelerated silting of the Huang He is one of the most dangerous and, at the same time, most intractable environmental problems facing China, and it has few equals, even in global terms.

Effective control of the river will be impossible without adequate control of the silt's source, that is, without a major environmental rehabilitation of the severely eroded loess region, which now contributes at least 1.1 billion tons to the river's silt load. The story of the

Sanmenxia dam is a costly lesson that illustrates this fact (Smil 1979a).

2.2.2 The Sanmenxia miscalculation

The grandiose plan for the complex utilization of the Huang He, approved in July 1955, had as its centerpiece the construction of 46 dams on the river to impound water for the generation of 110 billion kWh of electricity a year, to expand sevenfold the irrigated area in the basin, and to extend the navigable sections more than twentyfold (Berezina 1959). The dam at the gorge of the Three Gates— Sanmenxia, located in Henan approximately 120 km downstream from the rectangular bend near Laotongguan—was to be the largest and most important project of the original Huang He cascade.

Designs prepared with Soviet aid called for a 110 m-high and 839 m-long concrete gravity dam to create a 3,500 km^2 reservoir and to retain as much as 36 billion m^3 of water, one-and-a-half times the average annual volume of flow at the site. The project was to control 98 percent of the river's annual runoff, to cut the heaviest summer flood flow from 37,000 to between 6,000 and 8,000 m^2 per second, to provide irrigation for 2.6 million ha, and to allow the installation of 1,100 megawatts (MW) of generating capacity. The cost was a staggering sum for the China of the 1950s: approximately US$(1957) 700 million.

The planners were, of course, aware of the danger of rapid silting, but they thought that it could be controlled by a variety of measures. The control plan foresaw the mass construction of 215,000 works to protect the heads of gullies, 633,000 silt check dams, and 79,000 silt-precipitation dams as well as extensive afforestation, grassing, and terracing. The intent of the combined effect of all these measures was to extend the life of the reservoir to at least 50 to 70 years. As the experts confidently concluded, any "difficulties that may arise in power generation, irrigation, and navigation as a result of the silting up of the reservoir . . . will be comparatively easy to deal with" (Teng 1955).

This turned out to be—probably owing to both the faulty initial appraisal and the subsequently much higher rates of silting—an astonishing and potentially extremely dangerous miscalculation. Silting of the reservoir greatly exceeded the original projection; most of the incoming mud and sand was being retained in the lake, and this accumulation became especially worrisome as the deposits started to extend rapidly upstream to the Wei He above Laotongguan, elevating the inlet channel and seriously endangering the densely populated agricultural plain and the city of Xi'an, China's ancient capital and now her eleventh-largest urban area.

Of the reservoir's total storage (7.7 billion m³), 4.55 billion m³, or 59 percent, was silted up between 1958 and 1973; at such rates the reservoir would have been completely filled in just 24 years even without storing floodwaters every year. On two occasions when flood flows were intercepted by the dam as much as 90 percent and more of the silt was retained: between September 1960 and March 1962, 1.645 billion m³ of silt entered the storage, and 1.529 billion m³ (93 percent) was deposited; and between July and October 1964, of 2.724 billion m³ of silt carried by a heavy flood, 1.952 billion m³ (72 percent) stayed in the storage (Li Changzhe 1980). Clearly, with annual flood storage the reservoir's life would be just a few years.

Emergency adjustments were therefore necessary. Power generation had to be stopped because the lowest water intake for the turbines was still higher than the natural river level at the Wei He confluence; but the removal of the turbogenerators and abandonment of water storage did not solve the problem because spillway intakes were too high and the silt continued to accumulate. The only possible solution was to open large outlets at the bottom of the dam, lower the steel penstocks, and turn them into silt discharging tubes. This piercing of the dam tripled the discharge capacity, thus appreciably helping to move the silt downstream. Compared with the average annual storage capacity loss of 540 million m³ in 1960-1970 the current value is about 10 million m³, but all three key roles of the reservoir—storage of irrigation water, power generation, and above all, guarding against floods and prevention of damage to dikes downstream in Henan and Shandong—have been substantially compromised by the reconstruction. Because between July and October the floodwaters carry more than 80 percent of the annual silt load passing through Sanmenxia, summer flood impoundments had to be cut drastically to minimize silting, and water is now stored only between flood seasons when the river carries some 40 percent of its average annual flow but with only 10-20 percent of its silt load. Simply put, when the dam is needed most it can be now used least.

This miscarriage of Sanmenxia's mission is clear when winter and summer LANDSAT images of the reservoir are compared (Smil 1979a). On the one hand, winter (and spring) images show the gorge segment of the reservoir between the dam and the Huang He bend filled with relatively clear water, swelling in the least confined place to a width of more than 6 km and covering as much as approximately 250 km²; on the other hand, during the peak flood season the reservoir below Laotongguan shrinks to a narrow ribbon of heavily silted water with an area as small as 90 km² (Figure 9).

And Sanmenxia's predicament is repeated, on a smaller scale but often at faster rates, in reservoirs throughout the loess region. Some reports on impoundments in the Wei He basin mention losses of 20 percent of total storage capacity in just three years after completion, and a Shaanxi conference on antiflood work repeatedly issued warnings on blocked channels and silted reservoirs impairing flood drainage and control; provincewide, 512 million tons of sediment is deposited in reservoirs annually, corresponding to a staggering 15.3 percent loss of the total storage capacity (Li Chaobo 1980). The economic cost of turning Sanmenxia and hundreds of other reservoirs into hazardous storers of silt rather than useful water control projects is, needless to say, enormous. Sanmenxia now has an installed capacity of just 250 megawatts, instead of the planned 1,100 MW, and even so it must be idle most of the time, and its annual storage cost is estimated to be ¥30 million (Li Changzhe 1980).

The reconstructed version of Sanmenxia reservoir does little to eliminate the silting problem in Henan and Shandong where the Huang He, confined by dikes, flows 3 to 5 (in places up to 10) m above the surrounding countryside. Of the 1.6 billion tons of silt the river carries when it enters the North China Plain, some 400 million tons are deposited annually in its lower course through the two provinces, continuously raising the riverbed (the current rate is about 12 cm a year) and creating a major flood hazard. The ancient task of repairing and strengthening the dikes must continue. The magnitude of this effort— without which the North China Plain would become uninhabitable— can be illustrated by work done in Shandong between 1958 and 1976 (NCNA, March 18, 1977, *SWB* 921). More than 300 million m³ of earth and almost 7.3 million m³ of stone—virtually all of it dug or cut, lifted, moved, and placed by human hands alone—went into the dikes. The volume of earth and stone that went into raising and strengthening 1,800 km of the Huang He dikes in Henan and Shandong during the 30 years between 1949 and 1979 totaled 480 million m³, a result of annual water and spring reinforcement carried out by 300,000-400,000 people (Henan provincial broadcast, January 30, 1980, *SWB* 1072).

Sanmenxia's failure and the continued hazardous elevation of the Huang He's lower course can be alleviated only by controlling the source of the problem—by moderating the erosion rates on the Loess Plateau.

2.2.3 Controlling loess erosion

The seriousness of the environmental degradation on the Loess Plateau

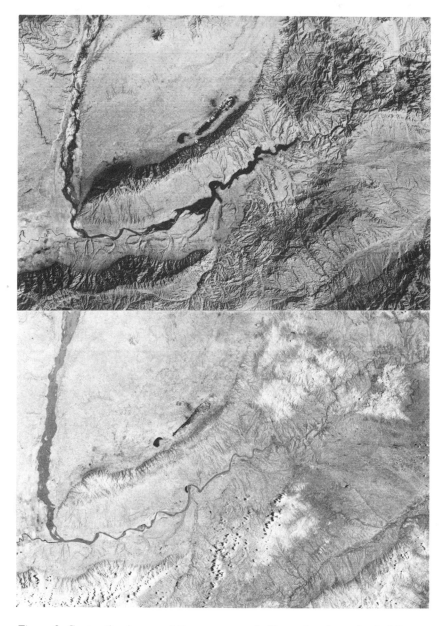

Figure 9. Contrasting images of Sanmen reservoir illustrating the project's failure. The top image, acquired on February 14, 1977, shows substantial storage of
clean water (dark color in spectral band 7) in the reservoir during low water
flows; when the high flows come, heavy silt loads make storage impossible, and
during the summer Sanmen reservoir is nearly empty, its waters silted (light
gray shade in the bottom image, acquired on July 13, 1976).

and its dangerous downstream consequences have led to increased scientific and public policy concerns and to proposals for viable long-range strategies. Since 1973, repeated high-level meetings have put forward plans to ameliorate the destruction by extensive application of traditional remedies: planting trees, planting grass, and terracing. A gathering in Xi'an in March 1979 proposed to partition the whole plateau into four development zones, each stressing a different land use but still retaining a considerable measure of field cultivation even outside the specialized agricultural region.

This region, concentrated on grains, cotton, and edible oil production, would include northern Shanxi, western Gansu, and central Shaanxi as far north as southern Yan'an Municipality. The forestry and animal husbandry region would cover the hills and gullies of southern Gansu, southern Ningxia, and northwestern Shaanxi north of Yan'an; here the planting of trees and grazing herbages would have priority, with some grain cultivation along the rivers and on the terraced riverbanks. Central Gansu, southern Ningxia, northwestern Shanxi, northern Yulin Prefecture, and some parts of Nei Monggol would specialize in animal husbandry while also planting windbreaks and grazing forests as barriers against further erosion. Finally, the forestry region would embrace higher-lying areas in the counties around Ziwu, Long, Huanglong (Shaanxi); Lao, Jiao, Liupan (Gansu and Ningxia); and the Lüliang Mountains (Shanxi)(Xinhua, March 20, 1979, *SWB* 1026).

Tong Dalin and Bao Tong (1978) were the first influential decision-makers to argue persuasively for a more radical and ecologically appropriate approach: in the long run most of the area is not suitable for field crops, and hence an appreciable portion of the farmland should be reconverted to pastures and forests that would not only bring higher economic returns but also safeguard the Huang He's lower course against further rapid rising.

Tong Dalin (1980) singled out the region's large fossil fuel (especially coal) and hydroenergy resources and its great potential for animal grazing as the two essential advantages, and large-scale planting of pasture plants (above all perennial legumes), shrubs, forests, and fruit trees and construction of dams and water conservancy projects as the key preconditions for success in alleviating the plateau's current misery. Sun Hua of the Northwest Agricultural College, quoted by Tong (1980), argued that the plateau with its countless hills and slopes could support very extensive orchards, including red dates and grapes in

Ningxia and northern Shaanxi, olives and citrus fruit in the southern part of Shaanxi, and apples in Gansu. Planting of vigorous bush fruit trees and vines, such as raspberries, gooseberries, and pomegranates, should also be encouraged.

Tong and Bao (1978) illustrate the benefits of a grazing-forestry orientation with two cases, one historical, the other recent. They note that although in the course of the more than 2,100 years from the Qin dynasty to 1950, 973 major dike breaches occurred in the lower course of the Huang He, there were only two major breaches during the 580 years from Wang Mang (AD 9-23) to the beginnings of the Sui dynasty (581-618), a time when the Loess Plateau was primarily grazing area with a few crop fields.

Their contemporary example cites the benefits brought about by changes in Gaoxigou Village of Mizhi County in northern Shaanxi, whose farmland used to yield starvation levels of around 200 kg of grain per ha. From the late 1950s on they cut the cropland by two-thirds (increasing the total yield substantially) and concentrated on planting grasses and trees. A record rainstorm in the summer of 1978 (which brought 300 mm, or as much as the total precipitation in 1977) washed away the topsoil of new fields into reservoirs in neighboring villages, but Gaoxigou emerged unscathed. Although the authors may be indulging in some hyperbole when they describe "crystal-clear-water streams" around the village, there is little doubt that very substantial micro- and meso-scale changes can be effected by protective plantings.

The Gaoxigou example is wholly consistent with the measurements made by the Northwest Water and Soil Conservancy Bureau in 1973 when the total rainfall in Shaanxi averaged 346 mm: the exposed fallow land lost 6,750 kg of soil per ha, and farmland erosion reached about half of that value (3,570 kg/ha)—but on the grasslands only 93 kg was lost, and the water erosion in forested area carried away a mere 60 kg of topsoil—two orders of magnitude less than on the fallow land (of course, during prolonged summer droughts, much cropland turns into *de facto* barren land as the plants wither away!).

Afforestation may often be difficult, however, owing as much to the harshness of the area as to the lack of experience (see section 2.1.1 for more details). Many more people in the area know how to grow grazing herbages—different grasses, alfalfa, sweet clover—and that is why Shi Shan (1980) of the Support Agriculture Office of the Chinese Academy of Sciences made a proposal for a major conversion of crop fields to pastures. He estimates that 15 kg of seed and a month of work are needed to plant one ha of new pasture, which should be, from the third year of growth, sufficient to feed 15 sheep or 600-750 rabbits. After 8 years the pastures have to be reseeded.

The arguments advanced by Tong, Bao, and Shi have not been universally accepted. Stubborn advocates of the grain-first policy maintained that only the land in excess of 2 or 3 *mu* of grainfields per capita capable of providing 400-500 kg/capita of food grain should eventually be converted to pastures or afforested. Simply put, as long as there is no local grain self-sufficiency, it would be impossible to develop animal husbandry or to afforest. What a fine example of putting abstract, ideologically influenced guidelines ahead of simple economic realities and inescapable environmental imperatives! Naturally, in the short run the conversion may (but not at all necessarily) mean the loss of some foodgrain—but in return the country would gain valuable forest and animal products, much needed wood and meat, plus, a no less critical consideration, downstream protection and alleviation of the Huang He's silting.

By 1980 the rational approaches respecting natural conditions and pointing to inevitable specialization finally gained the lead. They were supported by hundreds of local studies and scientific reports, and in April 1980 a Xi'an symposium, organized by the State Scientific and Technological Commission and the Chinese Academy of Sciences, reached, after an emotional debate, a consensus on turning the eroded loess areas into pastures and woodlands (Xinhua, April 16, 1980, *SWB* 1080). Fourteen counties were selected as pilot areas for implementation of extensive environmental conservation programs to be executed with the state's financial and technical help. One of the major innovations of this program is aerial sowing of forage grasses, which is to be performed yearly over thousands of ha of eroded slopes.

New studies of the erosion process and river silting should be also helpful in the control effort. For example, Chen Yongzong (1976) discovered that statistically the most important determinant of the erosion rate is the slope gradient rather than the intensity of rainfall or the depth of runoff. In practical terms this means that before grassing or planting young trees an effort should be made to change the slope gradient to greatly lessen the erosion. Qian Ning, after analyzing the records of 103 Huang He floods between 1952 and 1960 and between 1969 and 1978, concluded that most of the silt consisting of coarse particles originated in two areas totaling 100,000 km² along the river's course through Shaanxi, Nei Monggol, and Shanxi. This finding allows the concentration of the anti-erosion effort to be more specific and more highly effective (NCNA, March 29, 1980, *SWB* 1077).

As with the giant northern tree shelterbelt, at least 5 to 10 years will be needed before the pace and the success of the conversion and control program can be appraised: its direction is undoubtedly correct; its execution will depend not only on the state's sustained financial and professional aid but equally as much on the maintenance of the newly introduced private incentives, which make the conversion to woodland and grazing very appealing from the monetary viewpoint alone. Another campaign condemning a private woodlot on a slope beyond a peasant's house, two scores of rabbits in cages in his courtyards, and a dozen sheep in a pasture as the "last vestiges of capitalism" and the bold new program will go the way of Shaanxi's topsoil in a July thunderstorm.

As long as the Huang He receives large amounts of silt from the Loess Plateau, new ways will also have to be found to control the changes in the river's delta in the Bo Hai. Currently the sediment adds an average of 23 km² annually, and during the years 1855-1972 the coastal zone (there is no sharp delimitation between the silty shallows and the low-lying sedimentation deposits) advanced seaward at a rate of 150-420 m a year (Figure 10). Lengthening of the estuary decreases flow velocity and aggravates silting, and the addition of new land thus necessitates extending the protective dikes about 40 km and digging new channels to control the water and silt movement (NCNA, March 29, 1980, *SWB* 1077).

Obviously, there are no easy, shortcut solutions to China's loess erosion and Huang He silting. Filling countless gullies, building small dams on streams to check the silt flow, leveling fields, and terracing slopes are essential steps in cutting down the rapid soil erosion, and the Chinese are both experienced and skillful in these endeavors. The conversion of fields to grazing should also prove relatively uncomplicated, although grassing on steeper slopes will be more difficult to accomplish. Afforestation is the critical step—and the most difficult: survival in the arid climate with pronounced hot-cold fluctuations and months-long dry spells has been appallingly low, and a great deal of research and testing will have to be done on the selection, planting, and management of the most suitable tree and shrub species.

I believe that loess erosion is one of the most intractable environmental problems, even in global terms, and it will demand much

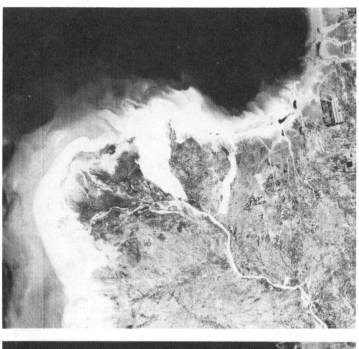

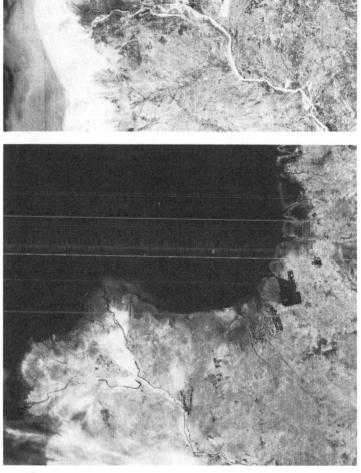

Figure 10. The Huang He's mouth during Cean winter-spring flow (left image, May 14, 1978) and heavy silted summer flow (right, August 31, 1976). During low water months the river channel is narrow, the stream relatively clear (thin black lines at left); during flood months the stream is swollen and full of silt: the white color of silt in the right image spills far from the shore into the Bohai Bay.

greater and deeper attention than it has been given since 1949. Such attention, costly and only slowly rewarding, is absolutely necessary not only to ameliorate the environmental degradation in the region itself, and thus to improve the meager livelihood of its nearly 50 million inhabitants, but also to protect the low-lying plain in Henan and Shandong from the excessive silt accumulation that is still raising the river's yellow waters above land inhabited and tilled by more than 50 million peasants.

2.2.4 Spreading erosion

Serious erosion and silting is far from limited to the Loess Plateau and the middle and lower Huang He: it now blankets 1.5 million km², or about 15 percent of all China (Ma and Chang 1980). In the Huang He's upper course, the Longyangxia hydroelectric project in Qinghai, China's second largest hydro powerplant, is now threatened by rapid wind erosion (Li Wei 1981). Conversion of grasslands and hilly forest land to grainfields raised erosion rates from Heilongjiang in the northeast to Yunnan in the southwest. But certainly the most disquieting recent news regarding erosion outside the Loess Plateau has been the disclosures of the magnitude of the problem in the Chang Jiang basin.

There, large-scale deforestation, especially during the 1970's, has been responsible for rapid topsoil losses (in Jiangxi as much as 4 cm a year), a decline in crop yields (in parts of Hunan cereal harvests are down to just 750 kg per ha), and widespread stream and reservoir silting. The following details on the basin's erosion and silting problems are taken from recent papers by Guo Tingfu (1980), Li Changzhe (1980), Liu Haifeng (1980), Wang and Chen (1981), Huang Yongshi (1981), and Wang Ganmei (1981).

Serious soil erosion now affects 360,000 km² in the Chang Jiang basin, or about 20 percent of its 1.8 million km² area, with 2.4 billion tons of topsoil eroded every year, 50 percent more than in the Huang He watershed. In the Jinsha Jiang section of the basin in Yunnan, erosion rose from 130 million tons in 1958 to 290 million tons in 1974 (Wang and Zhou 1981). Sichuan and Guizhou formerly had low erosion rates, but the recent increases resulting from deforestation have been rapid. In the basins of three Sichuan rivers—Jialing Jiang, Tuo Jiang, and Fu Jiang—the erosion is extremely serious, with annual losses of over 250 million tons, the equivalent of a 12-cm-thick topsoil layer over 100,000 ha of farmland. Water erosion in the hilly and mountainous terrain of the deforested regions along the river's upper course is compounded by gravitational erosion (mud and rock flow frequently stripping the thin soils to bedrock). In Guizhou many locations now have barren rock patches on badly eroded slopes; erosion cones and deposits cover the foothills and farmlands and make the cultivation of previously good soils impossible. In this sense erosion in the mountainous region of the Chang Jiang basin is much worse than on the Loess Plateau, where even severe erosion still usually leaves thick layers of loess for eventual revegetation.

Most of the eroded soil is deposited in the rivers and lakes, continuously elevating their beds, blocking their outlets, lowering their storage capacity, and increasing the dangers of severe flooding. Dongting Hu in Hunan, a major regulating water body in the basin, lost over 1,600 km^2 to heavy silting, and it now measures only little more than 2,700 km^2; Poyang Hu, China's largest freshwater lake, in Jiangxi, now contains 29 percent more sediment than it did in the 1950s.

In flood-prone Hubei Province 178 reservoirs in Huanggang District lose 6 million m^3 of storage capacity each year to silting, many small reservoirs had to be abandoned after just two or three years, and some larger hydroelectric stations had to be taken partially out of operation. A recent survey of 33 large and medium-size storages in the basin revealed that 16 are already more than half filled with silt, and the average useful life will not surpass 13 years. Even Danjiangkou, China's most voluminous reservoir on the Han Shui in Hubei, is silting rapidly: 115 million tons of mud and sand are now entering the storage each year, and in just over a decade it lost 580 million m^3, or one-seventh of its total capacity. And there are fears that the useful life of the Gezhouba hydroproject, China's largest power station, now under construction on the Chang Jiang in Hubei, will be considerably shortened (see section 3.2.1 for details).

Silt content of seven other major rivers in the basin increased by 23 percent in the years 1966-1975 compared with the 1956-1965 level, and shallow waters have made navigation impossible on 977 km in Jiangxi Province since 1957, and on 6,455 km of 214 rivers in Hubei since 1960. During the more frequent flooding, waters carrying sand and pebbles deposit this debris on the farmland or scour the fields. In Xishui County near Wuhan, one-seventh of all arable land has been thus affected. In terms of fertility losses, the topsoil currently eroded in the Chang Jiang basin contains nitrogen equivalent to the output of 50 medium-size (500,000 tons a year) fertilizer factories. And there is a mounting direct human and economic toll as the floods, aggravated by the losses of water retention in forests and of storage capacity in lakes, reservoirs and rivers, appear to become ever more destructive. There can be little doubt that the devastating Sichuan flooding in the summer of 1981, in which 15 million people were affected and when the peak flow recorded in Chongqing was the highest since 1949, was intensified by the massive deforestation and erosion in the Chang Jiang basin (see also section 2.1.3).

Of course, the Chang Jiang is still much less turbid than the Huang He: normal suspended loads of the two rivers are, respectively, just around 1 kg/m³ and over 30 kg/m³, but this large difference is owing to the Chang Jiang's much larger water flow (see section 3.2.1). In absolute terms the difference is now only 2.5-fold (640 vs 1,600 million tons), and the rapid increases of the Chang Jiang's silt load have led many Chinese scientists to dramatize the worsening situation by stating that the river is becoming a second Huang He; even the premier, Zhao Ziyang, has picked up the phrase in his exhortations for accelerated afforestation.

Afforestation provides the only practical solution, and interesting comparisons published by Li Changzhe (1980) show how effective it can be. During a torrential rain in August 1975 parts of southern Henan received 800-1,000 mm in just three days, and, on the one hand, two reservoirs in the area with only 20 percent forest cover were breached, exacerbating the downstream flooding; on the other hand, two nearby reservoirs, in whose basins 80 percent of the land was forest-covered, survived the flood undamaged. Long-term comparison of silting rates shows that in the former case 20 cm of silt a year (and up to 40) are deposited on the bottom; in the latter case the new layer is mere 1.5 mm, a 133-fold difference!

Another outstanding illustration of the anti-erosion effectiveness of forests is Fengman reservoir on the Songhua Jiang (Sungari River) in Liaoning. Surrounded by forests, in 27 years it lost only 142 million m³, or a mere 1.3 percent of its 10.78 billion m³ storage capacity; at that rate, therefore, even after 1,000 years it would be only half silted. In this case, however, an argument can be made that the Changbai Shan surrounding the reservoir are covered with natural climax forests (though cut over) and that new plantings would be far from so effective. Generally this is true in the short term, but in just a few decades such plantings can afford excellent anti-erosion protection, especially in the south where a variety of fast-growing trees can be used. In the 23 years since the construction of Ting Jiang reservoir in Fujian, 85 percent of the barren land surrounding the storage was afforested, and the annual silting rate is now a mere fraction of a percent of the total volume (Li Changzhe 1980).

Urgent and extensive action is needed in virtually every region of the country to moderate the rapid erosion rates. Nationwide figures are quite alarming: topsoil loss is now at least 5 billion tons per year, and with this mass go millions of tons of principal macronutrients, nitrogen, phosphorus, and potassium, as well as precious micronutrients—China's annual synthetic fertilizer production provides less soil nutrition than that lost to erosion! And if only larger reservoirs (over one million m^3 storage capacity) are counted, China has recently been adding 260 million m^3 of new water storage each year—but 80 million m^3 per year have been lost to silting (Qian Ning et al. 1980).

2.3 Desertification

In arid lands everywhere, erosion is one of the principal causes of desertification, a severe environmental degradation affecting globally nearly 50 million km^2 on all continents (about 35 percent of this total is in Asia) and directly influencing the lives of more than 600 million people. In the 1970s there was concentrated research and public attention when this problem was brought into worldwide focus by the Sahelian drought of 1968-1974, and culminated in the United Nations' Desertification Conference in 1977 (United Nations 1977). The general consensus blames poor land management rather than climatic changes as the principal cause of desertification, and the southerly advance of China's large interior deserts provides clear support for this view.

China's deserts, extending over an area of 1,095,000 km^2 (about 11.4 percent of the total territory), are overwhelmingly concentrated in the Northwest and North, west of 106°E (Figure 11, also Appendix A.4.c, A.5.a). Takla Makan, with 327,000 km^2, by far the largest, is made up mostly of huge composite dunes usually 100-150 m high. Nationwide, the sandy deserts, including the true *gobis* as well as sand dune areas in the desert steppe and steppe zones, constitute 59 percent of the total; the rest is largely gravel-covered (Department of Desert Research 1978). Most Chinese deserts receive less than 200 m of precipitation annually, while evaporation typically ranges between 3,500 and 4,000 mm, and aridity indexes, generally above 4.0, reach as high as 20-60 in the Tarim Basin. Only in the smaller deserts and sandy

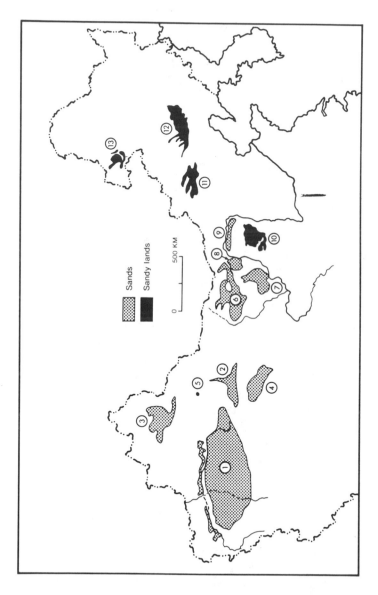

Figure 11. The deserts of North China are numbered as follows: 1. Takla Makan Shamo, 2. Kumutage Shamo, 3. Gurbantunggut Shamo, 4. Qaidam Shamo, 5. Turpan Shamo, 6. Badain Jaran Shamo, 7. Tengger Shamo, 8. Ulan Buh Shamo, 9. Hobq Shamo, 10. Mu Us Shadi, 11. Ortindag Shadi, 12. Horqin Shadi, 13. Hulun Buir Shadi. Map according to Lanzhou Institute of Desert Research (1979).

lands of the Northeast does the summer monsoon bring up to 450 mm of rain and keep the aridity index between 1.5 and 4.0. The survival of grasslands bordering these deserts is thus precarious even without human interference, and anthropogenically induced desertification of northern China is an ancient phenomenon, with large parts of Mu Us Shamo in Nei Monggol and nearly all of Horqin sandy land in Jilin as the two most extensive examples of the advance. Both areas used to be fairly rich grasslands, the former with rainfall in excess of 400 mm and with marshes and thickets in sheltered areas. Gradual reclamation of grasslands for fields, tree felling, and overgrazing destroyed the stabilizing plant cover and the sands began to shift: a 60 km wide belt along the Great Wall between Shaanxi and Nei Monggol and the large sandy stretches in the bend of the Xiliao He (Xiliao River) have been so desertified over the past 200 years.

The very same processes have accelerated since 1949: like spreading erosion, most of China's current desertification can be clearly ascribed to human actions, above all to widespread and indiscriminate reclamation for grainfields as well as to frequent overgrazing and tree felling. Between 1949 and 1980 about 65,000 km² (an area roughly equivalent to twice the size of Belgium and Luxembourg) in 207 counties in 11 provinces was desertified, and 91 percent of this large loss was caused by improper land use; an additional 160,000 km² is in danger of desertification (Ma and Chang 1980; Wang Lichao 1981; Wen and Liu 1981). The country's extensive northern and northwestern grasslands bordering the large interior deserts of Mongolia, Ningxia, Gansu, and Xinjiang have suffered most heavily. Nei Monggol offers the most drastic examples. Of the region's 86 banners and counties, 66 are affected by desertification, and windblown sand now encircles 33,000 km² of farms and grasslands (Ma Wenyuan 1980). In the Ih Ju league 12,000 km² of grasslands turned sandy between 1957 and 1972, and during the late 1970s more than 2,000 km² became sandy each year. Forty percent of the Ju Ud league's 47,000 km² of grasslands has become sandy. Similar widespread losses have occurred in Ulanqab and Xilin Gol leagues.

Still, the losses may seem minor compared with the nearly 2.87 million km² of true grasslands (of which 2.2 million km² could be used for pasture) in the semi-arid northern regions. However, only 15 percent of this total is abundant long-grass meadows, and while outright desertification destroyed only some 65,000 km², according to one source about 460,000 km² of pastures has qualitatively degenerated—

and the statistics revealed at a 1979 national conference on grassland development show that more than one-quarter of China's usable grasslands, that is, at least 550,000 km², has deteriorated owing mostly to desertification or alkalization (Xinhua, July 29, 1979, *SWB* 1044).

The effects are predictable. First, the advancing desertification cuts down both the quantity and quality of the grass available for grazing and drastically lowers the amount of hay for winter feeding. Consequently, in the northwestern part of China as much as 2 ha of pasture are needed to support a single sheep (Ma Wenyuan 1980), and large numbers of cattle die not only of cold but of plain hunger, a harsh reality best illustrated by the fact that animals dying as a result of chronic spring shortages of fodder far surpass the number of cattle delivered to the state by herdsmen (Xinhua, July 29, 1979, *SWB* 1044). The resulting decline of cattle herding in Nei Monggol (although not all of the drop can be ascribed to desertification!) is shown by the published growth rates: while between 1949 and 1958 animal husbandry output rose by an average 9.2 percent a year, the rate dropped to 2.9 percent between 1959 and 1969, and average animal production *decreases* of 0.7 percent prevailed between 1970 and 1978 (Xinhua, December 3, 1978, *SWB* 1018).

Second, when the formerly grass-protected, water-retaining surfaces become barren, the frequency of droughts increases and the strong anticyclonic winds cause more frequent sandstorms, further expanding the desert area. Beijing's Meteorological Observatory recorded an average of three sandstorm days a year in the early 1950s (Watts 1969); during the 1960s the number rose to 17; in the years 1971-78 the mean frequency was 20.5 days annually (Anonymous 1979b); and between 1974 and 1980 it reached 26 days (NCNA, July 10, 1981, *JPRS* 78623).

Third, the reclaimed fields have suffered from extensive erosion and evaporation, with grain yields quickly deteriorating. Thus, in spite of Nei Monggol's large-scale reclamation of arable land—each person now has 0.355 ha compared with the nationwide average of 0.106 ha —per capita grain availability declined considerably in comparison with the mid-1950s, and the region's average cereal yield is now less than 1,500 kg per ha, a mere one-third of the all-China figure (Hu 1981).

A long overdue restitution is now under way: further conversion of grasslands into fields has been banned; the orthodox, and unachievable, requirements of local grain self-sufficiency have been dropped; animal husbandry enjoys its former priority, and an effort is being made to rationalize its operations; private woodlots on desert fringes are encouraged; and new research centers have been set up to study the techniques of controlling the drifting sands. One of these new centers, at Dongsheng in the Ih Ju league, will concentrate on the Mu Us Shamo and Hobq Shamo in the Ordos Bend, while the Dengkou station will work on the Ulan Buh Shamo west of the Huang He. The Desert Research Society of the Institute of Geography was established in October 1980 (Hou Renzhi, honorary president, Zhu Zhenda, president), and several scholarly journals are now being published.

Research and experiments conducted in many of China's desert areas have selected the most suitable trees and established many effective sand-controlling techniques (Department of Desert Research 1978). For planting inside or on the fringes of oases as well as for shelterbelts, the following trees and shrubs have the most widespread utility: various poplars (*Populus cupidata, bolleana, diversifolia, simonii, nigra*), willows, (*Salix matsudana, cheilophila, flavida, microstachya*), tamarisks (*Tamarix chinensis, ramosissima*), saksaul (*Haloxylon ammodendron*), and Russian olive (*Eleagnus angustifolia*). Approaches found useful for controlling the shifting sands include a variety of fringe shelterbelts, combined tree-shrub-grass structures, and the establishment of sheltered enclosures (so called "grassy *kulums*") to protect pastures.

By far the most important recent development in China's attempts to control desertification is the start of work on a huge forest shelterbelt system which is to eventually span some 4,000 km. The project was approved by the State Council in 1978, and it is intended to be a key strategic measure to check advancing desertification and to improve the conditions for farming and animal husbandry. The shelterbelt is to extend over three northern areas (hence its Chinese name *san bei*): the Northwest, the northern part of North China, and the western part of the Northeast. A total of 324 counties (or banners) in Xinjiang, Qinghai, Gansu, Ningxia, Nei Monggol, north Shaanxi, northwest Shanxi, the Bashang area of northern Hebei, and in the western parts of Liaoning, Jilin, and Heilongjiang will be involved. Their combined area is about 2.6 million km² (nearly one-quarter of China's territory), of which almost half is deserts, and more than 200 counties in the combined area with 13.3 million ha of farmland and pastures are being damaged by sand. The livelihood of 44 million peasants in the area is very poor, with low grain rations, insufficient fuel, and miserable housing.

The first stage of what the Chinese call the "great green wall" is to be completed by 1985. About 5.3 million ha of trees are supposed to be planted to increase the forest coverage of the desert fringe areas from the present 4 to about 10 percent and to give what the Chinese term "initial protection" to 13 million ha of farmland and pastures (Xinhua, June 1, 1979, *SWB* 1041). Existing forests and shelterbelts will be incorporated into the project which, the Ministry of Forestry urges, should be carried out through measures "suitable to local conditions" without "practicing formalism or demanding uniformity in everything" (Xinhua, June 7, 1979, *SWB* 1041).

These are encouraging guidelines insofar as in the past large afforestation campaigns were too often implemented in a simplistic manner by planting one tree species regardless of its suitability for local conditions. The planting of bushes and grasses is also an important part of the effort, as is the strengthened protection of existing vegetation to be enforced by special units of forest police and by new forestry courts set up in the *san bei* area (Xinhua, June 17, 1980, *SWB* 1100). Even in the best of circumstances such a grandiose undertaking would not be easy to manage and to bring to a reasonably effective conclusion. To bring about visible positive results in just a matter of years in the harsh environment where even the existing trees have difficulty surviving would rank among the most notable successes in environmental improvement anywhere. Initial claims of sapling cultivation and tree planting have been most encouraging, but only by the end of this decade will we be able to judge the extent of the accomplishment.

2.4 Reclamation of lakes

The grain-first policy destroyed, above all, many forests and grasslands, but it also seriously affected the country's aquacultural resources. Fresh-water fishing and breeding of aquatic species are ancient Chinese traditions, with the first comprehensive instructions, by Fan Li, preserved from the year 473 BC, and with a wide variety of practices (Gu 1975; FAO 1977a; Ryther 1979; Pritchard 1980). Over 500 fish species reside in China's fresh waters, and although at least 200 are suitable for human consumption, the catch is dominated by four cyprinid species (family fish or Chinese carps): grass (*Ctenopharyngodon idella*), black (*Mylopharyngodon piceus*), silver (*Hypophthalmichthys molitrix*), and bighead (*Aristichthys nobilis*) carps. Other carps, including the golden (*Carassius auratus*) and the common carp (*Cyprinus carpio*) and shads, perches, breams, and *tilapia* are also widely bred, as are several crustaceans and water plants, above all lotus (*Nelumbium speciosum*), water chestnut (*Trapa natans*), and prickly water lily (*Euryale ferox*).

These traditions and tastes were carried on after the establishment of the PRC, and in the late 1950s no less than two-fifths of the nation's aquatic harvest came from inland waters, with 70 percent supplied by natural catches and 30 percent by aquaculture (Cong 1979). Since then the irrational Maoist policy of "planting crops in the middle of lakes and on the tops of mountains" has drastically reduced the size of many of those natural water bodies that were best suited to intensive aquaculture. There have been other damaging effects: blocking of migration routes by dams and locks while failing to provide special passages or installing improper fish ladders (in the Chang Jiang basin, over 50 large lakes have had their outlets to the river cut); growing urban, industrial, and farm pollution (see section 4.2); as well as appalling overfishing, including dynamiting and poisoning. Most crippling, however, has been the massive reclamation of lakes and ponds.

Examples from all around the country abound. In Northern Jiangxi's Poyang Hu, China's largest fresh-water lake (originally 565,000 ha), 331 embankments were built during the 1970s to reclaim close to 90,000 ha of fields, and the area devoted to aquaculture shrank by half, to just 26,000 ha; Dongting Hu in northern Hunan was, with 435,000 ha, China's second largest fresh-water lake, but land reclamation reduced its surface to only 282,000 ha (see also Appendix A.5.b); half-moon-shaped Tai Hu in Jiangsu was diminished by more than 10 percent to 213,000 ha (Cong 1979). Even in arid Nei Monggol where any water surface is precious, Ulansuhai Nur was reduced to 22,000 ha, or only one-third its original area (Tian and Liu 1979). Shanghai Municipality lost 30 percent of its fish breeding area, and in Zhejiang Province nearly 3,000 ha of fish ponds were turned into fields. But Hubei, the proverbial "province of a thousand lakes," has been affected most of all: of its 1,056 lakes larger than 1,000 *mu* (66.6 ha) less than 400 remain, and the total provincial lake water surface dropped by 75 percent between 1949 and 1978 (Hu and Tian 1981). Major lakes that completely or largely disappeared in eastern Hubei include Chen Hu, Diaocha Hu, Xi Hu, and Bei Hu; Hong Hu was reduced to 40,000 ha, or half its original size, and much of the remainder is so shallow that people can wade across (Figures 12 and 13). For China as a whole incomplete statistics for 1949-1978 show a loss of over 20 million *mu*,

Figure 12. This outline map shows the Chang Jiang lakeland around Wuhan in eastern Hubei as it appeared about fifty years ago. The map was compiled from two 1:1 million sheets (NH-49 and NH-50) published by the U.S. War Office in 1943 and 1946.

or at least 1.33 million ha, of waters suitable for inland fishery (Xinhua, March 17, 1979, *SWB* 1026).

The effects have been predictable. The natural inland catch in 1978 was only half of that in 1954, and it constituted only 30 percent of the total fresh-water harvest (compared with 70 percent in the 1950s). In spite of the massive extension of reservoirs (for hundreds of large and tens of thousands of small hydrostations as well as for irrigation) and pond breeding, the total fresh-water harvest was down from 40 percent of the aggregate aquatic output in 1959 to just 23 percent in 1978 (Xinhua, April 11, 1979, *SWB* 1030). In some leading fresh-water fishery provinces and counties the decline was even more precipitous.

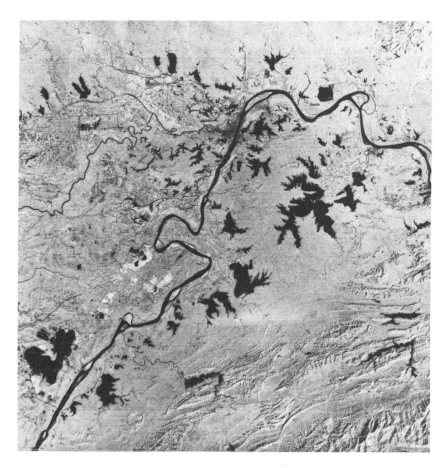

Figure 13. In October 1978, when this LANDSAT image was scanned over the same area as Figure 12, Hubei's lake surfaces had been drastically reduced. Comparison of the two figures clearly shows the extent of the lake reclamation, and the LANDSAT image contains many details of drainage canals and newly established fields on the bottoms of former lakes.

Guangdong's annual catch went from 20,000 tons in 1966 to just 10,000 tons in 1978; the output of Hong Hu County in Hubei fell 60 percent between 1975 and 1978 (NCNA, December 24, 1979, *SWB* 1064). Fresh fish, a traditional delicacy enlivening an overwhelmingly vegetarian diet, has become scarce even in the locations previously famous for their rich catches. In Wuxi Municipality on the shores of Tai Hu, in the very midst of Jiangsu's "rice and fish country," annual consumption of fresh-water fish amounted to just 4.5 kg per capita per year (Xinhua, March 1, 1978, *SWB* 979). In 1979 in the Zhu Jiang

(Pearl River) delta, and in Chang Jiang lakeland Xinhua correspondents often heard people saying that "it is now very difficult to get fish to eat" (NCNA, December 24, 1979, *SWB* 1064). In Hubei the provincial annual average of fresh fish consumption per capita stood at only 2.5 kg in 1979 (Hubei provincial broadcast, April 2, 1979, *SWB* 1030). And China's total fresh-water fish output of 1.11 million tons in 1979 translated into a nationwide average of a mere 1.1 kg per capita (Xinhua, November 14, 1980, *SWB* 1110)—this in a country with a chronically precarious food balance where fish offers perhaps the most appropriate opportunity to increase the consumption of essential high quality protein.

Naturally, not only fish catches were lost: the harvests of water plants for food, waterweeds for fertilizer and feed, and reeds for various manufactures have also declined substantially. For example, in Nei Monggol's Ulansuhai Nur reed cuttings plummeted from 20-25,000 tons annually to a mere 3,400 tons (Tian and Liu 1979). And, most ironically, after freshwater breeding, spawning, and feeding grounds were destroyed truly *en masse*, a large part of the reclaimed land surrounding the lakes is now reported to be wasted and empty, unsuitable for cropping after a few harvests. But the water surfaces are gone, and with them their moderating influence on local climate, above all on the extension of the frostfree period (a critical consideration in all colder double-cropping regions of populous eastern China), and their floodwater retention capabilities. And it is also beyond any doubt that the recent floods in the Chang Jiang valley were intensified by the severe loss of lake storages there.

The costly irrationality of all this is striking. On the one hand, there is the waste of much heavy labor, investment, and scarce materials (iron, cement) for massive reclamation of land from waters that could yield valuable protein, regulate water supplies, and moderate local climate; on the other hand, there is the cultivation of rice or wheat in the newly reclaimed land with often very low yields, and not infrequently for just a short time. On the one hand, there is the destruction of natural water surfaces and freshwater fisheries; on the other hand, there are continuing mass campaigns to build more water reservoirs, to dig up new fish ponds, and to set up new aquatic breeding centers. Indeed, it is the perfect image of towering inconsistencies and pervasive mismanagement of natural resources so characteristic of China for the past few decades.

Nevertheless, given the proper incentives and conditions, the potential for China's aquaculture is undoubtedly impressive. The country's lakes, rivers, reservoirs, and ponds cover 26.7 million ha (lakes alone account for more than 6 million ha), of which at least 5 million ha could be used for fish breeding but only 48 percent of which is so used (Xinhua, April 15, 1979, *SWB* 1033). The opportunities are especially favorable in more than 80,000 reservoirs, but only less than two-thirds of their 2 million ha is now being used for aquaculture, and the average yield has been very low, a mere 85 kg per ha (Xiao Peng 1981). In contrast, the average yield in lakes is about 140 kg per ha, and in 7,400 ha of China's extensive fish ponds it was about 1,000 kg per ha in 1979 (NCNA, January 4, 1980, *SWB* 1066). Yields at Hubei's Hong Hu used to be around 4,000 kg, *Tilapia* bred in southern lakes could bring up to 18,000 kg, and raising fish in nets cast into reservoirs and lakes can provide (of course, only from small areas) harvests as high as 70 tons per ha (NCNA, December 24, 1979, *SWB* 1064). Careful management, scientific approaches, and priority attention to pond cultures could thus bring impressive nutritional benefits, with up to 5 million tons of fresh fish produced annually (Cong 1981).

What is being done to stop the further destruction of inland water surfaces? For one thing, new regulations governing the breeding and protection of aquatic resources, issued on February 10, 1979, by the State Council, do not explicitly forbid any new conversions but prescribe that "in reclaiming land from sea or lakes, it is necessary to make overall and systematic arrangements to ensure that aquatic resources are not damaged" (Xinhua, March 27, 1979, *SWB* 1030). Perhaps even more important is the disappearance of bureaucratic pressure to convert to grainfields, as most of the reclamation arose from the central directives rather than from the wishes of local peasants. As a result, in some areas much of the reclaimed land was reflooded, and with the return to diversified farming most villages traditionally specializing in aquaculture have made a strong comeback.

Incomplete statistics for 1980 show an increase of 200,000 ha in fresh-water fishing grounds and about an 8 percent growth in total catch (NCNA, November 15, 1980, *SWB* 1110). In Hubei the increases were stronger: 16 percent more fish caught, 18 percent more fish fry bred (Hubei provincial broadcast, September 18, 1980, *SWB* 1110). For 1981, catches were expected to be at least 10 percent higher than in 1980, and in most provinces, peasants are now allowed to dig fish ponds on their private plots, an opportunity seized by 1.2 million southern households on 24,000 ha by the end of 1981 (NCNA, December 26, 1981, *SWB* 1168). Should the current rural development policies continue, environmental damage caused by the reclamation of lakes and the destruction of fresh-water aquaculture may be substantially reversed in a relatively short period of time.

The same should apply to reclamation of coastal areas where grain-fields displaced beaches traditionally used for the breeding of marine species. Between 1959 and 1978 nearly 70,000 ha of such beaches were turned into fields, incurring the loss of thousands of tons of fish, shrimp, oysters, and mussels. As with fresh-water production, the loss was not balanced by grain production gains: it took years to wash the reclaimed fields clean of salts, and former fishermen could not farm well. Even when they were relatively successful, their incomes suffered: for example, the average annual output value of one *mu* of oysters is equivalent to the gain from two outstanding crops of rice on two *mu* of land; for seaweed or mussel breeding the ratio is 1:5 (Yang Haiqun 1979).

Again, such conversions, including a massive plan in Fujian that would have displaced 100,000 fishermen in 13 coastal counties dependent on mussel breeding, were largely halted after 1978, and labor intensive mariculture is now also promoted as an excellent means of earning foreign exchange: after all, one ton of prawns can buy 56 tons of wheat, and one ton of dried oysters can buy 44 tons of wheat on the foreign market. Such comparisons make the grain-first policy and the demands for local grain self-sufficiency patently losing propositions!

2.5 Losses and deterioration of cultivated land

Preceding sections have described how the understandable Chinese preoccupation with rising grain production found unfortunate and environmentally disruptive expression in the irrational mass land reclamation campaigns, leading to deforestation, filling of lakes, erosion, and desertification. There is now general agreement among Chinese farming experts that the price paid in terms of ecosystem degradation has been too high and that such efforts must not be repeated—especially in view of the fact that most of this reclaimed land is relatively unproductive, coming nowhere near the yields of old fertile farmlands. For example, Weng and colleagues (1981) state that on the average 3-5 ha of such land still produces less than the output of one ha of established cropland.

In a country that has to feed nearly a quarter of mankind this alone would be a most regrettable result: destroying valuable ecosystems for a dubious low-quality, often just temporary, gain. What makes the situation truly tragic is that the destruction of natural ecosystems and the creation of poor quality cropland has been accompanied by almost incredibly large losses of prime arable land—a diabolical combination of processes that ruins the irreplaceable natural heritage, negates the immense labor sacrifices of the peasants, and puts China farther away from the cherished goal of comfortable food self-sufficiency.

2.5.1 Losses of arable land

Given its physical endowment and large population, modern China never had the luxury of abundant farmland. In 1957, the last year of the 1950s for which official figures are available, China's cultivated area was 1.677 billion *mu*, or 111.8 million ha (State Statistical Bureau 1960); in per capita terms this translates to just 0.172 ha. In spite of the official information blackout from the late 1950s on, much had been inferred about the country from a variety of fractionary sources, but nothing indicated the magnitude of the change that was revealed in the late 1970s.

The first clear admission of the loss, contained in a document on agricultural development issued by the Central Committee of the CCP (1979), was that between 1957 and 1977 "more than 100 million *mu*," that is, some 7 million ha, of cultivated land was requisitioned for various capital construction projects. This loss alone implies that China's arable land in the late 1970s was no more than about 105 million ha, a decline of at least 6 percent in comparison with the late 1950s. On many occasions in 1979 and early 1980, however, a variety of Chinese sources, including the Soil and Fertilizer Institute of the Chinese Academy of Sciences (1979) and official Xinhua releases, were referring to just 1.5 billion *mu* of arable land nationwide, that is, only 100 million ha.

Finally, in April 1980 Zhang Zhenming (1980), writing in *Renmin ribao*, revealed the complete statistical dimensions of the losses and gains for the two decades, an account of astounding damage: between 1957 and 1977 China lost, to urban and rural construction and to natural disasters, 500 million *mu* or 33.33 million ha, an incredible 29.8 percent of the 1957 total. This is a truly frightening figure whose full import is not easily comprehended: the world's most populous nation with already scarce farmland losing nearly a third of its prime cropland in just one generation! The losses were partially made up by the previously mentioned reclamation campaigns: 21.33 million ha (320 million *mu*) were added in this way so the net loss was 12 million ha, or 10.73 percent of the 1957 total.

Slightly different figures were offered 18 months later by Yi Zhi (1981) in *Hongqi*: a total decrease of 440 million *mu* (29.33 million ha) and reclamation of 260 million *mu* (17.33 million ha)—the resulting net loss of 12 million ha, however, is identical with Zhang's figure. Even when looked at in strictly quantitative terms—ignoring the inferior quality of most of the reclaimed land—it is an awesome drop, equivalent to the disappearance of *all* cultivated land from Sichuan (China's most populous province, with some 100 million people), Guangdong (60 million), and Guangxi (about 36 million) combined.

This farmland, capable of sustaining some 200 million people (the equivalent of both Germanies, the United Kingdom, and France put together!), is gone—while China's population grew during that period by about 300 million people. Consequently, per capita availability of farmland dropped from 0.172 ha (2.59 *mu*) in 1957 to 0.104 ha (1.57 *mu*) in 1977—a 40 percent decline—and it is now no more abundant than in Bangladesh or Indonesia, and about 2.5 times less than in India or Brazil (FAO 1980). Naturally, in many provinces and localities the losses have been even more rapid. In Liaoning, with the massive expansion of heavy industrial concentrations and settlements, farmland available per capita shrunk by almost 60 percent, in Shaanxi by nearly the same amount (Yi 1981).

Perhaps most striking has been the loss of suburban farmland, traditionally planted mostly to several crops of vegetables (Figure 14). Beijing Municipality had 607,000 ha of such land in 1949, and only 427,000 ha by 1980, a 30 percent loss brought on by the state taking over two-thirds of all vegetable areas in close-by suburbs for new housing and factories instead of rebuilding the decaying city itself (Zhang Zhenming 1980). During the 1970s these farmland withdrawals proceeded at a rate of 20,000 *mu* (1,333 ha) a year, and should this trend continue for another decade, the equivalent of all of Haidian, the city's principal vegetable producing district, would be gone. Yet even now, in spite of priority deliveries for the capital, vegetable supply is strained because China has no long distance vegetable transport like North America or Europe, and suburban cultivation is thus decisive: while for each of the capital's 2.03 million inhabitants there were 0.3 ha of vegetable plots in 1949, today there are only 0.05 ha for each of the city's nearly 9 million people, and a decline of this magnitude is difficult to reverse even with intensified multicropping and higher yields.

Figure 14. New office and apartment buildings taking over vegetable fields on the outskirts of Chengdu, Sichuan's capital, a picture repeated in every suburb of a country whose arable land per capita is already less than that of Bangladesh.

Similarly, in Shanghai over 650 ha of vegetable plots were confiscated in 1979 and 1980, and in Wuhan some 2,000 ha, representing one-third of all suburban vegetable fields, were diverted to construction uses (Qui Yuan 1981). In all Xi'an suburbs, cultivated land is now less than 0.02 ha per capita, making the continued survival of farming families impossible (Anonymous 1981b).

Serious as the losses of suburban land are, they could be slowed or even reversed if the city and provincial authorities redirected growth from outward expansion to urban reconstruction. Controlling the waste of farmland in rural areas will prove to be much more difficult, however. The huge rural losses can be attributed to three main processes: the activities connected with farming, the indiscriminate expansion of small-scale industries, and the building of new houses. Surprisingly, the first category is a relatively minor contributor: new roads, irrigation canals, reservoirs, and grain storage and processing grounds usually do not eat away excessive areas. Tractor stations, however, have been taking too much land: where just 0.33-0.40 ha would be entirely sufficient for a six- or seven-machine enterprise, up to 1.3 ha of land are taken (Feng and Li 1980).

But small rural industries and housing have been the main offenders.

The frenzied construction of small factories to provide local self-sufficiency in many industrial products has been often hailed by Western
admirers of Maoist China as a splendid contribution to a "small is
beautiful" world. In reality, these enterprises, with primitive technologies, shoddy management, rampant duplication, prodigious waste of
resources, and huge production inefficiencies, have been an overwhelming economic loss and burden to the countryside. Built in response to erratic decisions during dubious campaigns, they have taken
over much flat, easily accessible prime farmland. Yi (1981) describes
the process succinctly: "Why could an enterprise leader advance a
proposal to use cultivated land by a snap of his fingers after he got out
of a jeep which had just carried him to the countryside?"

Small industries are now deservedly out of favor, but the newfound
prosperity of many rural areas and the greater room for individual
initiative—those precious gains for which the Chinese peasants have
waited so long—promise only further destruction of farmland by the
peasants' pursuit of that universal symbol of well-being, a new family
house. Between 1978 and 1980 more than two-fifths of the cropland
taken out of cultivation in the southern provinces was used for new
rural housing. Disaggregated figures for Hangzhou Prefecture in
Zhejiang, a province with losses of 13 percent of arable land between
1957 and 1978, show that in 1979 new housing took away 90 percent of
the lost farmland, state capital construction the rest (Wang Weizhang
1980). In some counties the demand for new houses affects up to 150 ha
a year, and up to twice that area is taken by brickworks (Yi 1981).
Every household in the North now occupies about 80-90 m²; in the
South, 70-80 m²; but some new buildings, yards, and walls often
appropriate 400-500 m² (Feng and Li 1980).

The construction of lavish houses and country villas by the leading
local Party bureaucrats sets an example for their subordinates, and in
violation of repeated recent injunctions against it, the practice thrives.
Zhang Zhenming's (1980) most incredible admission, coming as it did
in the official Party newspaper, is the bleakest possible assessment of
future prospects: "The state has, in fact, lost control over the use of
land in villages." This appraisal must be combined with the realization
that the pent-up demand for better rural housing to replace the old
homes will intensify over the next generation with the rising demand
for new housing to accommodate the record numbers of newlyweds,
whose families, even with strictest population controls, will add at least
200 million people to China's one billion by the year 2000. Clearly,

some heavy taxes on the private requisition of farmland, and especially on suburban lots, should be enacted and enforced, and the state itself should set an example in conserving land in its new contruction projects. The dilemma is well defined by Yi (1981): "The housing problem must be solved, but not at the expense of solving the food problem."

The continuation of past trends for even just another two decades is unthinkable: with the population growing to 1.3 billion, per capita availability of farmland would slip to a mere 0.068 ha (680 m², a square of 26 × 26 m), and a 30 percent yield increase from every cultivated field would be required just to maintain nutrition at its current barely sufficient level. Even if the annual losses were brought to just one-third the rate prevailing since the late 1950s (that is, to some 550,000 ha a year), and even if continuous reclamation could match past achieve- ments and add another 20 million ha in two decades—both very opti- mistic assumptions—the net addition would be just 9 million ha, and even with a population of only 1.2 billion—again a highly optimistic assumption—the per capita farmland availability would still go down to about 0.091 ha.

2.5.2 Qualitative deterioration

High future production gains from every planted field, however, are totally unrealistic because the quantitative decrease of arable land has been accompanied by the widespread qualitative decline of soils throughout China, a process that imposes serious limitations on con- tinuing yield increases. To begin with, 40 percent of the current 100 million ha under cultivation is on soils already belonging to the low- yield category: 20 percent are hillside fields with relatively thin soils prone to erosion, 8 percent are waterlogged lowlands and saline- alkaline fields, over 9 percent are sandy soils, and the remaining nearly 3 percent are poor paddy fields (Yi 1981). These poor soils typically yield no more than 0.75-1.50 tons of grain per ha (100-200 jin/mu), and not infrequently the harvests fall below half a ton per ha (Soil and Fertilizer Institute of the Chinese Academy of Science 1979). The best illustration of how widely these poor soils are distributed is that fact that 16 of the country's 26 provinces and regions have grain yields lower than the national average (Hu 1981).

And, unfortunately, many recent cropping practices are seriously degrading the previously good or excellent soils. Careless irrigation is spreading the area of saline and alkaline soils throughout the Huabei

Plain, and it creates bog or gley soils in many intensively cropped parts of Jiangnan: for example, no less than 40 percent of the cultivated area (1.2 million ha) in Hunan has been turned into bog soils whose lowered air content and lowered temperature slow down the absorption of nutrients and impede plant growth. Tai Hu lakeland in Jiangsu is also seriously affected, as are large areas in Guangdong. Continuous cropping of rice throughout Jiangnan has been responsible for the spreading formation of "blue asbestos mud," an approximately 10-cm-thick clay layer about 20 cm below the soil surface that retains water and fertilizer, prevents root growth, and causes frequent rotting (Xi 1979). Crops grown in these degraded soils, shallow and deficient in organic matter, do not respond properly to higher (and costly) water and chemical fertilizer inputs; many southern paddies now yield annually just 2.25-3.0 tons per ha, and peasants talk about hybrid strains bringing misfortune because of their fields not being able to surpass the record yields set in the 1960s (Qiu 1979).

The continuous double- and even triple-cropping of rice, the improper application of synthetic fertilizer and lower quantities of organic fertilizers, and the failure to rotate wet and dry crops (especially decreased green manure and legume planting) have been greatly accelerating soil degradation. Rice multicropping has been promoted as a component of the simplistic Maoist policy of indiscriminate expansion of grain growing, and more irrigation and more chemical fertilizers were thought sufficient to bring repeatedly higher harvests. Proper crop rotation had been neglected. As a result, Jiangnan's area planted to green manures decreased from 8.4 million ha in 1972 to 7.7 million ha by 1977; Shandong's soybean fields shrank from 2 million ha in 1949 to 0.73 million ha by the mid-1970s (Soil and Fertilizer Institute of the Chinese Academy of Science 1979). The cultivated area of various edible beans has been steadily declining for years (Zheng Zhouje 1981). Fewer green manures and legume crops and the diminished application of organic fertilizers have recently caused a rapid decline of organic matter content in soils and further exacerbated phosphorus and potassium deficiencies, now one of Chinese agriculture's most intractable obstacles to additional yield increases.

Domestically produced and imported synthetic nitrogen fertilizers surpassed the nitrogen theoretically available in organic wastes in 1975-76, and the ammonia and urea output has since risen sharply with the construction of 13 large, modern plants imported from the United States, Western Europe, and Japan. Total synthetic nitrogen applications now average about 106 kg per ha of farmland or, taking into account the extensive Chinese multicropping (the index now stands at 150), nearly 70 kg per ha of sown land. This is a very respectable performance—the European average is just about 100 kg, the U.S. mean is some 55 kg, and the Soviets apply only around 35 kg of nitrogen per ha of farmland (FAO 1981)—yet the yield returns on applications have been diminishing nevertheless.

These decreases are not owing, as in some countries with very intensive fertilization, to the virtual saturation of plants' needs but rather to a widespread disregard of an essential ecological tenet, venerable Liebig's law of minimum limiting nutrients. In the early 1960s, the application of one kg of standard nitrogen fertilizer (20 percent nitrogen content) increased the production of rice by 4 to 5 kg, of wheat by 2 to 3 kg, and of cotton by 2 kg—while in recent years all of the returns have been a mere one kg or less (Liang, Lin, and Li 1980). At that time, the nitrogen/phosphorus application ratio was an appropriate 1:0.6, but since then the described expansion of nitrogenous fertilizer output has not been matched by proportionate increases in phosphorus applications, with the disparity being especially acute in the northern provinces. Widespread phosphorus deficiencies lead to phenomena well described in soil science literature: poor root development, reduced or no tillering, short stems, retarded blooming and fruition, poorly developed grains, overall low yields.

Phosphorus deficiencies have been noticeable for some time in some parts of China, but potassium shortages are fairly recent. Formerly, extensive recycling of crop residues and animal manures was able to meet all of the potassium demand in traditional farming, but with increased applications of nitrogen fertilizers, higher unit yields and higher multicropping, insufficient straw recycling, and the virtual absence of potassium fertilizers, shortages of this essential macronutrient have started to slow down yield increases, especially in southern China. Extensive burning of crop residues for fuel (see section 6.1.2 for details) takes away annually at least 3.2 and perhaps as much as 4.9 million tons of potassium, as well as around half a million tons of phosphorus and about 1.5 million tons of nitrogen. With intensified farming and higher nitrogen use, micronutrient deficiencies are also bound to spread, and many cereal crops, and above all rice, may be more susceptible to lodging unless more silica, previously returned with recycled straws, is applied to stiffen the straws.

The remedies are straightforward but costly because the current

Chinese macronutrient disparities are considerable: instead of the desirable nitrogen:phosphorus:potassium (N:P:K) ratio of 1:0.6:0.2, current applications average 1:0.2:0.002 (Liang, Lin, and Li 1980). Large deposits of phosphorous ores have been discovered in the southwest and central-south part of China, but without first concentrating these ores through expensive production of compound fertilizers the poor Chinese railway network could not handle the voluminous northward shipments. Potassium fertilizer production is now a mere 30,000 tons, and as with most of the world's nations, China's verified reserves of suitable ores are not large. Prospecting for new sources together with appropriate utilization of fuel ashes and recycled crop residues are imperative.

Most regrettably, however, the use of organic fertilizer—be it green manuring or the recycling of plant, human, and animal wastes—has declined to such an extent that negative effects are already clearly evident (see also section 7.4). For example, Zhen Xiazheng (1982) cites numerous instances from Zhejiang Province where a sharp decline in the spreading of organic wastes and a heavy reliance on synthetic fertilizers has led to widespread micronutrient deficiencies and to related plant diseases.

Boron deficiency in rape, cotton, and wheat is marked by the plants flowering but not bearing seeds; potassium deficiency in cotton leads to spreading stem blight; and silica deficiency in rice causes easier stalk lodging. Crops fertilized by chemical materials also appear to have lower pest resistance, and outbreaks of stripe rust, leaf blight, and spike neck pests have become more common. While 80-90 percent of cotton fields used to be planted in rotation with green manures, only 15 percent now have their organic soil content so renewed, and this, combined with repeated heavy chemical fertilizing, has led to worsening soil crusting and a 50 percent drop in yields. As a peasant saying aptly sums it up: "How can you expect a good harvest if cotton is planted on hard-surfaced highways?"

About the impressive effects of green manures on soil structure, fertilizing, and subsequent crop yields there can be no doubt. Some persuasive illustrations have come from three years (1977-1979) of controlled experiments conducted by Xiao Shuxian (1980) in Guangxi. Compared with winter cultivation of wheat with double cropped rice, winter planting of Chinese vetch (*Astragalus sinensis*) increased the number of soil granules greater than 0.25 mm in diameter by nearly 50 percent and pushed the subsequent rice yields 50 percent higher than those following ordinarily fertilized wheat. Yields in wheat-rice-rice rotation could be, of course, increased by higher fertilizer applications, but the economic benefits are poor, and the demands for seasonal labor exertion are very high. And the soil structure continues to suffer.

The maintenance of good soil structure thus leads to a conclusion directly contradictory to the Chinese cropping policies of the recent past: "Only in those places where the double cropping of rice has a very high yield . . . and where labor and fertilizer are sufficient can the triple cropping system of rice-rice-wheat . . . be used" (Xiao Shuxian 1980). In all other cases an omission of green manure from the triple cropping cycle will cause the soil structure to deteriorate and soil fertility to decline.

Soils with higher organic content also retain moisture much better. Zhang Qinwen's (1981) calculations for Shanxi show that each ha of green manure plowed under can hold up to 1,950 m³ of water so the aggregate retention on 2.7 million ha of the province's dry fields would total 5.2 billion m³, sixfold the volume of all water stored in Shanxi's reservoirs! As for yield improvements, the incorporation of 15 tons of green manure in southern rice fields usually increases unhusked yields by over 20 percent (Lin Yin 1980).

3

WATER

The wise man delights in water,
The Good man delights in mountains.
For the wise move;
But the Good stay still.
The wise are happy;
But the Good, secure.

Confucius
Lun Yü VI, 21

Moreover, is not water, whether trickling,
flowing, spraying, foaming, splashing, or in rivers
or oceans, the very blood and marrow of
Heaven and Earth?

Mustard Seed Garden Manual
of Painting (1679)
(in Mai-mai Sze translation)

Art mirrors, succinctly and admirably, the human perception of the environment. When European painters looked at a landscape, various elements would prevail. Light from the high clouds in Jacob van Ruisdael, majestic trees in John Constable, shimmering colors in Claude Monet. In contrast, the Chinese painters have always seen their landscapes as *shan shui*—mountain-water—the term containing all the tension and harmony of *yang* and *yin*, evoking whole sets of analogies, lending to landscape painting "a worshipful attitude, making it a ritual act of reverence in praise of the harmony of Heaven and Earth" (Sze 1959). Water, the first of the ancient five elements, the Black Tortoise of the Five Regions of the Heavens, has thus always had a pivotal place in the Chinese culture—and in everyday Chinese life (Smil 1979b). One does not have to agree with Karl Wittfogel's (1957) historical thesis about the emergence and institutionalization of hydraulic despotism in China to appreciate the close relationship between water and the country's civilization, a link both beneficial and destructive, and a link very much enduring.

Vagaries of precipitation, drought, and flood still determine the size of harvests; the arid north still has to endure month after rainless month, while typhoons may be smashing southern dikes. And new dimensions have been added with rapidly progressing industrialization and urbanization and with expanded irrigation and chemicalization of agriculture: much higher uses of water in general, frequently straining the available resources and leading to shortages of even drinking water; drastically increased extraction of ground waters followed by sinking water tables and surface subsidence; and widespread water pollution of all major streams, lakes, and coastlines. All of these problems (to be treated separately below) are often related to those critical Chinese environmental constraints—relatively small volume and irregular distribution of the country's water flows.

3.1 China's water resources

Each year some 6 trillion m^3 of precipitation, or an average of 630 mm, falls on China. This is only about one-fifth less than the global average of 800 mm, and in absolute terms certainly does not make China a particularly dry country. About 56 percent of all the total precipitation is absorbed by soils and vegetation, to be evaporated, transpired, or stored in the ground so that the runoff (including the underground portion equal to 600 billion m^3) amounts to around 2.64 trillion m^3, placing China fifth globally after Brazil, the USSR, Canada, and the United States (Chen Zhikai 1981). The average depth of this annual overland and river runoff is 274 mm, slightly higher than the world average, although below Asian, Latin American, and European means.

What makes the Chinese situation unfortunate and difficult to manage are the spatial and temporal distributions of the precipitation, on the one hand, and the very low amount of water available in per capita terms, on the other. As stressed in the opening chapter (section 1.1), in the densely inhabited eastern third of the country the North is much drier than the South, and both of these regions are prone to extended and, owing to massive deforestation, recently worsening spells of drought and flood. Also, aridity in the North is in most locations more of a distribution problem (with up to one-fifth of all yearly moisture coming down in a few peak summer downpours), rather than an absolute scarcity—although the region *is* dry, especially as far as crop farming is concerned: the basins of the Hai He, the Liao He, and the Huai He have 28 percent of China's farmland but a mere 4 percent of its runoff! (Chen Zhikai 1981).

The relative smallness of China's runoff is the irremovable function of the country's huge population. Currently the runoff amounts to about 2,700 m^3 per capita a year, which is only one-fifth the global average of

12,900 m³ and less even than West European or Japanese means. Perhaps the most striking way to illuminate this critical environmental constraint is to point out that China's per capita runoff is just about the same as the current actual per capita water usage in the United States, about 2,600 m³ per capita each year.

Of the rivers' runoff, about 410 billion m³ is currently utilized (that is, one-fifth of the available amount), and over 50 billion m³ is pumped from underground (for more on ground waters see section 3.3). The aggregate utilization of some 460 billion m³ is about 17 percent of the total runoff, about the same share as in West Germany but only about half of relative water withdrawals in the United States. In per capita terms this translates into just 460 m³, nearly six times less than in the United States, about one-quarter of the typical European utilization, and about two-fifths of the Japanese utilization (van der Leeden 1975).

The regional distribution of water utilization is, of course, extremely uneven: in the basins of the Hai, the Liao, and the Huai as much as two-thirds of the runoff is tapped, in the Chang Jiang basin it is no more than 15 percent, and in the basins of large southwestern rivers the rate is far below one percent. Similar regional differences apply in the use of ground waters (see section 3.3) and, in reverse, in the distribution of artificial storages: the south has considerably more reservoirs than the North.

In spite of the ancient tradition of intricate waterworks (see section 3.4), the large-scale storage of water in China became important only in the past three decades. In 1949 there were only several reservoirs with capacities exceeding 100 million m³; now there are some 300 such storages, more than 1,500 medium-sized ones (10-100 million m³), and about 80,000 small ones (NCNA, March 10, 1980, *SWB* 1075). Interestingly, some earlier listings of water conservation achievements put the number of reservoirs at 100,000 (for example Xinhua, July 27, 1978, *SWB* 993)—reflecting perhaps both the inflated earlier statistics and the attrition of many small projects that silted up or fell into disuse not long after their completion.

In any case, the overwhelming majority of reservoirs are very small, and the total capacity of water storage to regulate runoff is around 400 billion m³, or no more than one-sixth of the annual runoff (Shen 1981). However, the improper management of the storages (''empty belly'' reservoirs full just once in a decade are not uncommon) and their silting means that only 7.7 percent of total runoff is actually stored (Chen Zhikai 1981), a share lower than the global average and yet another example of China's impressive quantitative achievements hiding serious qualitative shortcomings.

As in all other nations with significant irrigation, China's agriculture is by far the heaviest user of water, accounting for 87 percent of the total (Chen Zhikai 1981); for comparison, the Soviet irrigation share is 75 percent, while U.S. agriculture uses about two-fifths of the total withdrawn (van der Leeden 1975). Industrial consumption is only 6.6 percent (in rich countries it is much higher owing to large water usage in thermal power generation), and the rest, 6.4 percent, is for municipal and drinking water use. Trend estimates indicate about a 50 percent increase in the total water demand by the year 2000, or about 700 billion m^3. Theoretically, this volume could be easily accommodated because it represents no more than about 26 percent of the runoff, or a smaller share than the United States withdrew during the 1970s.

In reality, the regional shortages, especially along the Huang He, the Liao He, the Hai He, and the Huai He, will worsen, with annual deficits in these four basins adding up to perhaps as much as 70 billion m^3, or more than the Huang He's total flow. Which of the two possible likely solutions will prevail—rationalization and greatly increased efficiency of surface water use in irrigation (see section 3.4) and in cities, combined with better storage and scientifically guided ground water exploitation (see section 3.3), or massive interbasin water transfers from the south, bearing with them not inconsequential environmental dangers (see section 3.2.2)—is difficult to guess. The desirability of the first course is obvious, but it demands countless small-scale measures, changes, and adjustments and thorough and ongoing management and follow ups no less than a permanent high-quality operation. Nickum (1981) correctly observes that the Communist Chinese have displayed a pervasive bias toward project construction rather than good management. Although efforts to usher in better management are now fostered everywhere in China, one cannot be overly optimistic about the outcome: the mobilization mass project mentality may yet again prevail. In any case, the utilization of China's surface and ground waters, north or south, is bound to become an even more critical consideration in economic planning and in everyday human life.

3.2 Surface waters

Fresh-water surfaces cover 26.7 million ha of Chinese territory, about 2.8 percent of the total or an equivalent of roughly one-quarter of the area now occupied by farmlands. There are other slightly or substantially different estimates, however, the lowest one being only 16.7 million ha (NCNA, March 28, 1979, *SWB* 1024). Natural lakes are estimated to cover 6.3 million ha—although it is unclear if the figure refers to the extent before the mass lakeland reclamations of the late 1960s and 1970s (see section 2.4) or to the actual recent value—and man-made reservoirs of all sizes occupy at least 2 million ha (Xinhua, May 30, 1979, *SWB* 1033). The rest, that is, at least 8.4 or as much as 18.4 million ha, is presumably taken up by river and stream surfaces.

Despite the growing importance of artificial storages in the Chinese economy (see the preceding section), rivers remain the principal sources of municipal and industrial water supplies as well as, in most regions, of irrigation water. The next section will deal with some opportunities and constraints in this utilization by focusing on the two rivers that are in so many ways the embodiment of the Chinese environment and civilization—the Huang He and the Chang Jiang.

3.2.1 Rivers

Large parts of China's arid interior have no permanent rivers—and no drainage to an ocean—with seasonal streams disappearing in the sands (Figure 15). But the rest of the country has more than 50,000 rivers with basins exceeding 100 km², and 1,200 of these have drainages surpassing 1,000 km². The size of the river, be it measured by its length, discharge, or basin area, has been in most cases less important for the stream's place in Chinese civilization than the river's location and the density of its surrounding settlements. Many large rivers such as the Himalayan and Xizang Plateau streams flowing southward—the Yarlung Zangbo Jiang (the Indian Brahmaputra), the Nu Jiang (the Burmese Salween), and the Lancang Jiang (the Indochinese Mekong)— and northeastern border streams—the Heilong Jiang (the Amur) and the Wusuli Jiang (the Ussuri)—have been of marginal economic importance compared with the Wei, the Hai, and the Huai, streams that long molded the environment of Chinese civilization.

Yet any examination of China's few key rivers should not, I feel, start with any stream other than the Huang He (the Yellow River). Few of the world's major rivers had such a profound effect on a major civilization as the Huang He had on China. The two core areas of the emerging Chinese state—one in the Wei He valley in Shaanxi, and the other between Luoyang and Kaifeng in Henan—were harbored in the Huang He basin; frequently, however, the river also had a destructive

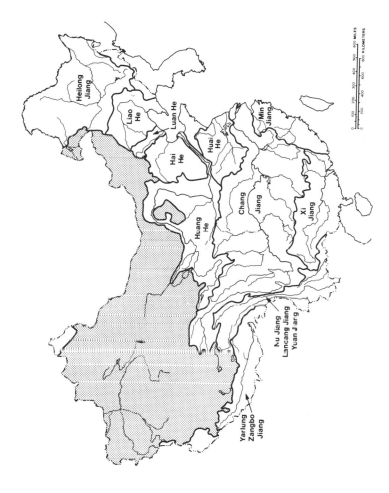

Figure 15. China's principal river basins; the dotted area is without outlet to oceans.

effect. In more than two-and-a-half millenia of recorded Chinese affairs it had a major course change every century (flowing into either the Bo Hai north of the Shandong Peninsula or the Yellow Sea south of Shandong) and on the average it broke the dikes in its lower course every two out of three years. Throughout history hundreds of millions of peasants and the fates of changing dynasties were affected by the overflowing, silty waters.

The distance between the river's source on the high Qinghai Plateau and its mouth at the shallow Bo Hai is 5,464 km; the total descent is 4,300 m; and the basin is 752,443 km². The average water volume of 48 billion m³ is no more than one-twentieth of the Chang Jiang's mighty flow, but the seasonal fluctuations of the Huang He are extreme: the record flood flow at Zhengzhou in Henan was 22,000 m³ per second, 88 times the winter minimum of 250 m³ per second in the same year, while the mean annual discharge at the mouth is 1,600 m³ per second (Smil 1979a).

Although it has a relatively dry drainage basin and an uneven flow, the hydrogeneration potential of the Huang He and its major tributaries is still a considerable 32.2 Gigawatts (GW), or about 6 percent of China's total, and eight major hydrostations with more than 4,000 Megawatts (MW) of installed capacity are now on the river, including Longyangxia in Qinghai (with 1,600 MW; now under construction, it will be China's second largest hydroelectric project) and the failed Sanmenxia between Shanxi and Henan (see section 2.2.2). The Huang He's water is also used to irrigate some 3.3 million ha (compared with 800,000 ha in 1949), or just 7 percent of China's watered land (Henan provincial broadcast, January 30, 1980, *SWB* 1072).

The large power generation and irrigation gains of the past three decades notwithstanding, the river remains a far from controlled environmental problem. While there have been no serious flood disasters in the lower stretches of the river during the past 30 years—a great relief to tens of millions of peasants in Henan and Shandong and clearly a major flood control success—the river's influence on China's fortunes remains strong as its potential for destruction has, in fact, grown greater with the faster erosion on the Loess Plateau and with heavier silt deposits on its bed in two plains provinces and in its delta into the Bo Hai (see sections 2.2.1 and 2.2.2).

The prodigious control efforts of strengthening and raising the embankments between which the river is confined in Henan and Shandong with 480 million m³ of new earthwork and stonework since 1949 have treated the most dangerous symptom of the problem—the riverbed's yearly 12 cm rise above the surrounding landscape—but have had no effect whatsoever on the cause, the accelerated devegetation and erosion of the Loess Plateau. And as this problem will not be effectively controlled, even under the most optimistic scenarios, for decades to come, the risks of catastrophic flooding along the lower course will remain high. And naturally, if the destruction of trees and grassland on the Loess Plateau is not radically reversed, the danger will intensify.

There is yet another worsening problem in the Huang He basin: the increasing imbalance between the availability of water, on the one hand, and the demand for water for irrigation, industrial, and urban uses, on the other, a situation which has led to the resurrection, near adoption, postponement, and finally the approval of a large-scale interbasin water transfer from the south, that is, from the main stream and some tributaries of the Chang Jiang.

The Chang Jiang (the Yangtze River) is not only China's longest river but one of the world's longest and most voluminous streams. In the past the river's length was put at 5,500 or 5,800 km, but new Chinese investigations on the Qinghai-Xizang plateau in 1977 changed the total to 6,300 km because the Tuotuo He is now considered the main headstream (NCNA, January 14, 1978, *SWB* 965). From the source to Yibin in Sichuan the remeasured length is 3,496 km; below Yibin it was shortened by 80 km to 2,804 km owing to the straightening of the two large bends in the Jing Jiang section in Hubei. This new value makes the river the world's third longest stream after the Nile (6,650 km) and the Amazon (6,437 km) and puts it ahead of the Mississippi and the Yenisei (van der Leeden 1975).

The river's 1.8 million km² basin comprises nearly a fifth of China's territory, and as most of it is in relatively rainy areas the annual runoff surpasses 1.1 trillion m³, translating into an average discharge of some 35,000 m³ per second, placing the river, again, third globally, after the Amazon (over 200,000 m³ per second) and the Zaire (about 40,000 m³ per second). The total descent of the main channel, 5,060 m (0.8 m/km), gives the river an outstanding hydroelectric potential of 230 GW, which is about two-fifths of China's total. However, 95 percent of this descent occurs between the source and Yibin, an additional 4 percent between Yibin and Yichang (a section including the famous San Xia, the Three Gorges), and the river descends a mere 40 m during the last 1,800 km of its flow.

In this lowland section the river meanders extensively and is prone to major flooding. The worst segment is in Hubei, where it snakes in chains of S-shaped bends, some of them curved to such an extent that navigation covers distances four to nine times as long as the straight course. As noted above, two highly curved bends were straightened between 1966 and 1969, but the overall danger of flooding remains high with protective dikes containing the river's crest up to about 10 m above the densely populated plain north of the Chang Jiang (NCNA, March 30, 1980, *SWB* 1977).

Recent large increases in silt content caused by extensive deforestation, especially in Sichuan, will further intensify this danger and require additional raising and reinforcement of dikes not only in the Jing Jiang section but also elsewhere in Hubei, Hunan, Jiangxi, Anhui, and Jiangsu; after all, the Chang Jiang has a much longer system of dikes— 3,100 km—than the Huang He. Similarly, flood diversion projects with a total capacity of 50 billion m³ were built during the past three decades along the Chang Jiang's course through the central China lakeland, but the widespread silting of lakes, including the largest ones (Dongting and Poyang) has actually worsened the situation in many locations along the river.

Although many of them have already yielded to siltation, some 20,000 small reservoirs built throughout the basin for power generation have been the principal source of rural electrification, and many have also helped with irrigation water or doubled as fishponds. Judgment on China's largest hydrostation now under construction on the Chang Jiang, and even more so on the planned giant San Xia project, can hardly be overwhelmingly positive. Undoubtedly, China has acute shortages of electric energy, and these structures will be able to regulate frequent floodwaters (during the past two millenia the river overflowed once in every ten years) before they reach the perilous lakeland stretch but, as with any large dams and reservoirs, the environmental and other problems are far from negligible.

Gezhouba, the station now under construction, is, in terms of generating capacity, twice as large as China's second largest hydroproject (Longyangxia on the Huang He); it consists of a 2,561-m-long and 70-m-high concrete gravity dam built to hold 1.58 billion m³ of water at a point, near Yichang in Hubei, where the average annual flow is 14,000 m³/sec and the designed flood flow is 86,000 m³/sec; the power plant will have an installed capacity of 2,700 MW to generate 13.8 billion kWh (Zhou Zheng 1981). San Xia, about 40 km upstream from Gezhouba, would be, with 25,000 MW, the world's largest hydrostation—or the second largest if the giant Inga project on the Zaire is eventually developed to its full capacity of more than 30,000 MW. Currently by far the largest hydrostation under construction, Itaipu on the Parana between Brazil and Paraguay, will have an installed capacity of 12,600 MW.

Wei Tingcheng, deputy director of the planning office of the Chang Jiang basin and one of the leading designers of Gezhouba, claims, predictably, that the dam "has not changed the ecological equilibrium" (Zhou Zheng 1981), but even he acknowledges that the important unresolved question is how to protect some rare species, above all the Chinese sturgeon. Significantly, no consensus has been reached about a passageway for aquatic creatures, and therefore the dam does not have one, a further, and in this case truly insurmountable, obstacle to the maintenance of natural aquatic life in the Chang Jiang basin: it will become impossible for the rare Chinese sturgeon, as well as several common carp species, to migrate (Zhang Guanzhong 1981). However, for the sake of the higher public good—flood protection and power generation—one could argue that the extinction of several fish species is a mild penalty to bear.

Indeed, there is a much costlier and immeasurably more important problem arising with the dam's construction: the silting of its reservoir. Compared with the Huang He, the Chang Jiang is not particularly silty, but because of its large volume the annual mass of suspended matter it carries is already quite considerable. Moreover, as discussed in section 2.2.4, rapidly advancing erosion in the Chang Jiang's basin in Yunnan, Sichuan, and Guizhou is steadily raising the river's silt content. Naturally, the project's designers took into account the voluminous flow (an average of 14,000 m³ per second) and built silt-checking dikes and a silt-discharging gate to cope with the mean silt load of 1.19 kg per m³, equivalent to an annual inflow of 525 million tons of suspended matter.

These assumptions, however, appear to be low in light of the latest available evidence. Xu Dixin (1981) states that surveys by the Wushan hydrological station (at the easternmost tip of Sichuan where the Chang Jiang leaves the province) show that each year 640 million tons of silt are now transported oceanward. Hardly any of this load will be deposited by the fast-flowing stream in the gorges the river traverses before it enters onto Hubei plain, where Gezhouba is located. Consequently, the silting rates of the reservoir will be at least 20 percent higher than anticipated by the design, and unless the erosion in the upper Chang Jiang basin is checked rapidly and effectively, the silting is bound to worsen. Not surprisingly, some Chinese scientists have already started to talk about Gezhouba as the second Sanmenxia.

Although the total silt influx of 640 million tons is, and even if steadily rising will for a long time to come remain, much lower than Sanmenxia's 1,600 million tons, the economic losses inherent in the decline of water storage capacity and reduction of flood control ability will be hardly less costly and dangerous in the case of this much bigger and costlier project. And Gezhouba itself would be utterly dwarfed by the San Xia station, whose construction, so ardently promoted by the top managers of the Chang Jiang Valley Long-range Planning Commission, would bring challenges and consequences of unprecedented magnitude.

Situated at the end of Xilingxia, the third of the three Chang Jiang gorges, the project would consist of a 200-m-high dam housing turbogenerators with 25 GW of installed capacity to produce 110 billion kWh a year (Anonymous 1981c). Useful capacity of the reservoir would surpass 100 billion m^3 (Gezhouba's is only 1.58 billion m^3), and the newly created lake would extend up to 100 km upstream from Chongqing for a total of about 700 km! Naturally such a vast storage would greatly facilitate navigation, with ships of up to 10,000 tons passing all the way up to Chongqing—but it would also necessitate the resettlement of nearly 4 million people and the flooding of more than 80,000 ha of arable land. These factors alone might be sufficient cause to abandon, or at least substantially scale down, this project whose other environmental impacts would involve major changes in natural aquatic biota and the uncertainties of silt accumulation and earthquake dangers. Most likely, however, the staggering cost of the project will be the key to repeated postponements.

No other rivers in the densely populated eastern third of China rival the preeminence of the Huang He and the Chang Jiang, but many much shorter and less voluminous streams have always shared a critical place in the country's history, owing both to the destruction wrought by their frequent floods and to their crucial role in crop irrigation. Perhaps the two foremost examples are the Huai He and the Hai He.

The Huai He gathers its water in a 165,000 km^2 basin in Henan and Anhui, and even before it enters Hongze Hu (Hongze Lake) in western Jiangsu it must be confined by dikes. From there eastward its extremely small gradient causes serious drainage difficulties, naturally exacerbated by flooding. Mass construction started in the 1950s was aimed at comprehensive control of these problems. A group of large reservoirs was built in the mountains of western Anhui, and more than 5,000 small storages were constructed between 1951 and 1976; dikes were added and strengthened along the basin's rivers, along the low-lying Hongze Hu and Gaoyou Hu, as well as along the seacoast in Jiangsu; and several major new outlets (the longest being about 200 km) were dug to speed up the outflow of flood waters to the Huang Hai (the Yellow Sea). These measures have been fairly successful in reducing the basin's flood and waterlogging problems.

Mass work in the Hai He basin started in 1963, and up to a million peasants working every winter and spring in 10 years completed 80 large and 1,500 small reservoirs; 34 trunk waterways with a total length of 3,700 km; 4,300 km of flood-prevention dikes; and 60,000 bridges, water locks, and culverts (Ho 1975). New outlets to the Bo Hai increased the discharging capacity fivefold in comparison with the early 1960s, and Tianjin gained a much higher degree of safety from floods. However, no waterworks within the basin are capable of solving the chronic water shortages in the area, which contains 3.6 million ha of irrigated farmland as well as Beijing and Tianjin, two of China's three largest industrial centers.

Tianjin's water supply is precarious even in normal years; during dry spells the situation becomes so critical that interbasin water transfer is necessary, and a part of the Huang He's flow is diverted through a series of irrigation canals from Henan and Shandong to the Hai He. This had to be done three times in the years 1972-75 and again in 1981, when a total of 340 million m³ of water was channeled through three canals, 850, 600, and 480 km long. The widening and dredging of the canals and the cutting of new shorter links took six weeks of the massed labor of 400,000 peasants and also involved the relocation of some settlements. These labor intensive measures will not be necessary when another interbasin transfer is completed in 1984, a 135-km-long permanent canal from the Panjiakou reservoir (2.9 billion m³) on the Luan He northwest of Tianjin. Both of these large interbasin water transfers to Tianjin are minuscule in comparison with the contemplated South-North diversion between the Changjiang and the Huang He basins. If accomplished, this would be the greatest human intervention in China's water cycle; as such, it clearly deserves at least a brief discussion.

3.2.2 Water transfer

The idea of channeling the waters of the Chang Jiang northward to the Huang He basin is not new: it was first suggested, under Soviet influence, in the early 1950s, and a major survey of water resources and routes involved in such a grandiose scheme was completed in 1959. Then the plan lay dormant for nearly a generation, yet another victim of China's internal political upheavals and unsettled economic strategies. It was revived in the summer of 1978, and since then discussions on the need, extent, and execution of the project have been a frequent topic of public and scientific debates.

The need seems to be self-evident. China's north and northwest have half of the nation's cultivable land, but the basins of the Huang He, the Huai He, and the Hai He have but 7 percent of the total river discharge; in contrast, the Chang Jiang basin, with a third of China's cultivable land, has 76 percent of the aggregate runoff. As explained above (section 1.1), the availability and reliability of northern precipitation are extremely precarious: most of the Huang He basin has less than 500 mm of rain and snow annually, and between 45 and 68 percent of this low total comes down in erratic summer downpours between June and August. On the other hand, China south of the Chang Jiang has more than a meter of rain annually with a much more even frequency distribution. The Chang Jiang's flow—about one trillion cubic meters a year compared with the Huang He's 48 billion—thus seems to be a ready and inexhaustible source of water for the moisture-deficient North. A massive transfer of the surplus southern flow northward offers a logical solution to the dilemma of recurring droughts and water shortages in a region that must increase its food production substantially.

Studies from the late 1950s identified three principal diversion routes (Greer 1979). The western course, channeling the Jinsha Jiang's waters from Sichuan through tunnels and canals to Gansu, is plainly unrealistic. The middle route was endorsed, though not without qualifications, by a national forum on diversion schemes held in Tianjin between March 29 and April 11, 1979 (NCNA, April 23, 1979, *SWB* 1031). It would involve linking Beijing with the Danjiangkou reservoir on the Han Shui via a 1,000-km-long canal (which would cross the Huang He near Zhengzhou) and joining the reservoir with the Chang Jiang through a canal starting near Yichang. This scheme would annually divert an average of 10 billion cubic meters (an equivalent of the yearly flow of the Hai He)—and irrigate 4.66 million ha of cropland, mainly in the Hai He basin. Most of the flow along this course would be by gravity.

The eastern version, which would not be amenable to gravity flows, would follow the Grand Canal through Jiangsu, Shandong, and Hebei.

This plan was revealed in some detail in August 1978, after three months of intensive new surveys and planning (NCNA, August 25, 1978, *SWB* 996). The length of the main conduit would also be 1,000 km, and the Grand Canal would have to be dredged, widened, and partially rerouted to enable it to move the anticipated 30 billion m³ a year that would be withdrawn from the Chang Jiang by giant pumping stations at a rate of 1,000 m³ a second.

The total irrigated area would eventually extend over 4 million ha in Jiangsu, Anhui, Shandong, and Hebei; drainage would be improved for 18,000 km² of low-lying land; and industrial and public water supplies for Tianjin and other cities would be rendered much more reliable. About half of the total volume would be used south of the Huang He, and the rest would be channeled across the elevated river to flow by gravity toward Tianjin on the Bo Hai (Chen Shangkui 1978). The power requirements of 30 large pumping stations arranged in a 15-stage staircase would total 1,000 MW, nearly equal to the rating of China's largest power plant in 1979.

After years of debates this eastern route was approved in the spring of 1983, and the first stage of its construction, widening and deepening of the Grand Canal's middle section, is to be completed before 1990, when the total volume of diverted water should reach 2.1 billion m³ a year, only a fraction of the originally intended 30 billion m³. The decision to proceed with the transfer but only on a modest scale appears to be a compromise between the proponents of the project and its numerous critics. As the project would be an unprecedented engineering feat with potentially serious ecological consequences, it was encouraging to see serious discussions of its implications, including the questioning of the very need for any massive water transfer. The severe drought that afflicted the Chang Jiang's middle and lower course in 1978 provided a persuasive argument for the opponents of the diversion: Jiangsu and Anhui drew away so much of the river's water for irrigation that sea water advanced into the Chang Jiang's estuary where it surrounded Chongming Island, a major supplier of farm products for Shanghai, for months and forced Shanghai's population to drink salt-contaminated water for several weeks. The Suzhou and Nantong regions of Jiangsu were similarly affected. Obviously water diversion would only aggravate this already serious situation prevailing during dry years.

Opponents of the transfer—their arguments have been summarized in two special sections devoted to the problem by *Guangming ribao*

(Guangming Daily) on August 16, 1978, and August 1, 1979, and further bolstered by the consensus of a conference convened by the Ministry of Geology in 1980 (Anonymous 1980b)—make four principal criticisms of the project. First, there is a relative abundance of ground water sources in the North, and large-scale water storage and regulation is still possible within the region, providing everything is done in a rational, efficient manner. Improvements in the prevailing irrigation practices, which operate without recycling while wasting more than half of the available flow, could also go a long way toward increasing northern self-sufficiency. Reforestation and the establishment of good grasslands, the key long-term strategies to reduce soil erosion, would enable more dams to be built on the now exceedingly silty streams of the loess region, thus further improving the northern water balance.

Second, if water is really needed, why not divert the Huang He's flow? Again, with rational management up to 30 billion m^3 could be so used. Third, there is no clear scientific basis for making the fundamental decision of how much water can be annually withdrawn from the Chang Jiang without affecting irrigation and industrial and municipal water needs along the river and further worsening the backflow of sea water into its estuary, a most troubling phenomenon for the economic and human well-being of one of China's most densely populated regions. And, finally, the ecosystemic implications of the transfer are potentially no less damaging. The 1950s' experience with large-scale surface irrigation on the North China Plain shows a rapid water table rise and extensive salinization and alkalization; this led to the abandonment of the practice and the leveling of irrigation canals. Diverting water north would probably have the same result and additionally bring new aquatic species northward, upsetting the existing biota and possibly extending the danger of schistosomiasis (interestingly, the dangers of new species introduction are among the leading arguments in the current dispute about North America's largest planned interbasin transfer, the Garrison project in North Dakota).

The huge cost of the transfer and the persuasive arguments of its opponents, who were allowed to challenge the official promoters of the project (above all the Ministry of Water Conservation and Electric Power, which pushed the diversion so aggressively that it became part of the official 10-year economic plan in 1978), have resulted in a most welcome attitude of "caution and more caution," and the approved first stage of the eastern diversion—a relatively modest project aimed as much at improving the navigability of the Grand Canal as at the eventual larger water transfers—should be seen as the first partial but still significant victory, and one hopes not only a temporary one, of scientifically based prudence over the factional wishes of a partisan bureaucracy in a major environmental dispute in China.

3.3 Ground waters

Hydrological surveys, which covered all of China except the Qinghai-Xizang plateau, have established aggregate extractable underground water reserves of 800 billion m^3 a year, with 500 million m^3 per year in the South. But the smaller northern reserves are the most intensively tapped today. Of the present nationwide consumption of about 460 million m^3 per year, 55 billion m^3 (or 12 percent) is underground water, and of this total, 40 billion m^3 (or some 73 percent) is pumped out in 17 northern provinces and regions—and the nationwide usage is expected to double, perhaps even triple, by the year 2000 (Li Weiya 1981).

Ten cities in this arid or drought-prone zone are critically dependent on ground-water pumping for basic municipal supply (household and industrial) and suburban vegetable gardening: Beijing and Tianjin, Shenyang (Liaoning), Baotou and Hohhot (Nei Monggol), Xi'an (Shaanxi), Taiyuan (Shanxi), Jinan (Shandong), Harbin (Heilongjiang), and Wulumuqi (Xinjiang). Irrigated crop farming on the North China Plain would also be impossible without ground water: on the Hebei plain over 400,000 wells have been sunk since 1960 to tap 10 billion m^3 a year for watering 20 million ha, or 60 percent of the area's irrigated land (Li Weiya 1981).

As a result, while the nationwide average of extracted underground water is only a bit less than 7 percent of available reserves, on the North China Plain 25.6 billion m^3 is tapped annually from pools of 47.5 billion m^3 of verified shallow fresh water—or nearly 54 percent. In the Hai He basin the share is 70 percent, and in the Beijing region, situated at the northernmost fringe of the plain, the proportion is even higher: 2.6 billion out of the 3 billion m^3 available, or fully 86 percent, and in the city itself 750 million m^3 is withdrawn annually, although the sustainable reserve is only about 600 million m^3. Excessive pumping goes on in many other northern urban areas as well: in Jinan (Shandong) the extracted volume surpasses the allowable amount by 60 percent; in heavily industrialized Shenyang (Liaoning), by nearly 90 percent. Not surprisingly, such intensive pumping has led to the widespread lowering of the water table, to the formation of underground funnels, and even to surface sinking over a steadily expanding area.

In Beijing Municipality, where extraction from wells for suburban housing, industrial, and farming uses now surpasses 400 million m^3, or over 100 times the 1949 flow, an underground funnel has formed over an area of 1,000 km^2, with the water table dropping as much as 20 m in its center and 4.3 m on the average (Anonymous 1981d). The effect is especially serious in the southeastern suburbs, where the water table recedes by one to 1.5 m a year (Yuan and Zu 1981). In Shenyang 20 underground funnels are gradually expanding (some by as much as 7 km^2 a year) and will eventually link together. In Tianjin's Baimiao district the water table is sinking by 4.4 m each year. In Shijiazhuang (Hebei) it is sinking 3 m a year. Near Changzhou, in Jiangsu, just south of the Chang Jiang, the drop has been almost 50 m in three decades.

Similar figures could be cited for Xi'an, Taiyuan, and Baotou. Indeed, the Environmental Hydrology Group of the Ministry of Geology (1980) concludes that "the continuous reduction of the ground water table is a general problem of China's urban water supply." The effects of excessive utilization are also widespread in the Hebei countryside, where continued pumping of underground water during recent years of consecutive droughts resulted in "the water table falling everywhere, and the number of funnel regions ceaselessly increasing" (Hebei provincial broadcast, August 7, 1980, *SWB* 1099). Hydrological surveys have revealed 28 funnel regions of different sizes covering a total of nearly 12,000 km^2, or about one-tenth of the province's plains.

Surface sinking accompanies the ground water table drop in all cases where the extracted water is a part of the load bearing structure. Among large Chinese cities, Shanghai was the first to experience the problem, but because the city is not critically dependent on ground water it moderated the extraction rates and since 1963 has been replenishing the aquifers with 17 million m^3 of surface water a year, basically controlling the problem. In northern cities heavily reliant on ground water, however, the subsidence has been increasing. In the eastern suburbs of Beijing it has been quite serious, averaging 20-30 cm a year since 1950 (Zheng Jingshan 1981). Probably the worst situation is in Tianjin where the drop amounted to 1.5 m a year after 1959 and now is 10 cm a year. In many places the subsidence is rapidly accelerating; for example, in Xi'an it averaged 4 mm a year between 1959 and 1972 (total of 5.4 cm) but rose to 18 mm a year between 1972 and 1976, and now it is over 20 mm annually.

The consequences of sinking water tables and surface subsidence are predictably costly: new and deeper wells must be drilled, new water pumping equipment needs to be installed, and costs per extracted m³ (in both monetary and energy terms) are higher. Competition for this increasingly scarce resource leads to indiscriminate drilling of deeper wells by neighboring factories dependent on underground water supplies for their production and thus exacerbates the problem. And, no less important, the quality of the underground water used for urban supply has been deteriorating appreciably.

Environmental Hydrology Group (1980) data show that of 44 major cities relying heavily on underground water 41 draw on contaminated supplies, and in 9 cases (Beijing, Xi'an, Shenyang, Taiyuan, Baotou, Jinzhen, Baoding, Changchun, and Jilin) the level of pollution is serious. The most common pollutants are phenols, cyanic compounds, arsenic, mercury, chromium, and nitrates; water hardness has also been increasing steadily in most cases. The danger of ground-water pollution is especially serious in all instances of shallow sandy or pebbly aquifers where percolation is easy; unfortunately, Beijing, Shenyang, and Baotou have precisely this type of water-bearing strata.

In several coastal cities, Shanghai, Tianjin, and Dalian, for example, any extensive mining of ground waters is threatened by salt-water ingress into fresh water aquifers. Another problem is the irrigation of suburban farmland with polluted underground water, which leads to impermissible levels of heavy metals in vegetables sold in many northern cities. For example, in Shenyang, where polluted water has been used repeatedly for suburban irrigation, there have been "numerous instances" when several tons of harvested vegetables were unfit to eat, with chromium concentrations reaching up to 5.2 mg per kg of cabbage and 6 mg per kg of spinach (Ma Junfeng 1981). International, including U.S., standards prescribe the rejection of water as unfit when chromium (Cr) exceeds 0.05 mg per liter, or one-hundredth of the above values. Some rice harvested in the Shenyang suburbs irrigated with polluted well water has had more than one mg of cadmium per kg—the international standards for cadmium (Cd) are just 0.01 mg per kg.

With proper management, however, it is possible not only to turn the existing ground waters into a sustainable asset but also to extend the current water supplies through a technically ingenious and environmentally most appropriate way of storing more water in underground reservoirs in areas of prolonged dry spells. In the South this could be done easily enough in countless limestone caverns in extensive karst regions, but this approach is perhaps even more appealing in the North, where the construction of surface reservoirs is much more expensive and where the storages suffer owing to high evaporation and frequent seepage (Zhang Dachang 1981). Geologically, the most appropriate structures for underground reservoirs are ancient river channels formed by crustal sinking; their gravel strata have high porosity (generally in excess of 20 percent), and if the banks and bottoms and sunken riverbeds are composed of impermeable or poorly permeable clays, storage can be very effective—all without digging canals, destroying farmland, or exposing water to evaporation. Not surprisingly, many experts advocate these structures in preference to the South-North water transfer or to surface reservoirs.

The first large underground storage on the North China Plain uses a 20-km-long, 10-km-wide stretch of ancient riverbed filled with sand, and it is capable of holding 480 million m^3 of water, of which more than 100 million m^3 can be pumped out. When fully replenished by temporary water diversion from nearby streams, the reservoir will irrigate over 30,000 ha of farmland. Hydrogeological surveys in Hebei have revealed 7,000 km^2 of sunken riverbeds and more than 20 sites suitable for underground storage (NCNA, March 18, 1980, *SWB* 1076). In Shijiazhuang Prefecture, Hebei Province, several counties have been injecting surface water into the ground over an area of 100,000 ha to force up the sinking water table by one-half to 3 m (NCNA, March 19, 1978, *SWB* 977).

3.4 Waterworks and irrigation

China has an unparallelled tradition of constructing intricate waterworks on a grand scale (for many fascinating details on the country's ancient hydraulic engineering see Needham 1965 and 1971). Rivers of the North China Plain were first regulated 4 millenia ago. Waters of the Huang He have been used for irrigation for nearly 2,500 years, and the origins of the Grand Canal are in the same period. By the end of the thirteenth century (Yuan dynasty), one could sail directly from Beijing to Hangzhou, 1,782 km away.

Perhaps the most admirable example of perfectly integrated ancient hydroengineering is the Dujiang Yan irrigation system on the Chengdu plain of western Sichuan, where recurrent flooding by the swift Min Jiang was controlled after 230 BC by the ingenious designs of Li Ping and his son Li Erhlang and by the massed labor of generations of peasants. A rock-walled riverbed was cut at the stream's entrance to the plain, the flow was subdivided by building successive arrowheads midstream, and the water was diverted into 520 branch canals totaling 1,165 km, its course further regulated by some 2,000 dikes and dams. Dredging and dike repairs during the low-water season have kept the system working for over 2 millenia, and the Dujiang Yan now irrigates some 530,000 ha of fertile land (Figure 16).

The traditional ways of building waterworks were continued and greatly expanded after 1949. Vast masses of peasants (during the 1970s as many as 100 million worked on repairs or new construction during off-season winter months) converge on the sites and toil without the benefit of any machinery—with just shovels, picks, chisels, rods, hammers, weigh-beams, straw or bamboo baskets, wheelbarrows, pull-carts, and locally made explosives. The list of waterworks built during the first three decades of the PRC is impressive.

Besides the already discussed small and large reservoirs, Chinese peasants also dug nearly 100 large drainage canals, strengthened many thousands of km of protective dikes along major rivers, sunk more than 2 million pump wells, installed over 70 million horsepower of pumping machinery, built more than 6,500 new irrigation networks (each capable of watering 600 or more ha of fields), and thus extended the total of China's irrigated farmland from 16 million ha (31 percent) in 1949 to 47 million ha (47 percent) by 1980 (NCNA, March 10, 1980, *SWB* 1965; see also Appendix A.5).

Most of the irrigation water is withdrawn from rivers, lakes, and reservoirs, and in about two-thirds of the cases the work is done by liquid fueled or electrical pumps; the numbers of these pump wells have been increasing rapidly, from less than 100,000 in the early 1950s, to 1.2 million by 1973, and to more than 2 million by 1980. The total power of China's irrigation and drainage equipment rose from just one million horsepower in 1949 to about 9 million horsepower in 1965, and it topped 75 million horsepower in 1982 (State Statistical Bureau 1982).

All this might easily lead to conclusions of enviable success in securing water for nearly half of the nation's crops and putting into place a modern irrigation infrastructure with profound environmental and economic benefits. While the quantitative advance is undeniable, however, the qualitative deficiencies are widespread, and in most instances of intensive irrigation the environmental benefits are decidedly mixed. To begin with, the claimed capacities are far above actual performance. More than 6,500 new large irrigation projects should be

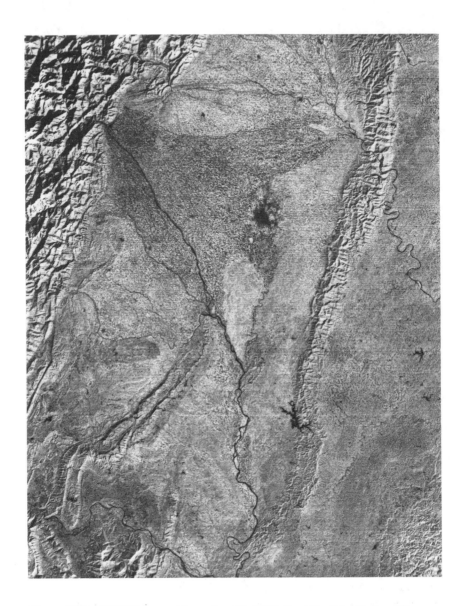

Figure 16. LANDSAT image (November 26, 1975, band 7) of the Dujiang Yan irrigation scheme in Sichuan. Chengdu, the province's capital, is the dark blot at the easternmost edge of the irrigated area which fans out immediately from the Min Jiang's entry into the plain. Few other farming areas in the world are so intensively cultivated.

able to water some 29 million ha, but only less than 20 million ha are efficiently watered. Leaks and seepages from irrigation canals, ditches, and culverts are so common that average losses of the channeled water amount to 40-50 percent, and in many localities 70-80 percent of the carried water is so wasted (Xinhua, July 27, 1978, *SWB* 993).

Similar quantitative-qualitative disparities apply to irrigation wells, of which there are now nearly 2.5 million (typically 30-40 m deep with 10-30 cm pipes). An average well waters no more than 2 to 6 ha. While the best Chinese arrangements can irrigate 20 ha (Nickum 1981), the center-pivot sprinkler on the North American plains can water up to 55 ha from a single well. The inefficiency of the former is caused by a combination of factors, ranging from faulty pump design and poor management (not unique to China: improper scheduling wastes plenty of water in most countries) to a lack of surface preparation (no or insufficient land leveling) and energy shortages. The last constraint is especially serious in China: electricity shortfalls are chronic, and official statistics show that for each horsepower of farming machinery just a bit more than 50 kg of fuel are available, enough for no more than 50 days of operations annually (Shangguan 1980). Frequent overexploitation of underground water, discussed in the preceding section, is another obvious reason for poor performance.

Chinese irrigation problems would be helped by technical modernization, most notably by the substitution of wasteful canal-fed systems by various sprinkler arrangements which allow a highly efficient distribution of water (with options to add fertilizer or pesticides) while minimizing salinity buildup and conserving good soil structure. Sprinkler irrigation has been tried out on smaller plots in a least half of all Chinese counties, but any extensive dissemination will long be hampered by the relatively high capital cost of different sprinkler systems, above all of the well-fed center-pivot irrigation system, which would be ideal for grain-growing areas of the northern and northeastern plains.

An interesting irrigation innovation that is raising crop yields in some parts of the Huang He valley is the use of water with high silt content. The usual practice in Shaanxi has been to close irrigation systems once the sediment content reaches 167 kg per m^3, but now the waters of the Jin He, the Luo He, and the Wei He are being diverted to irrigate some 330,000 ha in the Guanzhong area even when the sediment content is as high as 35 percent by weight, or about double the previous limit. Experimental U-shaped troughs with an adequate gradient and used at flow rates that prevent excessive silt sedimentation are to carry a slurry containing 820 kg of suspended matter per m^3 (one can hardly call this water) for distances of up to 50 km (NCNA, April 6, 1979, *SWB* 1030). And tests have also shown that muddy waters with a sediment content of up to 60 percent can be used to flood plots of alkaline or saline land to create a new fertile soil layer. Water and soil conservation in irrigation are much more amenable to technical fixes than the fundamental environmental problem increasingly plaguing all of China's water utilization—serious organic and inorganic pollution. This problem will require very heavy and sustained investment—not to achieve zero discharges but merely to bring the appalling situation within acceptable limits after decades of no control.

3.5 Water pollution

First, some summary statistics. According to a 1979 survey, daily discharges of polluted water amounted to 77.8 million m^3, or 28.4 billion m^3 a year (6 percent of the total volume utilized), with each m^3 of waste water contaminating the average 14 m^3 of natural water, and the annual economic loss caused by this massive pollution was put at about ¥5 billion (Qin 1980). Of 78 monitored rivers, 54 were polluted; 14, including all the major streams, were seriously polluted (Shen Gangqin 1981). Undoubtedly, the worst situation is in China's largest cities, where both municipal sewage and waste waters of numerous industries are dumped largely untreated into rivers, lakes, and reservoirs and onto soils, or where the polluted water is used for irrigation in suburban, predominantly vegetable, fields.

3.5.1 Urban wastes

Nothing is more illustrative of the state of Chinese urban waste-water treatment than the fact that in 1980 in a country with some 200 million city dwellers there were only 35 small municipal treatments plants (Li Chaobo 1980), and that over 90 percent of urban waste water is discharged untreated (Ma and Chang 1980). China's first big waste-water treatment facility was put into operation in Beijing's eastern suburb only in fall 1980; in the same year a new secondary treatment plant was completed near the capital's international airport with a daily capacity of 15,000 tons, with the effluent destined for irrigation (NCNA, June 24, 1980, *JPRS* 76056). But these measures are mere beginnings: Beijing's sewage flow rose from 66,000 tons a day in 1954 to 1.8 million tons by 1980 (NCNA, June 24, 1980, *JPRS* 76056), and the

Figure 17. An open sewer in downtown Beijing. Only now, after decades of neglect, is the city getting higher investment into essential waste water infrastructure.

sewers, though extended to 1,270 km, fail to keep pace with the inflow
(Figure 17).

Shanghai's situation appears to be even worse. The daily discharge
of polluted water now surpasses 5 million tons, but only 200,000 tons
are treated; and despite the recent substantial increases in waste-water
treatment capacity, the city is worse off than it was in the mid-1970s
because in the same period new sources of polluted water have added
nearly twice as much waste volume (*WHB*, November 11, 1980, p.1).

And the sewers in older parts of the city are not only totally inadequate but the city is unbelievably lax about their breakdowns, as illustrated by the following story from *Wenhui bao* (Chen and Zhou 1980). In the densely inhabited Huangpu district, 107 sections had raw sewage leaking onto streets in the winter of 1980, but it was only after a letter of complaint from a resident was published in the paper that repair crews were sent out. Yet actions like these are temporary stopgaps at best; the district's sewage pipes were laid in the 1920s and 1930s, when the population was a fraction of today's. Pipes and septic tanks have never been enlarged, and thus there is no way for the sewers to handle so much waste. And, curiously, the article also complains of shortages of repair crews and drainage workers—in a city with tens of thousands of unemployed.

The situation is similar in just about any large Chinese city. In Tianjin, which together with Beijing and Shanghai is one of the three cities directly under central administration, 1.26 million tons of untreated waste are dumped daily, and the Hai He is seriously polluted not only with the usual urban and industrial wastes but also with sea water flowing upstream, especially during dry years when the Hai He's volume is so low that interbasin transfers are necessary to provide the city with a minimum of water (Tianjin city broadcast, September 2, 1981, *JPRS* 79122; see also section 3.2.1). In Wuhan, Hubei's capital, formerly scenic Dong Hu (Dong Lake) in the southeastern suburbs, owing to the extensive disposal of industrial wastes and feeding of fish with human wastes, has been turned into a smelly cesspool (Li Xinghuai 1980). In Xi'an, only one-fifth of the daily discharge of 300,000 tons of polluted water is treated, and then only by natural settling.

If overloaded big city sewers are a symptom of China's rapid urban growth, how are urban wastes treated in the smaller cities? Most Westerners have been persuaded by repeated visitors' writings on the almost fanatically thorough recycling of nightsoil, China's precious and renewable fertilizer, that the buckets are emptied almost as soon as they are filled up and that the smelly wastes are turned into sweet vegetables (for a classical Western account admiring of the practice see King 1927; for recent descriptions see, for example, FAO 1977b). The image is not altogether false; indeed, to gather human wastes, the suburban villages have the cities and towns apportioned into wards and the collectors take (carrying, pushing, pulling, steering animals, or riding garden tractors) the nightsoil to the fermentation pits and into the fields—but not always regularly or on time, and increasingly with less enthusiasm (see also section 7.4). And Li and Huang's (1979) graphic description of the actual situation in Haikou, Hainan's largest city, is worth quoting at some length; very similar circumstances are to be found in many smaller cities around the country.

A stroll down of any of Haikou's streets, and even more so a glimpse into its backyards and alleys, reveals huge piles of garbage, and as "garbage trucks seldom come" to collect it, an "unbearable stench" suffuses the streets. "More serious is that the people removing excrement from Haikou are busy from morning till night. They remove it with carrying poles, bicycles, handcarts, oxcarts, and trailers. These nightsoil carts commonly leak their contents and splash them all over the roads they travel. Some carts, owing to carelessness, even tip over and spill their load in the streets, yet no one is concerned, waiting only for the rains to wash it away. In the city large and small hogs can commonly be seen wandering in the streets and defecating and urinating at will.

"Many residential areas are without sewers, and the residents can only dig small ditches into which they pour the waste water. . . . The Fangxiu residential area has about 400 households, or over 2,000 people, but to date there is not even one sewer, so that on rainy days the streets are flooded with sewage . . . making it hard for people to get around."

Three reasons are offered for this dismal situation. First, equipment and personnel are grossly inadequate: three available garbage trucks can collect some 40 tons a day, but over 200 tons of excrement and garbage are generated. The rest is the responsibility of peasant collectors, but because these have no strict removal schedules, pits often fill up and overflow. Second, funding is insufficient to cover even the operation of existing waste disposal units. Third, there is "leadership neglect and a lack of mass education and propaganda regarding sanitation." The responsible bureaucrats "take no interest" in the problem (an attitude all too frequently encountered in China) and see the preposterous sanitation "as a part of everyday life." And the people, knowing that heaven is high, trudge through the excrement.

The dismal state of Chinese municipal sanitation not only offends the city inhabitants with its smells and sights, but also polluted streams, reservoirs, lakes, and underground aquifers in, around, and underneath the cities are, almost without exception, the main sources of urban drinking water, and so it is hardly surprising that the quality of such liquids is often far below the prescribed standards. Here are just a few examples.

In Shanghai, where only 4 percent of the waste water is treated, 4 million m³ of unprocessed sewage is dumped daily into the Huangpu Jiang (Whangpoo River) and its branches, making the river one of the world's worst and largest sewers (Gao and Jin 1980). Yet it is Shanghai's principal water source, and eight water pumping plants are interspersed along the river with raw sewage outlets, with one intake, for Zhabei ward, a mere 40 m downstream of a large sewage opening! The heavy chlorophenol odor of Shanghia's water is distinct indeed!

The city's residents can get an acute sense of the water's quality just by walking along the river; every summer (May to September), when the irrigation water is used heavily upstream of Shanghai and the volume flowing through the city is substantially cut, the ratio of relatively unpolluted water to the dumped municipal waste falls to between 6:1 and 4:1, and in 1979 it sank to an incredible 2:1 and temporarily to 1:1 (Shen 1981). Of course, it was still the only source of drinking water, thus making half of every glass of water basically chlorinated sewage. During the summertime the "river" smells, with the malodorous periods getting longer; since 1964 there have been at least 20-50 such days, but in 1978, 106 were recorded, and in 1979, despite the doubled precipitation, there were still 99 (Gao and Jin 1981).

Tianjin's drinking water contains excessive concentrations of heavy metals, arsenic, and phenol (Rou 1980). Beijing's underground aquifers, the city's principal source of drinking water, are also contaminated with heavy metals, phenol, cyanide, and nitrates, the concentrations of the latter surpassing the standard severalfold (Li Xianfa 1980). The overall chemistry of the city's ground water has also changed, from strong carbonic acidity in the 1950s to sulfuric, chloride, and nitric acidity now, and in five of the six major aquifers water hardness has almost doubled in the past three decades.

From Chinese sources it is quite clear that as bothersome and environmentally harmful the improperly disposed organic municipal wastes are in most cities and towns, the most dangerous threat to the safety of drinking and irrigation water, and the most frequent danger to aquatic life, is posed by various uncontrolled industrial wastes.

3.5.2 Industrial pollution

The most frequent industrial water pollutants are different kinds of oil products, phenolic compounds, cyanide, arsenic, heavy metals (lead, chromium, cadmium, mercury), chlorinated hydrocarbons, nitrates, and sulfates. By far the heaviest concentration of industrial water pollutants is, of course, in larger cities in general, and in the highly industrialized cities of the North and Northeast in particular. However, as the sad example of Guilin shows, industrial water pollution is now a problem in just about any larger stream, save the remote Xizang rivers.

Guilin, in northern Guangxi, is the center of perhaps the most famous picturesque landscape in China. To many Chinese, and to an increasing number of foreigners who fly in, this is the most beautiful scenery the country offers: variously and wondrously shaped isolated hills carved out by water and wind in the karst region of the Li Jiang, the surprising shapes and colors of the rocks contrasting with the deep green vegetation and twisting streams, the landscape underlain by countless caverns and grottoes. Yet this is a badly flawed wonderland, although I have been surprised how many tourists appear to notice nothing awry. Plenty is.

The first public disclosures came in February 1979, telling of the Li Jiang being so heavily polluted by phenol, arsenic, chlorides, and cyanide that three factories had to be closed down and the operation of another one suspended. However, these measures came too late for most of the cormorants traditionally used for fishing on the river. In the past a cormorant used for fishing could catch over 5 kg of fish a day, and a fishing team could bring in 50 kg; now three out of four fishing teams in a small town near Guilin have had to take up other occupations, and the cormorants have died (NCNA, February 7, 1979, *SWB* 1022), a sad but inevitable result of the accumulation and concentration of toxic materials as they move up the food chain. More than a year later two Chinese dailies published detailed accounts of just how much the State Council's January 1979 orders on "speedy remedial measures . . . to protect the unsurpassed excellence of the Guilin scenery" had been implemented. The conclusion: the industrial pollution of scenic Guilin was still increasing (Wang and Gui 1980; Sun 1980). Here are some details.

In spite of the closing of the three polluting enterprises (a power plant, a smelter, and a paper pulp factory), and in spite of a government allocation of ¥ 7.83 million for control equipment, the pollution of the Li Jiang was worse in the spring of 1980 than in early 1979. Oil slicks and white scum floated on the surface, and the stench of the river, as well as of a few of its tributaries and Rongshan Hu, was "overwhelming." Cyanide and phenol showed no decline, while mercury concentrations rose more than 40 percent, and iron, fluorides, nitrates, and sulfides were also up. Dissolved oxygen declined precipitously, falling to zero downriver from the Longyin bridge, and more fish also died owing to an acute cyanide poisoning between January 17 and 18, 1980. And the Guilin rubber factory is dumping its wastes into grottoes, a sure way in the karst region to contaminate a wide area of underground waters.

There are other tourist attractions marked by polluted water. With China's opening to Western visitors, a variety of "high class" tour options emerged, among them a pricey boat trip (more than $3,000 without airfare) on the Grand Canal, the oriental counterpart of expensive French canal boating. The patrons would be perhaps interested in the following synopsis of the Grand Canal's health in Wujin County, Jiangsu, near the start of their journey (Anonymous 1980c). Of 4,700 ha of water surfaces in the county, 40 percent are seriously polluted, the county's Grand Canal section most of all, as an oil refinery, some chemical factories, a paper mill, and a print and dyeing plant discharge all their wastes into it without treatment.

The quantities of kerosene and, above all, phenol, are so high that the local fishery has been completely wiped out; desperate fishermen "marched collectively on the factories to protest and to demand food"; the plants were subsequently fined and started to compensate the fishermen with a fraction of their previous income—and kept on dumping the wastes. Western tourists willing to ply the sewers of east China are thus a clear boon for the local economy (Figure 18). But in other respects these waters are reasonably safe; at least I have not come across any report portraying the Grand Canal aflame—unlike the Ba He in Beijing.

Several factories in the capital's Chaoyang ward were dumping huge amounts of untreated oil waste into the Ba He, where it accumulated in a several-cm-thick layer. On December 16, 1979, some peasants working in a field on the southern bank of the river near Louzizhuang bridge were warming themselves by a small fire, and one of them tossed a smoldering piece of wood into the Ba He. The oil wastes immediately ignited and in 30 minutes the intense blaze destroyed nearby high voltage lines, melted five steel sluice gates out of shape, separated the surface cement layer of the bridge, thereby lowering its load capacity by a third, for a total loss of more than ¥80,000 (Anonymous 1980d).

Chinese rivers are also polluted by large volumes of solid wastes dumped by coal-fired power plants, mines, and metallurgical plants.

Figure 18. The Grand Canal, China's principal north-south water link, is full of transport and houseboats—and of heavy pollution coming from the vessels, millions of peasants, scores of cities, and numerous large factories on its shores.

Some 15 million tons of ash are dumped annually into rivers by power plants (Kinzelbach 1983), in Shaanxi stretches of some rivers are so filled with solid waste that the water "can no longer flow smoothly" (Shaanxi provincial broadcast, June 20, 1978, *SWB* 988), and slag dumping became a major threat to one of China's major archaeological sites. This unusual report comes from Anyang where the local steelworks have been dumping various residues into a local stream for more than a decade (Wang, Yang, and Zheng 1980). This dumping of slag and ashes created a 90-m-high pile in the middle of the river and squeezed the stream to mere two m width near the eastern bank, along which, in the Xiaotuncun-Houjiazhuang area, is China's largest Yin dynasty archaeological site, where more than 100,000 oracle bones and bronze and jade pieces were uncovered. The narrowed river is now eroding away this state-protected cultural site, and should serious flooding occur the area will certainly be much damaged as the blocked river now, as compared with the early 1960s, can handle only about a quarter of the flood-flow. Yet the most incredible part of the story is the proposed solution: not stopping the waste dumping into the river, not dredging the blocked channel—but cutting a new riverbed east of the old one, right through the protected site!

And then there is plenty of unspectacular water contamination by industrial releases, invisible and tasteless but very dangerous to human health: uncontrolled releases of heavy metals have been responsible for some astonishingly high cadmium and mercury concentrations in rivers and underground waters. At the entrance to Tianjin's largest water treatment plant the Hai He carried 17 times the allowed mercury content (*TJRB*, July 10, 1980, p. 1); at the main outlet of Xi'an's Lijiahao reservoir mercury concentrations are 440 times above the standard; and in the Songhua Jiang downstream of Jilin, organic mercury pollution in a stretch of more than 20 km reaches concentrations of between 2 and 20 mg per liter (Kinzelbach 1981), values up to five times higher than those recorded in Minamata Bay in Japan, the location of the world's most famous chronic mercury poisoning epidemic. (International mercury standards for drinking water specify no more than 0.001 mg per liter.) Fish in the Zhaoyuan Jiang have a mercury content up to 5.36 mg per kg of body weight, posing a direct threat to human health (Zhang Guanzhong 1981).

Industrial and urban wastes are eventually carried to the ocean, and among China's coastal seas the semi-enclosed Bo Hai—with sluggish water circulation, a large number of industries, ports and oil fields on its shores, and the waters of heavily polluted Hai He bringing into it the wastes of Beijing and Tianjin—has become so seriously polluted that in 1977 the State Council issued a directive to improve the situation (Xu Shangwu 1980). Shengli and Dagang oil fields are now finally treating most of their waste water, and heavy metal discharges have been lowered somewhat. However, the Bo Hai's waters are now the scene of (for China) relatively large-scale offshore drilling (a joint venture with the Japanese), and this will certainly add to the sea's pollution.

3.5.3 Controls

Since 1978 there has been no dearth of high-level decisions taken, orders given, special funds set aside, regulations created, letters of protest and exhortation published; the necessity to control China's widespread water pollution has been emphasized in numerous conferences, information meetings, and articles in dailies as well as in scientific journals. Any literate person in China should by now be aware of the magnitude and acuteness of the problem; no bureaucrat even just occasionally reading the Party daily could plead ignorance. And yet, there has been relatively little real accomplishment: some new primary waste-water treatment plants were completed in big cities (the largest in Beijing and Jilin), various industrial enterprises installed recovery systems to cut down their releases of pollutants, a few grossly offensive factories were even closed. On the whole, however, the quality of China's surface and underground waters has continued to slip. Why?

Certainly not for a lack of a legal or regulatory framework. The Law on Environmental Protection (Appendix D) is explicit in its injunctions against pollution and on behalf of needed waste controls and maintenance of good quality water (see above, and articles 11, 16, and 20 in Appendix D). Numerous local regulations based on the law can specify in detail any offenses and the penalties. For example, recent antipollution regulations enacted for Shanghai's port, where every day over 1,000 tons of sewage and 350 tons of garbage used to be dumped into the Huangpu Jiang by more than 4,000 ships (Gao and Jin 1980), are very comprehensive and stern. The 18-point regulations forbid any uncontrolled discharges of waste oils, refined oil products, and all other toxic pollutants, rinsing of ship decks into the river, redischarge of dredged bottom mud, use of chemical oil removers, etc., etc. (*JFRB*, July 1, 1980, p. 4).

Investment funds available for water pollution control have certainly not been adequate, even after the recent major increases, to start tackling the whole spectrum of accumulated neglect, but the situation has not been one of an absolute lack of money, or modern technology either. In fact, quite often the allocated funds have been relatively generous owing to the prominence of the location or the severity of the problem, yet the results have been very unsatisfactory. There can be no better example of this than the developments in Guilin. After the State Council issued its guidelines for the area's pollution control in January 1979, it provided a special fund of ¥5.915 million, the regional government added ¥43,000, monies carried over from the pollution control budget for 1978 amounted to ¥1.512 million, and finally ¥190,000 came from the factories' revenues for a total of ¥7.66 million, far from an inconsiderable sum. Yet only ¥2.077 million was actually spent, just a bit over one-quarter of the available sum (Wang and Gui 1980)—as if improvements were not urgently needed.

Discharges from a paper and dyeing mill in Yantai (eastern Shandong) have been polluting an ocean bay for years, often poisoning clams and other aquatic species. After strong protests by local fishermen the plant was given some ¥200,000 in 1975 to control the discharge, but by 1980 "this capital has not yet been used while pollution slowly grows" (Wu Guoguang 1980). And just one more of many similar examples is the lack of progress in controlling water pollution from the Zhanjiang mill on the Nanqiao Jiang (He Xibao 1979). The mill is releasing daily 4,000-5,000 tons of waste water, turning the river into a "huge polluted ditch with purplish-black water over which floats yellow froth and under which lie heavily polluted sediments." Some 10,000 people living along this smelly stretch must close their doors and windows in summer, and must eat vegetables irrigated by the water. Not surprisingly, the pressure to control has been strong, and since 1973 the mill has been given by the state ¥190,000, 23 tons of steel, 20 tons of cement, and 36 m³ of wood expressly to establish waste treatment; and the plant's technicians were sent to other provinces to study the installation and operation of the controls. Still, "these measures have been without result" (He Xibao 1979).

The reasons for the discrepancy between the new official attention paid to water pollution and the funds allocated for its control, on the one hand, and the sluggish introduction of efficiently operating technologies, on the other, lie in the very nature of the Chinese management structure. Writes Wu Guoguang (1980): "There are some plants that are not evaluated as Daqing-style enterprises because of noncompletion of one of the eight economic indicators . . . while there are some enterprises that have polluted whole rivers and endangered the health of millions of people, yet this has not affected their ranking as Daqing-style units." (For those who might never have heard the name of China's largest oil field in Heilongjiang, Daqing's production achievements in the 1960s and early 1970s became the regime's paradigm—dubious, as it turned out—of economic advance in industry.)

Anything that does not contribute to higher production and fulfillment of plan ahead of schedule (hence to special bonuses and rewards for the managers) is basically disregarded. More often than not higher layers of bureaucracy within the same resort will cover up and obfuscate on behalf of their inferiors to maintain their own aura of successful production supervision, and these attitudes and practices do not generate much fear of the new laws and regulations but do lead to feelings of arrogant nonchalance. When a fishing village at the entrance of Hangzhou Bay complained in a letter to a national newspaper (*GMRB*, October 22, 1980, p. 2) that yellow croakers had disappeared, that shark catches were down by 60 percent, and that in just four years jellyfish landings had declined by 80 percent, Shanghai's Main Petrochemical Plant, one of the principal polluters of the bay, extended "profound sympathy" to the fishermen in a letter, generous help indeed. Because there are no Friends of the Earth or Sierra Clubs in

China, or requisite laws and courts to which claimants may appeal, that is where the matter rests.

Because neglect is common, even now when the official line urges heightened attention, successful examples are not very many and, unfortunately, one of the greatest water pollution "successes" of the recent past turned out to be a cruel fake. Yaerh Hu near Echeng, a shallow lake of about 13,000 ha some 60 km east of Wuhan near the Chang Jiang, used to be one of the Hubei's major fishery areas and the source of drinking and irrigation water for 300,000 people living on its shores. The untreated discharges of three chemical plants built on the lake in 1959 led to heavy pollution, above all to high accumulations of organic phosphates. The lake's fish and shrimps died out, and the water became unfit for drinking and irrigation. After 1976, four oxidation ponds were set up and "pipes were installed to drain the effluent . . . thus avoiding the use of water-control channels" (NCNA, July 17, 1978, *SWB* 991).

The whole project cost ¥6.53 million and 6 million work units of "volunteer" labor. An expensive model of the installation toured various science and technology exhibits around the country, and starting in 1978 numerous news items, broadcasts, and articles portrayed the lake as pristine again, with fish catches surpassing the previous record levels, and claimed that "the physical health of the masses around the lake has been assured" (Ma and Yang 1980). But a writer for the Communist Party daily visited the region in the summer of 1980 and came away with a shocking twist to the success story.

He heard "peasants incessantly beseeching high heaven: 'Hurry and save us! Save our children and grandchildren!'" (Liu Hong 1980) The reason: as noted above, all sewage from the three large factories was to be drained to the oxidation ponds through pipes, but it flowed through the 9-km-long conduit for only one month after the work's completion! As the polluted water was not pretreated and the pipeline corroded rapidly, all the wastes were drained through an open canal alongside the pipe, a canal which was the only source of drinking and irrigation water for several tens of thousands of peasants. All food and water for these peasants was thus contaminated, and the *Remin ribao* reporter did not see any solution in sight.

China's water pollution controls, both quantitatively and qualitatively, are currently akin to those of rich Western countries of several generations ago: only the beginning of a long effort which is far from satisfactorily accomplished even in the United States, France, or West

Germany. The costs are, without exaggeration, enormous, and some exacting technologies and consistently able management are called for. But the rewards are many, and more so in China than in a typical rich Western country for the following reasons.

In rich countries most of the people live in cities, which are much easier to supply with properly treated water than hundreds of millions of peasants in tens of thousands of villages in the Chinese countryside who draw their drinking and cooking water directly from rivers, lakes, and ponds. Boiling this water will kill bacteria but does not affect the concentrations of heavy metals and numerous other toxic substances: here a proper waste-water treatment before release is the only solution, and it would contribute immensely to rural health. And the contribution of the improved quality of currently polluted irrigation water would be no less important. Except for Egypt, no nation has so much irrigated land as China, and productive Chinese farming is unthinkable without further extensions of watered land; yet, as already noted in several places in this chapter, irrigation with polluted water is causing economic losses and, more importantly, health hazards.

If China's waste waters were properly treated, more such liquids could be used for irrigation. Some 270,000 ha of farmland are now irrigated by treated sewage in China, and the area is expanding. The potential for using treated sewage for irrigation is large, however; it is calculated that if all municipal wastes were so used, about 80 percent of all water consumed by cities could be reused in farming, at considerable savings (Cao 1980). Of course, treated sewage is not particularly high in essential nutrients, and hence very large volumes must be applied if it is the only, or the principal, fertilizer. Technically, this is not an insurmountable problem if the liquid can be used within shorter distances of a treatment plant. In any case, treated sewage containing a high concentration of heavy metals is unsuitable for irrigation, and these, and many other pollutants, must be controlled at the source.

Again, this control could be very effective in both economic and environmental health terms; Beijing is a good example: citywide consumption of metallic materials for electroplating in 1978 was 1,100 tons, of which 600 tons was washed away with waste water, a loss of ¥25 million (Guo Zuyuan 1980). Recovery and reuse are undisputably rewarding, and Beijing's already considerably polluted water supplies would be spared further degradation. Throughout China there are scores of such heavy concentrations of electroplating wastes that would benefit equally from treatment.

Finally, the best applicable controls and recycling could go a long way toward helping to solve the current water shortages in many parts of North China, above all in the capital (see section 6.2.1), where today the industrial controls are weak, recycling is rare, often there are no usage fees, and the state keeps giving large subsidies for the development of additional resources without in any way managing the demand.

4

AIR

The setting sun shines low upon my door
Eve dusk enwraps the river fringed with spring
Sweet perfumes rise from gardens by the
shore,
And smoke, where crews their boats to
anchor bring.

Du Fu, "Wine"
(in H. A. Giles translation)

The wind so fresh, the sky so high
Awakes the gibbons' wailing cry.

Du Fu, "The Heights"
(in W. J. B. Fletcher translation)

When comparison is made by the numbers of people affected, China's air pollution is decidedly a minor problem compared with the country's water pollution. Rural areas in the South, where there is little need for household heating, only small-scale and scattered coal mining, and few fuel-intensive village industries, are virtually unaffected; and, of course, the vast stretches of the Northwest and Xizang are similarly unaffected. (However, the quality of inside air in these areas is often quite poor, with inefficient combustion of poor fuels in primitive stoves or in open fireplaces.) But in many northern and northeastern localities where villagers burn poor quality coal (dug out of small pits) through often very cold winters with heavy temperature inversions, even the rural air is seasonally heavily polluted with soot and sulfur dioxide. And in the country's larger cities, no matter in what region, air pollution is particularly troubling.

4.1 Pollution sources and effects

Inefficient combustion of low-quality coals in power plants, industrial boilers, steam locomotives, ships, and millions of households is by far the largest source of China's anthropogenic pollutants, accounting for about four-fifths of all emissions, and as such it will be described in some detail. Yet it is not the only important source. China's astonishingly inefficient iron and steel industry adds its share, as do the color metallurgy enterprises, refineries, and rapidly expanding chemical plants and cement factories. In some heavily industrialized parts of the Northeast, the combined emissions of many sources are extending several tens of km downwind from large cities and are easily seen even on LANDSAT satellite images. And throughout large areas of the North, westerly and northwesterly winds are bringing an unpleasant natural form of air pollution, small sand and soil particles from the deserts and eroded lands of Nei Monggol and the Loess Plateau.

The effects of air pollution on living organisms are always noticeable first in the place of the highest concentrations, and the recently reported rapid increases in the rate of lung cancer mortality in the country's large cities are especially disquieting. Plants and crops will be more affected by acid rain and photochemical smog, two of the potentially most dangerous imminent air pollution problems, which will be discussed separately later.

4.1.1 Chinese fuel combustion

China is now the world's third largest consumer of primary commercial energy behind the United States and the USSR and just ahead of Japan. Naturally, in per capita terms the country's energy consumption is just a fraction of these countries' levels: some 600 kg of coal equivalent (kgce) per capita a year in China vs more than 10,000 kgce in the U.S., over 6,000 kgce in the USSR, and 5,000 kgce in Japan. But unlike these three countries, and also unlike other large poor nations (India, Indonesia, Brazil), China is dependent on solid fuels to an extent almost unique in the 1980s: coal now provides 70 percent of all primary energy needs, crude oil only about 20 percent, and the remaining 7 to 8 percent is split about evenly between natural gas and hydroelectricity (Wu Zhonghua 1980).

A high dependence on coal will always be a major source of emissions, but the situation is made worse by the poor preparation of Chinese coals before combustion and by very inefficient conversion technologies. In general, Chinese coals are of reasonably good quality, with energy values around 29 megajoules (MJ)/kg, ash content between 2 and 20 percent (depending on the variety of bituminous coal), and sulphur content of 0.4-1.5 percent (Smil 1976). However, unlike in the other large coal-producing countries where most of the extracted coal is sorted, washed, and sized to remove impurities and prepare fairly uniform fuel, only 17 percent of Chinese coal output is cleaned or

Figure 19. Coal dust briquettes, here neatly staked in front of a coal shop in Guangzhou, fuel most of Chinese urban cooking and heating—releasing in the process large quantities of air pollution.

otherwise prepared before conversion. Naturally, combustion of mostly raw coal adds greatly to the generation of airborne emissions, ashes, and slag (Figure 19).

The other complication is perhaps even more important. In Japan, where virtually all energy must be imported and where oil products dominate consumption, average nationwide fuel conversion efficiency—or more precisely, according to the American Institute of Physics (1975), so-called first-low efficiency—is nearly 60 percent, and in the countries of North America and Europe it ranges between 40 and 55 percent; in China it is just 30 percent (Wu Zhonghua 1980). Seventy percent of the fuel burned is thus wasted, and emissions of air pollutants are, for the same quantum of useful energy, 50 percent higher than in Europe and twice as high as in Japan! Examples of energy use inefficiencies are ubiquitous, ranging from over two tons of coal equivalent and over 1,000 kWh of electricity needed to turn out one ton of steel (Western and Japanese means are below one ton of coal and below 500 kWh of electricity) to some nitrogen fertilizer plants consuming up to three times as much energy per kg of nitorgen as their Western or Japanese counterparts (Smil 1980c).

Peculiarities of Chinese sectoral energy consumption are yet another factor contributing to the country's considerable air pollution problems. Again unlike in most other countries, save the similarly oriented Communist societies, some two-thirds of China's primary energy is used by industries, while households and transportation each uses only about one-tenth of the total. This large industrial energy consumption is, of course, covered mostly by coal, and because it is heavily concentrated in about a score of large Chinese cities (with only half a dozen accounting for more than half the total industrial output!), power plants, iron and steel, metal-working, chemical, and other factories overwhelmingly equipped with outdated boilers and furnaces—there are about 200,000 of them, burning annually 200 million tons of coal and 25 million tons of oil with an average efficiency of just 50 percent (Zhao Zongyu 1981)—bring high emissions into all populous Chinese cities. And although household energy use is relatively small, the burning of raw coal in millions of small inefficient stoves is a very burdensome air pollution source through the colder half of the nation.

China's capital—where air pollution is "getting worse by the day" (Zheng Yijun 1980)—serves as a perfect example of compounded problems of high reliance on coal, heavy industrial concentration, and inefficient combustion in convertors, large and small. The city consumes over 8 million tons of coal a year, or no less than 76 percent of all fuel used in Beijing in 1980, and in turn, 70 percent of it is burned directly in several large power plants, some 10,000 small boilers in factories and offices, and in one million household stoves used for cooking and heating. The inefficient and uncontrolled operation of these stoves is the most intractable cause of high pollutant concentrations near the ground.

The combusion efficiency of small household stoves is usually no better than 15 percent, and most of the boilers do not surpass a 50 percent efficiency level. Typically, these devices emit 10-30 kg of soot for every ton of coal burned, together with 20 kg of sulfur dioxide (SO_2), so that the annual total reaches about 200,000 tons of sulfur dioxide and more than 300,000 tons of soot (Zheng Yijun 1980). Because these pollutants are emitted mostly from low chimneys, the always high ground concentrations are easily potentiated during periods of atmospheric thermal inversions, phenomena occurring during about 85 percent of fall and winter days, coinciding with the peak heating period (Tai 1980). Naturally, all industrialized cities in northern China are plagued by such frequent and strong winter inversions (as are their counterparts elsewhere in the temperate belt), which provide, in the absence of emission controls, a perfect setting for the repetition of acute air pollution situations made famous by the 1952 London episode.

In Beijing, measurements have shown SO_2 concentrations during inversions to be two to three times higher than during mixed air states; similar differences apply for particulate matter. The average SO_2 concentrations during the winter heating period are at least 20 percent above the national standard of 0.15 mg/m^3, while those for particulates exceed the standard (also 0.15 mg/m^3) about sixfold (Kinzelbach 1983). Dustfall should not exceed 8 tons per km^2 a month, but in the winter of 1978 the all-city mean was 38 tons, and Tai (1980) puts the annual average at 50 tons (with some 25 tons in ''clean'' summers still three times above the standard) and up to 80 tons in severe duststorms, the capital's other serious source of airborne solids (see section 2.3). Yi Zhi (1980) states that in the city ward near the steel plant the average is 285 tons a month and that in some industrial cities the local values frequently go up to 600 and even over 1,000 tons a month. Kinzelbach (1983) quotes Shen Baocheng's figure of 1,822 tons in one Shanghai location. Nationwide, dust concentration surpassed the norm in all 57 cities surveyed in 1979, and in 28 urban areas it was more than three times above the norm (Guo Huanxuan 1981).

As always with coal combustion, a significant fraction of solid particles (about half in Beijing) is smaller than 0.2 microns and therefore easily inhalable into the lungs, where it carries absorbed polycyclic organic matter (POM), a strong carcinogen resulting from incomplete combustion of coal, oil, and also wood. Usually measured in terms of benzo-a-pyrene, Beijing winter POM concentrations average 6.9 micrograms per 100 m³, two orders of magnitude above the acceptable standard (Kinzelbach 1981). Obviously, such relatively high concentrations of gaseous and particulate pollutants have many undesirable effects on atmospheric properties, human health, plants, animals, and materials. The next section will review some of this evidence.

4.1.2 Pollution effects

Relatively little Chinese information is available so far on the various effects of air pollution compared with many descriptions and studies of the undesirable consequences caused by water pollution (ranging from the disappearance of fish to the heavy metal content of vegetables irrigated by ground water). Why this is so I can only speculate: the cumulative effects of even relatively high concentrations of some air pollutants on vegetation or human health are noticeable and measurable only after some time, whereas in rivers turned anaerobic under indiscriminate dumping of oil and chemical waste all higher forms of life die almost instantly; epidemiological studies of air pollution effects are not only costly but must be undertaken with due caution and expertise.

In any case, we have some interesting information, and even if we didn't, the availability of ground concentration or dustfall values cited in the preceding section would be sufficient to deduce the effects on the basis of analogical Western or Japanese situations and the many detailed studies done in the area of air pollution effects mainly since the early 1960s. By far the most readily noticeable effect is, naturally, the reduced visibility in polluted areas, and in this regard I find poignant a plan for environmental improvement of the capital that speaks about the future goal of "a modern clean metropolis in which someone standing on the White Dagoba in Beihai park can see the Western Hills (25 km away)" (NCNA, September 28, 1978, *SWB* 1003).

This will require a complete reversal of recent trends. In Beijing the number of dusty days with greatly reduced visibility increased by 50 percent in the years 1971-78 compared with the decade of 1961-1970. This higher presence of condensation nuclei has been directly responsible for the increased frequency of heavy fogs (which, in turn, obstruct the dispersion of pollutants), whose number increased in the same period by 30 percent (Tai 1980).

Even setting aside the oppressive feeling of blurred, confined horizons—and all northern Chinese cities have them, especially in winter, although in summer the often heavy natural air pollution caused by advancing desertification may rival the cold months' loading of particulate matter—and looking straight up, one still cannot avoid a sun looking as dim as the moon. Large amounts of airborne particulate matter affect the incoming solar radiation through scattering and absorption, and the link between heavy air pollution and high frequency of rickets is, of course, a classic example of the indirect effects of suspended solids on human health. Perhaps I should note that although generally better nutrition, improved living conditions, and higher vitamin D intake in the food has basically eliminated the effect, a precisely measurable difference still remains: a series of Czech studies in the 1960s has shown statistically significant delayed bone maturation in children living in heavily polluted areas. I know of no comparable study in China (such studies are not cheap as hundreds of wrist x-rays must be taken in polluted control areas and compared), but an interesting historical-climatological study from Shenyang, one of the Northeast's most industrialized cities, documents a clearly significant weakening of solar radiation received on the ground during the past several decades (Han and Wang 1980).

While in the years 1933-34 dustfall per km^2 averaged 139.5 tons, during the 1955-1973 period, the average rose to 499.7 tons per km^2, and the incoming solar radiation was cut by molecular scattering and particulate and water absorption by as much as 33.3 percent in the worst years. Besides decreased insolation, annual discharges of 66.7 billion m^3 of waste gas, 190,000 tons of SO_2, 440,000 tons of fly ash, and 2.89 million tons of settling dust are highly correlated with the growing death rate caused by malignant tumors, which rose in Shenyang from 20/100,000 in 1957 to 80/100,000 in 1973, and to 120/100,000 in 1978, findings consistent with those elsewhere around the world. For China as a whole, lung cancer mortality is 4 to 5 cases per 100,000 inhabitants, but in cities it is between 17 and 31 per 100,000, a difference largely attributable to heavy air pollution (Kinzelbach 1981). In the northern cities, lung cancer is now the most frequent malignancy, and in Beijing its incidence grew by 30 percent during the 5 year period between 1974 and 1978, an alarmingly rapid increase (Tai 1980).

An estimate published by Qin Ling (1980) ascribes to the effects of air pollution in Beijing, Shanghai, Wuhan, and Guangzhou an annual loss of over some 3.5 million workdays (that is, an average of some 10,000 people incapacitated every day), as well as more than 6,000 premature deaths; these deaths occur, as clearly documented from Western epidemiological studies, predominantly among newborns and elderly people with chronic lung or heart diseases. And, naturally, chronic upper respiratory infections (rhinitis, pharyngitis) are much more common in heavily polluted areas (for a quantitative example see section 6.2.2 on Shanghai).

Local damage to plants and livestock must also be quite considerable near coal-fired power plants, refineries, and chemical works with no or only rudimentary controls. The few reported cases are, most certainly, just the proverbial tip of the iceberg. Xiong and others (1978) report that heavy industrial air pollution in Lanzhou's Xigu district has already destroyed all the fruit trees in nearby villages, dates flower but bear no fruit, and pumpkins fail to mature; livestock have oral cavities that ulcerate, perforate, and keep them from eating, causing high death rates. Xu and others (1980) mention that in 1974, 4,000 ha of wheat near Tianjin was damaged by chlorine escaping from a nearby factory. Scenic Guilin, featured above in a section on industrial water pollution (section 3.5.2), also has quite considerable air pollution problems. Various chemicals released from plants in the Dafeng Shan area have turned the rocks white, poisoned the trees, and "utterly destroyed" the sensitive karst ecosystem (Wang and Gui 1980). Of the 300 stacks in the area, 70 percent had no fly-ash control in 1980 (Liu Hongqi 1980).

And to close this list of examples, a report of a strange acute air pollution episode leading to human poisoning—an illustration as well of the casual neglect in waste disposal, an attitude that will take time to overcome. Somewhere in Liaoning Province in September 1980, workers at a chemical factory took a tank of 100 kg of chlorine to a riverbank and tried to dump it into the river (just like that); the container burst and the chlorine cloud seriously poisoned 78 patients in a nearby sanitarium (well located indeed!). The local hospital refused to treat them (as they were not local residents), and they had to be put into an army hospital. As if all of this was not incredible enough, the leading administrator of the sanitarium tried to interfere with the treatment of the stricken patients, and in the end nobody was even fined for the accident (Liaoning provincial broadcast, October 2, 1980, *JPRS* 76653).

If this episode exemplified typical Chinese attitudes toward air pollution control, prospects for future improvements would not be bright. Although I believe it to be far from an isolated example, I am glad to report that some genuine improvements have finally been initiated to reduce China's urban and industrial emissions of air pollutants.

4.2 Substitutions and controls

The overall magnitude of the control problem is staggering. On the one hand, the combustion of 600 million tons of China's inferior coal releases annually at least 120 million tons of ash, 20 million tons of fly ash, and 12 million tons of sulfur dioxide (Liu Hongqi 1980). On the other hand, there are no readily available, cheap hydrocarbons to re-place the coal (both crude oil and natural gas production have been stagnating for several years, and even sizeable offshore discoveries in the Nan Hai will not bring rapid relief), the cost of fully replacing the outdated conversion equipment is beyond China's foreseeable means, and even control methods well-established abroad, such as electric precipitation of fly ash, have the disadvantage of high capital and energy cost. What affordable and effective solutions are possible?

Large-scale substitution of direct coal combustion in urban areas by manufactured gas (usually called coal gas or town gas) has been per-haps the most favored idea among Chinese experts. Undoubtedly, it has the advantages of a good resource base, a relatively efficient and well-established technology of moderate cost, and the potential for bringing truly significant improvements of air pollution in China's large and medium-sized cities. Town gas, typically with about 18.5 megajoules (MJ) m^3 and only half as energetic as natural gas, has long been a nearly universal ingredient of energy usage in all larger European, American, and Japanese cities, while in China only about 10 million people in 60 of the country's 224 large and medium-sized cities have access to the fuel, manufactured in outdated gasification facilities, or to supplies of liquified petroleum gas (Zhao Zongyu 1981).

In comparison with current typical direct combustion rates, a coal gas plant with an annual capacity of 4 million m^3 could save about one million tons each year, thus obviating an investment of some ¥100 million for new coal mine construction or expansion; this benefit alone would amortize the plant's cost in only seven or eight years (Zheng Yijun 1980). There are, of course, considerable expenditures not only for the plant itself but also for distribution pipes and burners, heaters and stoves, but these, too, are soon repaid by greatly improved air quality and much higher combustion efficiencies. This solution would be especially appealing for the heavily polluted capital: within its mu-nicipal boundaries there are very large coal reserves, and the gradual development of coal gasification with an ultimate capacity of 10 million m^3 would enable all households and most industries to relinquish wasteful and polluting direct combustion.

How rapidly, indeed if at all, various gasification proposals become a reality will be a telling sign of China's advances in urban air pollution control because any large-scale introduction of other clean fuels—natural gas and electricity for heating and cooking—will be beyond China's capabilities for a long time to come. In any case, the other two strategies for reducing air pollution—increasing combustion efficiencies and installing control devices—should be pursued simultaneously.

In the first respect, the Chinese have enormous opportunities—witness their current huge lag behind industrialized countries—and since the late 1970s they have started to close the gap. In 1980 for the first time in the history of the PRC the total value of industrial output in the 32 largest cities went up by an average of 10 percent, while primary energy use actually went down by 4.6 percent as various conservation measures started to spread (Wu Baolang 1980). And for the country as a whole, industrial output rose by 8.7 percent, while primary energy consumption went up by merely a fraction of a percent. Naturally, it is in the best interest of the Chinese to encourage any efforts leading toward lower energy intensity of economic production because this lowers both the specific emissions of pollutants and output costs.

Reaching average Western levels in industrial combustion efficiency would save the Chinese at least 60 million tons of coal a year—and with it the emissions of millions of tons of ash and sulfur dioxide. News of the remodeling and upgrading of industrial boilers has been common since the late 1970s, and there will be outstanding opportunities for further improvements for many years to come. On the other hand, it must be realized that even with much better energy intensities and with greatly changed energy/GNP ratios (see section 7.5 for details) Chinese energy needs will rise substantially in the coming decades, and unless the Nan Hai drilling brings fabulous discoveries, coal will remain the principal source to satisfy this demand.

This will make air pollution controls more difficult: unlike hydrocarbons, coal cannot be economically desulfurized before combustion, and of course, burning will continue to generate large quantities of ash to be disposed of and fly ash to be captured by electrostatic precipitators. These control devices, mandatory on any larger Western coal-burning source, are now installed on only one percent of China's power plant capacity (Kinzelbach 1983), yet without them there can be no progress in eliminating most of the harmful particulates.

4.3 Coming problems

Even if the Chinese are very successful in eliminating much of their urban and industrial particulate matter air pollution by fuel substitution, combustion efficiency increases, and efficient controls, two new problems will be gaining prominence in the coming decades: acid rain and photochemical smog, both potentially very damaging and both difficult to control.

Acid rain—precipitation with pH well below the natural value of 5.6—is a phenomenon as old as the large-scale, concentrated combustion of coal, but only during the past two decades has its extent and effects been studied in detail in Europe, North America, and Japan (Husar, Lodge, and Moore 1978 is a fine survey). As long as the pollutants causing the effect, oxides of sulfur above all, are released in relatively small volumes and from low stacks the problem remains just a localized nuisance. Major difficulties arise when massive releases from tall stacks of coal-fired power plants or ore smelters are carried by prevailing winds, often for hundreds of kilometers, to affect large areas downwind from the source. As a result, previously unpolluted regions far from any major industries may turn out to have greater frequency of and more acid rain than the locations surrounding the pollution sources. Perfect illustrations of this occurrence can be found in southern Norway and Sweden, where the acid rain is caused mostly by English emissions carried across the North Sea, or in New England and the Canadian Maritimes, which are affected by pollutant releases from the industrial heartland of the United States and Canada.

Acute effects of acid rain are very rare. Only accidental releases of concentrated acids from chemical factories can cause the pH to drop so drastically that plant leaves will exhibit immediate damage, a rare case indeed. The real problem with acid rain is its cumulative effect on soils, vegetation, and aquatic ecosystems. Increasing acidity may lead to lower annual increments and finally to complete cessation of growth (coniferous trees are especially sensitive), to composition changes of terrestrial ecosystems (resistant weeds replacing climax species), and to gradual elimination of higher fauna from progressively more acid waters of lakes or ponds in all cases where the effect is not counteracted by naturally based substrate (i.e., acid rain's effects are especially pronounced in ecosystems on already acid soils, and are minimized on basic substrate).

Chinese acid rain has been, so far, either barely noticeable or very localized. A series of measurements during 1979-1980 showed that Beijing's rainwater was still close to neutral, with most values between ph 6 and 7, but that there was a heavy concentration of sulfate (SO_4) and nitrate (NO_3) ions, an average of 12 and 3.76 mg per liter respectively (Zhao et al. 1981). The investigators conclude that the high concentration of suspended matter neutralizes the acids and keeps pH up. On the other hand, measurements in Shanghai and Songjiang counties, started in March 1980, recorded the first acid rain episode in the Shanghai area between September 19 and 21, 1981 (Shanghai city broadcast, October 13, 1981, *SWB* 1106).

In any case, these are localized cases; more extensive regional impacts will not be felt until the Chinese substantially accomplish their planned expansion of coal-fired electricity generation in large modern power plants. To extract bituminous coal and, increasingly, low quality high-sulfur lignite from large surface mines and to burn it in so-called mine-mouth plants is a well-established, efficient approach extensively used in Europe and North America—but an innovation in China. In the late 1970s the Chinese started construction of a series of large mine-mouth power plants in Jilin, Liaoning, Hebei, Shaanxi, and Shandong (Smil 1981a). Continuing serious shortages of electricity and high costs and long lead times for hydrostation construction led to proposals for building a truly giant concentration of coal-fired stations in Shaanxi, China's richest coal province.

The realization of these Shaanxi plans would lead to a combustion of tens of millions of tons of bituminous coal a year, and the large sulfur dioxide emissions would be carried in a southerly and southeasterly direction in winter and a northerly and northwesterly direction in summer, affecting, in the first case, farmlands of the North China Plain and, in the second, Nei Monggol pastures. Moreover, the valley of the Fen He in Shanxi has very frequent periods of calm, over 30 percent of the time throughout the year, up to 70 percent in some locations (Wang and Dong 1980). This means reduced atmospheric mixing and more common and stronger inversions and hence a greater likelihood of higher ground concentrations of gaseous emissions.

Prevailing winds in lignite fields of Jilin, where another series of large mine-mouth stations is planned, would carry the summer emissions over the Da Hinggan, China's richest boreal forest, and increased SO_2 releases from coal combustion anywhere in China would have, in time, major destabilizing effects on aquaculture, which is now again expanding. Currently there are no reliable inexpensive techniques to control sulfur dioxide emissions from large sources, and the reluctance repeatedly shown by American and Canadian industries to commit themselves to stringent controls shows that even in rich countries SO_2 abatement is a difficult task.

Photochemical smog, encountered in any location with a combination of large nitrogen oxide and hydrocarbons emissions, sunny weather, and limited atmospheric mixing, has also already made its appearance in several Chinese cities, although automobile traffic, the principal source of pollutants needed to initiate complex photochemical reactions, is still relatively light even in such places as Beijing and Shanghai. The emissions of poorly made or inadequately maintained vehicles, however, are staggering. The Beijing brand jeep and Shanghai brand limousine, two vehicles accounting for about half of all Chinese light automobiles, consume, respectively, 17 and 20 liters per 100 km (Kinzelbach 1983). By comparison, a typical Western compact car of the early 1980s uses about 10 liters per 100 km.

According to the data of the leading group for Environmental Protection at the State Council, hydrocarbon emissions of Chinese-made cars are 13 to 55 times higher than those of comparable Japanese cars. Yet these are not the worst examples. Yu Guangyuan (1981) reports that many cars use 30 liters and some gulp as much as 50 liters per 100 km, releasing even more voluminous emissions of unburned hydrocarbons. Such prodigious emissions, congested cities under sunny summer skies, and stagnating high pressure cells limiting the air mixing are a perfect combination of ingredients for photochemical smog. In Lanzhou, a city with an unusually high concentration of chemical factories, photochemical smog is already forming 35 percent of the time (Xiong Yi et al. 1978).

In the early 1980s China had only 1.5 million civilian motor vehicles, of which just 180,000 were passenger cars and the rest trucks and buses. Although there is hardly any chance of private cars taking the place of bicycles and sewing machines as the desirable items for a typical Chinese consumer, millions of new vehicles of all sorts will be added before the year 2000, and the total volume of emissions and hence the potential for photochemical smog in China's large cities will increase accordingly. Judging by the situation in other industrializing poor countries afflicted by urban photochemical smog, no effective control measures will be taken in this respect for a long time, and tens of millions of Chinese city dwellers will continue to suffer from excessive concentrations of hydrocarbons, nitrogen oxides, ozone, and oxidants. Roadside accumulations of lead and its effects on children living near the busiest roads also will be increasing.

BIOTA

Methinks there is a genius of the hills, clad in wisteria, girdled with ivy, with smiling lips, of witching mien, riding the red pard, wild cats galloping in the rear, reclining in a chariot, with banners of cassia, cloaked with the orchid, girt with azalea, culling the perfume of sweet flowers to leave behind a memory in the heart.

Chu Yuan, "The Genius of the Mountain"
(in M. A. Giles translation)

Bears roar, dragons chant—the thundering cascade . . .
Tigers playing the zither and phoenixes drawing the carriages . . .

Li Bo, "Tianmu Mountain
Ascended in a Dream"
(in Wu-chi Liu translation)

The richness of Chinese biota is considerable. China has more than 30,000 species of higher plants belonging to over 2,000 genera and 300 families, including about 3,000 species of trees. The United States, with virtually the same amount of territory, has only 679 native tree species (Hsiung and Johnson 1981). Still incomplete surveys of China's fauna have counted up to 2,100 species of terrestrial vertebrates, including 1,167 species and 911 subspecies of birds, 428 mammalian, 299 reptilian, and 208 amphibian species (NCNA, July 10, 1980, *SWB* 989; September 17, 1980, *SWB* 1102; Lin Zi 1980).

Most of this variety is to be found in South China, where in a few locations the untouched climax ecosystems are among the most diverse living assemblies of Asia. Unfortunately, the different forms of environmental onslaught detailed in the preceding chapters have done away, singly or in concert, with much of the natural foundations requisite for such diversity. And deforestation, erosion, desertification, destruction of lakes, blocking of rivers, and pollution of many kinds have not been the only degradative factors: the uncontrolled hunting of mammals, massive catching of amphibians and birds, overfishing, and destructive fishing by dynamiting or poisoning have contributed to the serious decline of many common species and to extinction or near extinction of several scores of animals.

5.1 The disappearance of species

International wildlife organizations have focused the public's attention on the disappearance of endemic exotic animals such as the Nilgiri tahr and the Philippines eagle. Their obviously earnest motivation aside, I have never been comfortable with this approach. Applying this approach to Chinese affairs leads to pandas taking over—and as soon as one learns that they have been accorded fairly extensive protection and that the World Wildlife Fund, whose symbol that little black and white bear is, is now cooperating directly with the Chinese, one might be well satisfied: the popular symbol of Chinese wildlife is in no immediate danger of extinction. Other rare Chinese mammal, bird, and fish species are endangered, as will be detailed below, but even this appears to me to be less important than the massive disappearance of formerly numerous ecosystemically essential though hardly exotic foxes, carps—and trees.

Indeed, this is where the standard conservation appeals are misleading: an emphasis on heterotrophs at the apex of nutritional webs to the near exclusion of trees and herbs. Save the bamboos, of course, is the real conservation task, not save the pandas! Chinese deforestation—massive nationwide, astonishing regionally, and outright crippling locally—is thus undoubtedly the gravest process of ecosystemic impoverishment in China of the last three decades and a principal reason for the accomplished or threatened extinction of several endemic heterotroph species.

In Chinese sources I have not come across any mention of a rare tree completely disappearing in the last 30 years, or an imminent danger to any endemic genera such as *Cathaya, Cunninghamia, Fukienia*, and *Glyptostrobus. Gingko biloba* still also grows wild in China (Hsiung and Johnson 1981). Nevertheless, the extent of deforestation has been such that I feel certain that some of the rarer of China's 3,000 tree species have been seriously reduced in number, as were many more of its thousands of flowering plants, some of which certainly disappeared with converted grainfields, on eroded slopes, or under reservoirs. There is mention of the near extinction of Hainan sandalwood

(*Ormosia henryi*) and Hainan magnolia (*Manglieta hainanensis*), and *Cathaya argyrophylla* has to be protected in the Huaping forest reserve in Guangxi (Zhang Tianxiong 1980).

On the other hand, there is a good deal of specific information on the extinction or endangered state of numerous mammals and birds. Among the 603 species of animals listed worldwide for absolute protection, 85 can be found in China (NCNA, September 8, 1979, *SWB* 1051), and Ma and Chang (1980) claim that since 1949, 10 wild mammal species have become extinct and 20 are very near extinction; the first category includes Przewalski's horse (*Equus przewalskii*) and the high-nose antelope (*Saiga tatarica*). (A selective list of important rare, protected, and endangered species in China can be found in Appendix E.) Most of the endangered species are in southern China, where the country's richest tropical and subtropical forests have been indiscriminately cut, causing drastic declines of mammal and bird counts. In 1949, Hainan's tropical forests sheltered about 100,000 water deer (*Hydropotes inermis*) and more than 2,000 pileated gibbons (*Hylobates concolor*); today their respective counts stand at about 10,000 and less than 30, both clearly very near extinction (Zhang Tianxiong 1980).

Similarly, Yunnan's Xishuangbanna national reserve has more than 500 large vertebrates, about one-quarter of China's total, but several protected species, including gibbons (*Hylobates* spp.), langurs (*Pygathrix roxellana*), lorises (*Nycticebus concany*), wild elephants (*Elephas maximus*), wild cattle (*Bibos* spp.), and green peafowl (*Pavo muticus*), are near extinction. To the loss of habitat one must add widespread poaching; one village shot 39 wild oxen in 1979, and a local Party secretary killed 8 of them in one day. As a writer in *Guangming ribao* carefully remarks, when protected animals in the nation's richest reserve are treated like this, one can imagine the fate of fauna elsewhere (Yang Yuguang 1980).

A better indicator of the real impoverishment of Chinese biota is the disappearance of many common species, on land and in water, whose decline or extinction opens the way to undesirable, and often economically extremely costly, ecosystem changes. Pollution and overfishing have drastically affected the catches of many formerly common marine species. For example, in the Bo Hai, economically valuable fish are virtually nonexistent; huge seasonal migrations of hairtail and yellow croakers in the Dong Hai (East China Sea) can no longer be observed; yellow croakers caught recently in the Nan Hai have been immature fish (NCNA, April 22, 1980, *SWB* 1081).

Around Zhoushan archipelago, where one-tenth of China's fish are caught, landings of yellow croakers dropped by 88 percent between 1974 and 1978 (Xinhua, August 26, 1979, *SWB* 1048). The annual catch of this species in all of the Dong Hai fell from record levels of 350,000 tons to just 110,000 tons by 1977 (Wang Guichen 1979), and a meeting of the China Aquatic Products Society in Shanghai was told that both large and small yellow croakers would soon become extinct (Beijing home broadcast, November 15, 1978, *SWB* 1010).

The construction of 45,000 dams on Chinese rivers, as well as the erection of more than 7,000 floodgates, virtually all of them without fish passages or ladders, deprived many fresh-water species of their spawning and breeding grounds and resulted in a massive reduction of harvests. In the Chang Jiang basin all large lakes, with the exception of the two biggest, are now completely separated from the river (Zhang Guanzhong 1981), and the river's fish output was more than halved, from 450,000 tons annually in the 1950s to 200,000 tons in 1980 (Wang Zhongren 1981). Nationwide, the decline was from 600,000 tons to 300,000 tons. As related in section 3.2.1 above, the survival of several aquatic species in the Chang Jiang will be made impossible if the Gezhouba project is completed without any facilities for fish passage; eels (*Anguilla* spp.) in Sichuan will be completely wiped out, as will be the rare white sturgeon, which spawns in the upper reaches of the river. In economic terms, the loss of 60-70 percent of the spawning grounds for four carp species (black, grass, silver, and variegated) will be even more important (Wang Zhongren 1981).

Among the common amphibians, frogs have been in serious decline; they have been killed in huge numbers by peasants, mainly to be sold to cities for food or for export or to be fed to chickens and ducks. The extent of this practice became so alarming that the Ministry of Agriculture in August 1979 issued a special circular prohibiting the catching and selling of frogs throughout China and insisting, moreover, that when fields are drained and treated with chemical fertilizers or insecticides all possible care be taken to protect frogs (Xinhua, August 24, 1979, *JPRS* 74373). They are being protected because in South China's paddy fields frogs consume a considerable number of insects; thus pest infestation is lowered and crop yields increased, at no cost and with less insecticide pollution. Many species of snakes, eagerly sought in China for their purported medicinal properties and for multicourse snake dinners (capped by gulping gallbladder liquid dropped in a cup of spirits), have also been much reduced in numbers, especially in Guangdong Province.

On the land, deforestation and indiscriminate hunting have reduced the number of fur animals throughout the country: while in the decade of 1956-1965 animal harvests averaged 16 million skins, now there are just over 7 million skins (Ma and Chang 1980). A survey of Xinjiang, where three river valleys in Qinghe County are China's only beaver (*Castor fiber*) habitat, has found that since 1965 the number of animals has declined by 90 percent owing to widespread felling of willow trees along the rivers and uncontrolled hunting (Xinhua, August 27, 1980, *SWB* 1108).

A widespread and economically very costly phenomenon has been the extinction of the four principal rat predators: foxes, weasels, cats, and owls. This had led to local outbreaks of massive rat infestation with rat packs destroying crops in the daytime. For example, melon crops were nearly obliterated, and every inch of an 800-ha field of peanuts in Tenglian village (Shandong) was damaged by rats in 1980 (Zhai et al. 1980). The disappearance of predators has caused large rat outbreaks and ensuing damage to previously productive pastures in Qinghai as well. In the late 1970s some 8 million ha of pastures was affected (one-eighth of the province's total), and the annual loss of dry grass reached 2.5 million tons, enough to feed more than 5 million sheep (Zheng Boquan 1980). Rats are also causing increasing damage to forest seedlings because the number of their predators, such as sables (*Martes* ssp.) and weasels (*Mustela* ssp.), has been much reduced owing to the high prices paid for their furs (Xu Dixin 1981).

If this had been written in 1970 or 1975, there would be little encouraging news to report. But tangible economic losses and spreading environmental awareness, including the renewed stress on preservation of the precious national heritage, have led to new conservation efforts unprecedented in Chinese history. Not surprisingly, this attention is aimed at the most unusual and most endangered ecosystems, plants, and animals.

5.2 Conservation efforts

Encouraging progress in nature conservancy dates only to the latter half of the 1970s. As of 1980 China had 72 natural reserves—the oldest ones dating back to the late 1950s, with more added in the early 1960s, but 34 have been set up only since 1976—with a total area of 1.71 million ha, still a mere 0.17 percent of the country's territory (NCNA, September 17, 1980, *SWB* 1102), and just a fraction of the protected lands in the United States (U.S. national parks and wildlife refuges now encompass over 66 million ha). A national meeting in September 1980 adopted proposals to set up 300 new reserves before the end of 1986 with a total area of 9.6 million ha, or one percent of China's territory; these protected lands are to include representative areas of all principal ecosystems, localities with endangered animal and plant species, unique geologic formations (deserts, glaciers, hot springs), and fossil sites (NCNA, September 17, 1980, *SWB* 1102).

In 1980 three of China's natural reserves were also designated as international biosphere conservation areas by the Man and the Biosphere Program of UNESCO: Changbai Shan in Jilin, Dinghu Shan in Guangdong, and Wolong in Sichuan (Xinhua, March 27, 1980, *SWB* 1083). Changbai Shan, founded in 1960 with an area of 210,000 ha, in three Jilin counties on the North Korean border is largely a typical temperate forest with four distinct vertical belts. More than 1,300 species of flowering plants, over 300 species of terrestrial vertebrates, and some 200 kinds of birds can be found in the preserve. The rarest of the protected animals there are the Siberian tiger (*Panthera tigris altaica*), the sika (*Cervus nippon mandarinus*), and the leopard (*Panthera pardus*). A detailed ecological study of the forest is now under way (Qing and Huang 1980).

Dinghu Shan is the oldest Chinese natural reservation, established in 1956 on just 1,130 ha in Gaoyao County (Guangdong), 15 km north of Zhaoqing. This semitropical reserve has an unusual variety of higher plants, over 2,000 species of 278 families and 1,118 genera. Within the reserve there is a 270 ha patch of natural forest more than 400 years old, an ancient sacred Buddhist grove. Since 1979 the reserve has been the site of a permanent research station.

Wolong, in the southwestern part of Wenchuan County (Sichuan), on the eastern slopes of the Qionglai Shan, is the largest reserve in southern China; it was established on 20,000 ha in 1963 and expanded to 200,000 ha in 1975. The area spans several distinct ecosystems up to just under 4,000 m above sea level, and it contains more than 60 mammal and 300 bird species. Among the 29 rare animals are the golden monkey (*Pygathrix roxellana*), the white lipped deer (*Cervus albirostris*), the snow leopard (*Uncia uncia*), and the monal (*Lophophorus lhuysii*). Not one of these creatures, however, is as famous as the reserve's most valuable resident, the giant panda (*Ailuropoda melanoleuca*).

Wolong is the panda's most extensive protected habitat, and recently Chinese giant panda experts and representatives of the World Wildlife

Fund led by George Schaller set up a long-range study of the animals' life cycle and habitat in the reserve (Schaller 1981), the beginning of a permanent research center. Ying Xionggou panda farm on the reserve, an enclosure containing many arrow bamboo groves, had six pandas for breeding as of early 1981 (NCNA, January 13, 1981, *SWB* 1123).

Nine more panda protection zones, seven in Sichuan, one each in Shaanxi and Gansu, have also been set up so that the total of the panda's protected habitat reaches 560,000 ha (NCNA, May 11, 1980, *SWB* 1083). The best estimates put the total panda count at a bit over 1,000, and the current attention and protection should ensure their continued survival. One problem that will always remain is the peculiar life cycle of the umbrella bamboo (*Thamnocalamus spathaceus*), which is the panda's staple diet. A mature animal eats 10-20 kg of this bamboo each day, and when after a cycle of 90-100 years the plants bloom, bear seeds, and subsequently wither away *en masse*, the panda's survival in such localities is gravely threatened. The most recent large-scale occurrence of this phenomenon was in 1975-76 in the Baishui reserve on the northern slopes of the Min Shan in Gansu, when 138 pandas starved to death (Ge 1979).

The largest and certainly most spectacular reserve in the eastern coastal region is Wuyi Shan in northern Fujian, established in 1979. A moist subtropical forest, peaks up to 2,158 m high, a warm climate, and frequent rain are the setting for 2,000 species of plants, rare mammals such as the Fujianese variety of tiger (*Panthera tigris amoyensis*), 54 species of snakes, and an incredible density of up to 25 lizards per m² in some areas; also, of China's 32 orders of insects, 31 can be found there (Qing and Huang 1980).

Among the largest recent additions to protected zones are the expansion of Xishuangbanna in Yunnan, whose forests and mammals have been so badly damaged, from 57,000 to 200,000 ha; the establishment of the 154,000-ha Jingpo Hu preserve in the mountains of southern Heilongjiang, and the 33,000-ha Qixinglazi reservation in east Heilongjiang to protect China's less than 100 remaining Manchurian tigers (*Panthera tigris altaica*); and the setting up of the 40,000-ha Dafengding preserve in Meigu County (southwestern Sichuan), where nearly half of all state protected species can be found, including giant and red pandas (*Ailurus fulgens*), snub-nosed langurs (*Presbytis phayrei*), snow leopards (*Uncia uncia*), silver pheasants (*Lophura nycthemerus*), and black-necked cranes (*Grus nigricollis*).

Other interesting additions include a 27,000-ha reserve for brown-eared pheasants (*Crossoptilon mantchuricum*) in the Luya and Pangquangou areas of northern Shanxi; a mangrove ecosystem (2,600 ha) and gibbon (*Hylobates* spp.) protection area in Quongshan County on Hainan Island; a reserve for elephants, slow loris (*Nycticebus concany*), snakes, and various *Phasianidae* in Cangyuan County in Yunnan (8,000 ha); and a lancelet (*Branchiostoma* spp.) protection zone in the ocean waters near Xiamen (Fujian), the first instance of marine species protection (NCNA, May 5, 1980, *SWB* 1083; October 28, 1980, *SWB* 1112).

As encouraging as these developments are, they will not mean much without sustained enforcement. As already noted, the past record is hardly encouraging, as illustrated by the indiscriminate tree cutting rampant in the Wuyi Shan reserve and the uncontrolled slash-and-burn farming and illegal hunting in Xishuangbanna. A recent "emergency appeal" by a group of Chinese scientists (led by Yu Dejing, deputy director of the Botany Research Institute of the Chinese Academy of Sciences) concerns the rapid deterioration of Shennongjia, a large natural climax forest in western Hubei north of the Chang Jiang gorges, where deforestation and erosion are threatening the survival of the area's rare flora and fauna (Hubei provincial broadcast, May 22, 1980, *SWB* 1088).

Even if the new and expanded natural reserves are successful in protecting the selected ecosystems, a greater and incomparably more difficult conservation task will remain: assuring the survival of sufficient numbers of common essential plants and heterotrophs, from frogs to foxes, without whom the viable performance of China's agroecosystem would be much impaired, in the area outside the one percent of China's privileged territory.

Another formidable task is preserving functioning ecosystems in many locations of outstanding natural beauty that must also support the farming and industrial activities of local populations. Certainly the best-known case of this problem is Guilin, and reports of the worsening water and air pollution in and around China's prime scenic landscape in that region have already been detailed above (sections 3.5.2 and 4.1.2). The combined effects of these degradations, ranging from withered trees to smelly water, would be devastating enough—but there is more: the city's streets are dirty; residents dump their garbage indiscriminately, as do 108 factories in the area; trees have been cut, bringing enormous erosion; and many of the steep picturesque hills along the Li Jiang, which give the landscape its unique flavor, have been mutilated or even leveled in order to quarry stone. "At the present time, unbelievably, not a single undamaged peak exists in all of Guilin" (Wang and Gui 1980). If this is the way an "extremely precious treasure of the Chinese people" is dealt with, one can imagine the despoliation of less exalted landscapes.

Some of these famous places are now under twofold onslaught—by the local population and by the changes undertaken to cater to the growing hordes of tourists. Famous Lu Shan (1,474 m) between Poyang Hu and the Chang Jiang in northern Jiangxi is a perfect example of this dual degradation (Anonymous 1980e). Like anywhere else in China where a mountainous and forested region is near a farming plain, the scenic area has suffered extensive illegal deforestation (mainly for firewood) and also damage by fires. At Lu Shan a large sandstone company is dynamiting a mountainside, and some villages, undoubtedly as part of the new economic initiative, are organizing to open smaller quarries, in addition to the more than ten already in existence. Deforestation and the planting of crops on steep slopes has led to heavy erosion and the drying up of several famous springs. Uncontrolled air pollution is also quite objectionable.

The outsiders coming to see the vistas of rocks, plains, and clouds contribute to this despoliation. More than 2,000 buses and cars travel in low gear up the steep roads every day, discharging dense exhausts, blowing horns, and causing numerous accidents. The whole area is becoming urbanized, with many new permanent inhabitants; groups of buildings which do not respect the traditional architecture; meadows and paths surfaced with tar; and, in the absence of any sewage system, waste water, excrement, and garbage in ditches and canals. And the connoisseurs lament that the Lu Shan of old is gone forever—a far from unique case in the regrettable process of the accelerating degradation of Chinese environments.

6
CHINESE ENVIRONMENTS

Blue water . . . a clear moon . . .
In the moonlight the white herons are
flying
Listen! Do you hear the girls who gather
water chestnuts.
They are going home in the night, singing.

Li Bo, "Nocturne"
(in Shigeyoshi Obata translation)

The moon is above the city of Changan,
From ten thousand houses comes the sound
of cloth-pounding;
The sad autumn wind blows . . .

Li Bo, "Autumn"
(in Shigeyoshi Obata translation)

Here, with the four topical chapters behind us and the closing discussion of possible solutions and complicating limitations still to come, I want to offer a summarizing look at China's rural and urban environments. This affords an opportunity for synthesizing the already described specific degradative trends as well as for dealing with several important topics that could not be fitted readily into the preceding chapters, ranging from the high dependence of Chinese farming on renewable energy and nutrient inputs (and hence on an undisturbed environment) to urban noise. Sections on rural problems in this chapter will be more generalizing (with specific local examples where essential), while the urban part will concentrate on China's two largest cities.

6.1 The countryside

At the end of 1981, 86.5 percent of the Chinese lived outside large cities—some among them prosperous suburban vegetable growers and pig and poultry breeders, some rich herdsmen—but most of them, hundreds of millions, just peasants in an agroecosystem that provides them with little more than a bare subsistence. The past three decades have seen some notable general advances, some very substantial regional improvements in the living standards of Chinese peasants, but as documented in the preceding sections, almost every commendable move has had its degradative counterpart whose existence and extent the Chinese have been openly acknowledging since the late 1970s.

An image of new tree-lined irrigation canals leading clean water from a mountain reservoir, surrounded by afforested slopes, to newly reclaimed fields where crops growing in clever rotation (with green manure providing much of the needed nutrients), their pests controlled by biological methods and their soils cultivated by neat garden tractors that cart the bountiful yields away to be processed into delicious meals, was an appealing vista in Maoist propaganda and sympathetic Western reports. The reality in tens of thousands of villages around the country is heavily eroded hillsides from which the topsoil is carried away by rains into irrigation canals in which most water, often polluted by industrial discharges or nutrients leaking from fertilizers, is wasted before reaching the insufficiently diversified crops treated in an unsafe manner with persistent pesticides and cultivated largely by hard manual labor, with harvests providing just a bit more food than needed for bare subsistence and with virtually no fuel to cook the meals for most of the year. All of these points, with the exception of those dealt with previously, will now be taken up in the next three sections.

6.1.1 China's agroecosystem

Two critical environmental constraints, both already described in some detail, circumscribe China's agroecosystem: a relative shortage of arable land and a frequent regional lack or surplus of moisture. Significantly enough, since 1949 both farmland shortages and water supply fluctuations have been the targets of concentrated improvement efforts through massive land reclamation and water conservation projects; yet the available prime farmland is now sharply down, and while some of the recently increased flood-drought fluctuations are undoubtedly a part of long-term natural perturbations, a far from negligible part of the apparently worsening trends must be ascribed to large-scale deforestation, erosion, desertification, and reclamation of lakes. All of these changes cut down water storage capacity and affected local and regional agroecosystems through a greater proclivity for floods and droughts.

The stability of China's agroecosystem has thus in many ways been impaired rather than strengthened, and the recent growing awareness of this dangerous degradation has led to a vigorous debate and to many proposals on how the country should develop its farming in harmony with different environmental conditions (see also section 7.4). To do away with the uniformity that until the late 1970s promoted grain growing everywhere and to concentrate on afforestation and tree planting in any suitable place are two essential ingredients already stressed in these pages. Greater attention to aquaculture is another obvious need, but there will have to be many other changes and adjustments—some of them controversial and now debated in interesting exchanges in Chinese publications, some of them costly and difficult to achieve any time soon—to make Chinese farming as environmentally benign as possible while making it produce enough food for 1.2-1.3 billion people by the end of this century.

These changes are all the more necessary in view of the far from satisfactory performance of Chinese agriculture. Recent Chinese admissions show unmistakably that until the last few years of the 1970s the nutritional status of the Chinese population remained very precarious as famines did not occur only in the areas of major natural disasters but also as a result of mismanagement and the breakdown of social order. A document of the Central Committee of the CCP issued on January 4, 1979, admitted that in 1977 "more than 100 million people in rural areas suffered from a lack of grain" (Central Committee of the Chinese Communist Party 1979). Only after 1978, with the retreat from command farming, the gradual return to greater crop diversification, and the encouragement of private plot cultivation and animal husbandry did welcome nutritional changes come to a Chinese population whose food intake remained at the same, barely adequate, level for the two decades between 1957 and 1977 (Smil 1981b).

Annual averages of per capita food consumption in 1978, the first year of improvement, were a mere 2.4 kg of edible oil, 5 kg of fish, and 7.7 kg of meat, being, respectively, about one-half, one-third, and one-third the totals that Chinese nutrition experts consider desirable (Yan 1981). By 1982, continuing dietary improvements raised the per capita food availability by 15.4 percent compared with 1978 (*BR*, June 7, 1982, p. 2), to a level just above the average essential basal and work energy requirements of the Chinese population. Large cities and suburban villages are relatively better off, while the actual consumption in the countryside of many poorer provinces remains appreciably lower, just at or below the minimum subsistence need. Not surprisingly, then, the Party's theoretical journal, *Hongqi*, admits that "our country is still plagued by a very serious food shortage" (Yu Guoyao 1980a), and a noted economist warns that "so far we have not gotten away from the critical situation of finding enough food to feed the 800 million peasants" (Zhang Zhoulai 1981).

One of the key measures for improving Chinese food supply and diversifying the overwhelmingly vegetarian diet (plant foods account for over 90 percent of total caloric intake) is to expand meat, milk, egg, and fish production. Extensive aquaculture is not only very desirable nutritionally but also would be environmentally beneficial with larger water surfaces and storages; incentives not to pollute the streams, lakes, and ponds; and reduced eutrophication of water impondments owing to grazing herbivorous fish species. Turning the Chinese into heavy milk drinkers will be, at best, a long-drawn-out process, although the demand for milk has been rising even outside the pastoral areas of the North and Northwest.

On the other hand, meat consumption has a long way to go before reaching just one-half or one-third of the current European and North American levels (these are in general between 50-100 kg a year per capita). Not surprisingly, many Chinese experts have advocated a vigorous expansion of animal husbandry, pointing above all to the huge meat-producing potential of the northern grasslands, as well as to hilly southern regions. As will be shown in the next chapter, this strategy has a lower food output potential than is imputed to it by some simple calculations, and it brings with it significant environmental complications of its own.

Other characteristic features of China's agroecosystem are revealed by the study of its energy flows. Most inputs to Chinese farming are still traditional: human and animal labor continue to provide the essential flexible energies needed in intensive crop cultivation, transportation, and numerous auxiliary tasks; biomass fuels are indispensable for household cooking and heating; the organic fertilizers also continue to be irreplaceable. Modern energy inputs started to spread substantially only during the 1970s, and they are overwhelmingly concentrated in water pumping and nitrogenous fertilizers.

Using three different approaches to calculate human energy inputs, I have arrived at a representative mean of about 420 megajoules (MJ) of useful energy per working adult per year, or in aggregate some 170 petajoules (PJ) annually in the late 1970s; for working animals, analogical calculations yield some 75 PJ of useful energy (Smil 1981c). The only comparable calculations I have come across in the Chinese sources credit rural manpower with 155 PJ a year and draft animals with 122 PJ, for a total of 267 PJ (Zhao Zongyu 1981) compared to my estimate of 245 PJ. This is an excellent agreement for such inevitably highly approximate computations. Taking 250 PJ as the actual value and assuming that liquid-fueled machinery to substitute for this labor would work with 25 percent efficiency (a rather generous allowance), no less than some 23 million tons of fuel oil would be needed annually to displace all human and animal exertion: in contrast, the current farming consumption is just about 10 million tons of diesel oil.

Despite some considerable advances in farming mechanization, China's field machinery thus still delivers no more than one-half the useful energy provided by human and animal muscle. The ratio would be more favorable if the countryside were not affected by chronic liquid fuel shortages. Of the 200 million horsepower of agricultural machinery, one half is installed in combustion engines, the other half in electrical motors (Deng Keyun 1981). However, only a little over 50 kg of fuel is available annually for each machine horsepower, an amount sufficient for only 50 days of operation (Shangguan 1980). Similarly, there are widespread electricity shortages and, again despite extensive electrification campaigns, 400 million villagers (half of rural China) have no electric supply at all.

The energy cost of producing farm machinery prorates to about 100 PJ a year, while the synthesis of nitrogenous fertilizers consumes some 450 PJ. As stressed before (section 2.5.2), there are growing shortages of phosphorus and potassium in intensively farmed soils, and without organic fertilizers the situation would be intolerable. My estimates for the late 1970s (Smil 1981c) indicate a total theoretical availability of some 5 million tons of nitrogen (N), 1.6 million tons of phosphorus (P), and 5.2 million tons of potassium (K) in recycled animal manures, human wastes, crop by-products, green manures, and other minor wastes (oilseed cakes, mud and silt, city garbage, bones, fish wastes). In contrast, synthetic nitrogen applications totaled some 6 million tons, but those of P and K were, respectively, only about 700,000 and 40,000 tons, just fractions of the recycled sums.

Energy and nutrient flow analysis thus reveals the continuing critical dependence of China's agroecosystem on self-perpetuating inputs of animate energies and organic fertilizers, a dependence made even stronger by the extremely high reliance on biomass fuels for household consumption.

6.1.2 Village environments

Looking only at the nationwide statistical averages gives a clear impression of major improvements in rural living—especially when one passes over the destructive decade of the "Cultural Revolution" when, at best, most of the indicators stagnated, and when one leaves out the disastrous years of the early 1960s when the staggering economic chaos following in the wake of the Great Leap Forward combined with natural disasters to produce perhaps the worst famine of modern Chinese history, with deaths in the millions. This is a lot of time to sweep away for the sake of attractive comparisons: by Chinese admissions, for about half of the three decades of the PRC's existence things have been getting either worse or at least not any better. But there have been some relatively impressive gains in the 1950s and since 1977, so the comparison of the late 1970s or early 1980s with the early 1950s yields mostly substantial gains and improvements.

Peasants live longer (official figures for China's mean life expectancy are now 67 years for men, 70 years for women); they certainly have much better health care available (still rudimentary by Western standards but above average in the poor world's terms); sanitation has improved (with the massive adoption of covered latrines and better handling of organic wastes); new housing, especially since 1978, has proliferated; new wells have brought better drinking water; mechanization of water pumping and food processing has eased farm chores; electrification has spread; literacy has increased; and today's proliferating material possessions—watches, bicycles, sewing machines, and in richer places electric fans and TV sets—were unthinkable in the early 1950s.

All of these changes and advances have improved the living and working environment in tens of thousands of China's villages—but many degradative trends have made the overall picture far less bright than the juxtaposition of some national statistical means would indicate, which is also owing in no small part to substantial regional and provincial differences. Preceding chapters have dealt in detail with many outright destructive or gradually degradative changes that have contributed to a serious decline of natural, as well as man-made, environments throughout China: deforestation, erosion, desertification, losses of water storages owing to reclamation and silting, the staggering decline of arable land and its qualitative deterioration, the mismanagement of water resources, the exhaustion of ground water reserves, water and air pollution, the disappearance or reduction of animal species.

Furthermore, misguided government policies such as the grain first mania, the banning of family woodlots, and the reduction or abolition of private farm plots have brought additional hardships to hundreds of millions of rural families, above all a lack of improvement in inadequate diets (see section 6.1.1)—reversed only recently—and very serious shortages of fuels for household cooking and heating. This acute energy crisis will be treated separately in the next section (6.1.3); in this section I will provide some general quantitative and qualitative background as well as some specific remarks on shortages and quality of drinking water, on sanitation and health problems, and on contamination of food.

To begin with, nationwide statistics, as in all such cases, hide large spatial differences. Detailed disaggregated data for 1978 show an average per capita distributed income of ¥74.7 but the villages with a mean income below ¥50 constituted 29.6 percent of the total, while only 17.8 percent of basic accounting units had a per capita income over ¥100; when counties are used for analogical calculation, 548 of them (23.7 percent) are rich (annual per capita income in excess of ¥100) and 377 (16.3 percent) are poor (incomes below ¥50) (Shi Shan 1980). What is most interesting, however, is that the rich counties are heavily concentrated in the suburban regions of large cities (most notably, all Shanghai and Beijing suburban counties) or in border regions predominantly settled by non-Han peasants and pastoralists (Jilin and Zhejiang are the only exceptions). In contrast, the provinces with the highest frequency of poor counties (over one-fifth of the total) form a continuous area in the Northwest and North (Gansu, Ningxia, Nei Monggol, Shaanxi, Shanxi, Henan, Anhui, Shandong) and in the South (Guizhou, Yunnan).

As Shi Shan (1980) concludes, "The distribution of rich counties and poor counties makes one uneasy. . . . Poor counties are concentrated in regions where the natural resources and ecological equilibrium have been seriously destroyed. And this destruction of natural resources and environment has to date not yet been stopped. If it continues, the numbers of poor counties will increase further." In most of these cases environmental degradation has been the principal (though not the sole) cause of everyday hardships: little or no disposable income, substandard food rations barely sufficient for survival, incredible fuel shortages (see the next section), and in many instances even a lack of drinking water.

Nationwide it is estimated that some 40 million peasants suffer permanent and serious scarcities of drinking water (Xinhua, June 12, 1980, *SWB* 1100) and, as described in Chapter 3, the pollution of many ground and surface waters is endangering the health of large numbers of rural inhabitants because the overwhelming majority of the Chinese draw their untreated water directly from rivers, ponds, reservoirs, or wells. This problem is especially serious in suburban areas: monitoring in Shanghai County found pollution in 96 percent of the surface water test points, with water at 25 percent of the localities no longer drinkable (Gao and Jin 1980). One specific form of spreading rural water pollution not described in Chapter 3 is contamination by farm chemicals— the leakage of nutrients from chemical fertilizers and pesticide residues (Figure 20). Like anywhere else, in China the most common form of water polllution from chemical fertilizers arises from the application of nitrogenous fertilizers, which introduces growing amounts of nitrates into the waters. Nitrates may be converted by bacteria in the gastrointestinal tract of humans into highly toxic nitrites that are powerful reducing agents; they reduce hemoglobin into methemoglobin, thus reducing the blood's oxygen-carrying capacity and leading to symptoms of anoxia, dyspnea, tachycardia, headache, fatigue, anorexia, and vomiting. Infants are particularly susceptible to toxic methemoglobinemia, as are many farm animals.

In the United States, nitrate pollution of waters is highest in California's Central Valley and in the Corn Belt, areas of the highest fertilizer use. In China, the dangers are highest throughout the South, where nitrogenous fertilizers are used heavily in the multicropped wet fields. Problems would arise even with cautious use, but Chinese sources describe improper and blind application leading to huge waste of the fertilizers, which means their lower absorption by plants and more extensive leakage into the environment. Most chemical fertilizers in China are just spread on the surface and not incorporated into the soil, which leads to losses of at least 65 percent for urea and more than 70 percent for ammonium carbonate (Yu Futong 1980). Fertilizers are also applied excessively because most places have no soil testing done and therefore soil conditions are unknown.

Moreover, there is a staggering leakage in packaging, transportation, loading, and unloading: package breakage is estimated at 20 percent of the annual fertilizer mass produced, and further losses occur during improper storage. Consequently, there is little doubt that large areas of intensively cultivated (double- and triple-cropped) farmland in South China are experiencing increasingly worse surface and ground water nitrate contamination, a development posing significant health

Figure 20. Washing clothes in a ditch near Shanghai; virtually all of the municipality's surface waters are seriously contaminated with heavy metals, oil, and fertilizer residues.

hazards to tens of millions of infants and young children in the region.

There is another troubling health hazard in South China's wet fields. Although many readers may remember the awestruck accounts of naïve (and poor-sighted) China travelers of the early 1970s wholesaling stories of impossible feats of the total eradication of flies, mosquitoes, rats, and sparrows (just think of it: ''experts'' writing in all seriousness that there are no flies or mosquitoes in a country of nearly ten million km² and one billion people!), these four creatures are alive and well in China. But South Chinese peasants going to work in the wet fields, and drinking and bathing, do not find them to be the most abominable pests. What they fear is leeches, and an extensive quotation from a Hunan veterinarian's letter to *Renmin ribao* shows why.

"In the South, wherever there is water there are leeches; large numbers in reservoirs, and small numbers in drinking wells. During busy farming seasons, when we stop working very late and draw water in the dark, we sometimes carry leeches to our water vats. Unless we are careful, leeches will end up on the stove, be dropped into food pots, or even eaten, which is extremely harmful to human health. During the two busy harvest seasons, when temperatures are very high, after finishing work in the paddy fields, our bodies frequently covered with bits of rice and straw and dirt, we like to go to a pond and take a bath, but the leeches stick to our shoulders our neck, and even bore into our anus. Most nauseating are the leeches in the wet fields. A common saying is that 'leeches must not be allowed to hear water sounds,' for wherever there is a sound of water, they run in frenzied hordes of 10 to 20 biting our legs till the blood runs. This is a common sight. During the two harvest seasons last year about 60 percent of our brigade's manpower had infected legs and hands as a result of leech bites, and they could only recuperate at home to the detriment of production" (Zhang Songlin 1980).

While leeches are an ancient problem that has hardly gotten any better, a new danger to the health of Chinese rural populations arises from the growing use of synthetic pesticides. Various enthusiastic reports from the 1970s depicting admirable advances in biological pest control notwithstanding, the Chinese have started to rely heavily on chemical pesticides, and this dependence has brought its usual share of problems noted all around the world—as well as some specific Chinese complications. China is now the world's fourth largest pesticide producer, with an output of about 80 kinds of insecticides, herbicides, and fungicides totaling 500,000 tons a year. However, only 160,000 tons of this total are effective, and nearly half of all pesticides applied are organochlorines, which are only slowly degradable (Ke 1980). DDT, banned virtually throughout the Western world for nearly a decade, is still widely used in China. Another frequently used organochlorine pesticide is benzene hexachloride (BHC), usually labeled *666* in China; it too has a long residence time, but it is more volatile than DDT and imparts odor and off-flavor to crops even when added to the soil instead of sprayed on the plants. The accumulation of these long-lived pesticides in some livestock and aquatic products has already made them unsuitable for export (Xiong et al. 1978).

With the growing chemicalization of Chinese agriculture, the instances of pesticide poisoning have been increasing. An article in Jinan's *Dazhong ribao* (Mass Daily) labels the situation in Shandong serious, stating that by July 1981 already three times as many people had died of pesticide poisoning as during the whole of 1980; poor storage and improper application methods are blamed (Zhang Junjie 1981). A survey in Zhejiang showed that most pesticides are applied "at too great a strength and in too small a quantity" (Fan Defang 1980). Naturally, this creates a twofold problem: such applications are not effective on a large field scale, yet residual pollution is increased. One relative advantage that might be enjoyed in the South is that the decomposition rates of organochlorine pesticides such as DDT and BHC are greater in wet fields than in the open air. Consequently, a conversion to wet fields or rotational cropping of rice and cotton would appear to be an effective way of accelerating the breakdown of some pesticide residues in soils.

Pesticides cause health problems not only owing to their improper handling and application but also because they are, incredibly enough, used directly in the preparation or preservation of food! Several letters sent to the editor of *Nanfang ribao* (Southern Daily), and printed in the newspaper on August 23, 1980 (p. 2), indicate the kinds and effects of this dangerous abuse.

In the first reported case from Guangdong's Xinxing County, the local health department discovered that a food called "deep fat frieds," sold at 12 different private stalls at a county fair, was in all cases contaminated with Rogor pesticide. This highly toxic agricultural chemical is mixed with soybeans during frying to give the "deep fat frieds" a shine and an attractive color (!). Another letter, from Wenchang County (Guangdong), describes the sale of rotten salted fish in the markets during summer and the practice of vendors sprinkling the fish with organic phosphate insecticide or Rogor insecticide to prevent this spoilage. The letter recalls an incident from a local fair where nine people were poisoned in one day and two children remained in critical condition for ten days before the effects of acute poisoning subsided.

The contamination of food by pesticides—accidental or deliberate—

Figure 21. This handling of pork, common in China's markets, leaves a great deal of room for improvement from a hygienic viewpoint.

is just a part of the broader problem of the wholesomeness of food sold and consumed throughout the country (Figure 21). There are too few properly trained inspectors, and shortages of the necessary analytic instruments are even more acute. This is especially of concern at thousands of reopened county fairs and village and city markets, where peasants are privately selling their raw or prepared foodstuffs. While one hopes that the just described adulteration with pesticides for color's sake is the exception, sales of other poisonous and harmful foods are far from rare. For example, Li Yin (1980) mentions that in one year in just two markets in Shanghai's Putuo ward, 1,350 kg of such contaminated food was discovered on sale in 230 separate incidents. Obviously, there must be many more undetected cases.

This is, of course, hardly surprising when highly perishable products—meat, poultry, fish, eggs, some prepared foods—are transported, stored, and sold without refrigeration in subtropical temperatures. To avoid personal loss many sellers will retail spoiled or contaminated food and, not exceptionally, poultry or livestock that has died from sickness or poisoning will also be offered as freshly slaughtered meat. Another common danger arises from the sale of wild mushrooms and poisonous aquatic species, and contamination also comes from the frequent practice of packing food in handy plastic bags previously used for farm fertilizers or pesticides (banning the sale of these chemicals in small packages would solve this problem).

What is more interesting is the attitudes of many buyers. Yin (1980) complains of consumers who "do not believe in science and are not worried about poisonous and harmful food. Some even deny the facts of hygiene just because they do not get sick immediately after first eating spoiled food." As long as there are shoppers seeking bargains in spoiled food or risking their lives to eat puffer fish it may be difficult to eliminate the selling of unsafe food. Concerns about this spreading problem have led to the issuance of local proscriptions against the sales of certain foodstuffs; the Shanghai list from June 1980 (Appendix F) makes for interesting reading, ranging as it does from globefish to "seriously moldy" foods.

This is an appropriate place to note, although it is of more interest to urban residents, the considerable extent of dubious practices in commercial food industries as well. Recent biochemical reviews show "many cases of abuse" among 267 chemical food additives used in 500 foodstuffs during the 1970s (Qu Geping 1980). These practices have included the use of nonfood dyes for food coloring (in some instances ammonium sulfate fertilizer was used to prepare red-brown coloring), the repeated addition of long-forbidden ingredients previously proven to be poisonous, and the use of additives in quantities several dozen times, even more than 100 times, above the standards.

Yet no matter how inconveniencing, troublesome, or outright dangerous the contamination of waters or foodstuffs is, in terms of number of people affected, hardships created, and damage incurred, by far the most pressing environmental problem for the Chinese peasant is the incredible shortage of household fuel and the associated disadvantages.

6.1.3 Rural energetics

While China's countryside has seen very substantial increases of all forms of energy used in farming—directly as electricity and liquid fuels for water pumping, field operations, and food and feed processing, and indirectly as all fossil fuels and electricity for the production of chemical fertilizers, farm machinery, and pesticides—the availability of traditional biomass fuels for household consumption (cooking, feed preparation, heating) has shrunk drastically, creating hardships no less acute, and more widespread, than those encountered by poor nomads and villagers in the Sahel or in Bangladesh whose plight was frequently described in the burgeoning rural energy literature of the 1970s.

A survey of rural energy undertaken in 1979 credits the whole

Chinese countryside with consuming 390 million tons of coal equiv-alent (tce) energy, or 44.3 percent of China's total; some 60 million tce went into the production and operation of farm inputs (Shangguan 1980). Of the 330 million tce of household fuel, fossil fuels constitute only a very small proportion: the use of natural gas and refined oil products (mainly kerosene) is negligible, and although there is no breakdown available for the use of electricity—that more than four-fifths of it is used for water pumping and in local small industries is, however, certain—per capita consumption of all electric power in rural China is less than 40 kWh per year (Shangguan 1980). Even if all of this energy were used in households it would only be sufficient to keep one 50 W lightbulb per person lit for two hours each day of the year. Coal is the most important fossil fuel in the Chinese countryside, but still no more than 20-25 million tons of it are burned annually for household use (Li Shaozhong 1979).

Subtracting these supplies means that an equivalent of some 290 million tons of coal, or about 360 kg of standard coal per capita, has to be compensated for by the combustion of traditional biomass fuels; put differently, the Chinese countryside still depends for no less than 85 percent of its household energy on biomass, a share as high as in rural Bangladesh or Nigeria. The provision of nearly 300 million tce of biomass fuels is extremely difficult, and most manifestations of China's environmental degradation—large-scale deforestation, wors-ening erosion, desertification, soil quality deterioration, and local cli-matic changes—are directly tied to rural energy scarcities leading to an often desperate search for fuel and the removal of any trees, stalks, straw, grasses, roots, weeds, and dung for domestic cooking and house heating.

Crop residues—largely cereal straws, corn stover, and millet stalks, but also legume straws, potato vines, cotton stalks, and roots—are by far the most important source of phytomass fuels in China's deforested farmlands (Figure 22). Annual production has recently hovered around 450 million tons, and as at least 220 million tons are needed for animal feed and as raw materials for thatching and numerous household manu-factures, no more than 230 million tons, or an equivalent of 120 million tons of standard coal, is left for fuel (Chen, Huang, and Xu 1979). Other estimates, however, put the annual consumption of crop residues for fuel as high as 75 percent of the total harvest (Qu Geping 1980).

Even this highest value averages out to a mere 5.4 kg of crop residues per rural family a day, far below the 10-12.5 kg considered

Figure 22. Straw is by far the most important fuel in China's deforested farm-ing areas; here it is dried right after harvest to be stored for later use.

adequate for cooking three meals and preparing feed for a couple of pigs; and even when 70 million m³ of firewood, equivalent to about 28 million tons of standard coal, is added, the average daily availability is still only less than 3.3 kg (or only 2.5 kg with the lower total) of coal equivalent—while the surveys estimate that about 4.7 kg of coal equiv-alent (kgce) of biomass fuels are actually used by an average rural household each day. The difference, at least 1.4 or as much as more than 2 kgce per household a day, comes literally from any accessible source that can conceivably burn.

Trees in protected forests and along roads are cut illegally; bark is stripped off the living trunks; stumps and roots are dug out; branches are lopped off; leaves, fallen twigs, and other debris are raked; grasses are cut; pieces of sod are carved out; animal dung is collected—and when all other possibilities have vanished, peasants in the warmer regions grow sweet potatoes on odd patches of land and use dried tubers for fuel (NCNA, January 3, 1981, *JPRS* 77182). And even so, most of China's peasants are acutely short of fuel. Official sources acknowledge that of 800 million rural inhabitants, 500 million suffer from a *serious* shortage of fuel for at least three to five months a year, and in the worst-off provinces, 70 percent of the peasants lack fuel for up to half a year every year (Shangguan 1980; Wang Mengkui 1980).

The situation in thousands of villages in the arid Northwest is especially desperate. In Gansu's Yongjing County, food and fuel are both in short supply, but fuel shortages are so pervasive that "when housewives face the stove, tears come to their eyes" (Zhang Qinghai 1981). The county's grain harvest in 1980 averaged only 1,275 kg per ha, and only 50 kg of crop residues could be allocated for fuel per capita. A household of five persons thus had only 250 kg of straw to burn for one year, a supply good for no more than one month of average consumption! However, virtually all households keep at least one donkey which must be fed by crop residues, and so the people are forced to use dung or to take long treks to the mountains to scavenge for some wood, break branches, strip bark, and dig up roots and sod; some exchange their scarce food for even scarcer coal, one kg of potatoes for two kg of coal.

Here is human suffering and an environmental crisis of truly immense proportions: serious recurrent shortages of even minimum quantities of fuel needed for cooking and heating afflicts every three out of five rural families, about half of the inadequate supply coming from crop residues and dung which should not be burned but rather recycled to maintain soil tilth and fertility and to protect against erosion, and the other half secured at an even heavier environmental cost of stripping soils of their protective cover, fostering rapid erosion and nutrient loss, and rendering the sites unfit for eventual revegetation. As a Chinese researcher put it, dramatically but without exaggeration, these practices will "bequeath infinite calamities and misfortunes to posterity" (Wang Mengkui 1980).

What are the solutions? The substitution of scarce biomass fuels with modern energies is out of the question. China does not have enough coal, crude oil, natural gas, and electricity even for its cities and industries (at least a quarter of industrial capacity is idle owing to energy shortages), and even if these supplies were much more plentiful the country lacks the infrastructure to distribute them on the required scale, i.e., supplying 170 million families in more than 100,000 villages spread over some 3 million km² (leaving aside the sparsely inhabited western two-thirds of China).

Decentralized supply at this stage of development is thus virtually imperative in the overwhelming number of cases, and since the late 1950s the Chinese have tried to accomplish this with coal from small mines, electricity from small hydrostations, and biogas from anaerobic digesters (Smil 1977; Smil 1980d; Smil 1982; Jing Hua 1981; Chen, Xiao, and Li 1979; Zhao Zongyu 1981; Shi Wen 1982). None of these efforts has made a real difference. Low quality raw coal from small mines has gone predominantly to mismanaged and highly energy-inefficient local industries producing substandard iron, chemical fertilizers, or various manufactures (many of these wasteful enterprises are now being closed down); electricity from small hydrostations is used overwhelmingly in water pumping, the rest again in village industries, and despite large numbers of such plants (over 80,000), 400 million Chinese peasants still have no electricity supply (Deng 1981).

Biogas digesters are a clever multiple solution to problems of energy supply, crop fertilization, and environmental hygiene, but their construction had been imposed hastily through typical Maoist mass campaigns on peasants inexperienced in building and running these relatively simple yet demanding devices. Statistics from the National Methane Production Leadership Group show that of all the digesters built in the second half of the 1970s only about 55 percent can be used normally, and even among these working digesters "not too many" can be used to cook rice three times a day (Huang and Zhang 1980). Difficulties and failures experienced with poorly built and shoddily operated digesters have been discouraging peasants from building more units, and the grand plan to expand the numbers tenfold from the 1978 total of 7 million units was soon forgotten as the new rural development policies of the recent past supplanted the receding Maoist instant-benefit campaigns (Smil 1982).

Still, all three methods—small coal mines, small hydrostations, and family biogas units—should be worthwhile ingredients in China's long-term strategy for improving rural energy supplies. The only practical keystone of this effort, however, is the massive expansion of private fuel-wood lots, a policy which is finally being pursued with official encouragement and with obvious peasant enthusiasm (see section 2.1.4). If uninterrupted, this policy should start bringing appreciable benefits before the end of this decade. And, like anywhere else in the energy-short poor world, Chinese rural fuel supplies could be greatly extended, and hence the environment much conserved, if the poor combustion efficiency of primitive household stoves, now wasting about 90 percent of the fuel, could be improved by introducing better designed, yet relatively simple, clay or brick stoves capable of at least 20 percent conversion efficiency.

Chinese scientists have made the political leadership aware of the magnitude of the difficulties, the everyday frustrations, and the heavy environmental cost caused by rural energy shortages, and the resultant new policies contain all the right ingredients: private fuel-wood lots, which are to supply one-third of all needs by the end of the 1980s; improvements in stove efficiency (by 1990 about half of the rural families should be using more efficient stoves); orderly diffusion of biogas digesters (one-tenth of rural families, or some 20 million, should have them by 1990); doubling of small hydrostation capacities (achieved by building fewer but larger units); and promotion of solar heaters and stoves in the sunny interior (Shi Wen 1982). If these programs succeed, Chinese rural energy use will still be a frugal affair, but the worst shortages might be eliminated, general energy availability greatly improved, and environmental degradation considerably slowed down, checked, or in many areas even reversed.

6.2 Cities

The chapters on water and air pollution have made it clear that perhaps the closest analogy to China's urban environment today are the growing industrial cities of nineteenth century Europe and North America: largely uncontrolled combustion of poor quality coal is releasing huge quantities of particulate matter, sulfur dioxide, and carcinogens into the air, and waste waters are dumped untreated. Also, open spaces are rare, greenery is scarce, living conditions are crowded, and the places keep growing at fast rates, promising more congestion and degradation to come. One important difference in the comparison: modern Chinese cities are certainly noisier, in fact often unbearably so, and before going into some detailed descriptions of Chinese urban environments I should offer at least a few paragraphs on this astounding common denominator of all larger Chinese settlements.

The editor of *High Fidelity* magazine remarked after his visit to Beijing that it is the noisiest, if not the most polluted, city he has ever visited, and that it is filled "with such an incessant, insistent cacophony of car horns that one could almost imagine cars crowding the streets" (Marcus 1979). He timed beeps in taxis in Beijing and Shanghai at a fairly constant average rate of one per car every 1.2 seconds. Of course, not only the horns are responsible. Cars and trucks, some of which perhaps have never had a tune-up, and not a few mufflerless, rumbling through streets clogged by bicycles and people, their motors turned off at red lights and restarted to save gasoline; noisy metalworking factories with incessant banging and screeching situated smack in the middle of residential areas; blaring transistor radios; children playing in narrow alleys—all these add up to high noise levels.

Impressions of inordinate noise have been given quantitative confirmation by Ma Dayou, deputy director of the Institute of Acoustics of the Chinese Academy of Sciences; he stated that noise in Beijing is, on the average, greater than in Tokyo, a city with 15 times the number of vehicles and many times more factories and transport terminals (Xinhua, March 18, 1979, *SWB* 1025). Measurements in Shanghai, Tianjin, Wuhan, Hangzhou, Guangzhou, Chongqing, Nanjing, and Harbin showed the average decibel levels in all of these cities to be higher than in New York, London, Rome, and Tokyo. But Ma Dayou (1980) noticed a slight recent improvement. In 1979, 67.4 percent of Beijing's locations where measurements were taken still had traffic noise in excess of 70 decibels (dB), and 21.2 percent even over 75 dB, but the city's mean level had gone down to 72.1 dB from 76 dB in 1975. This is still unacceptably high, and it is hardly surprising that Beijing residents complaining to their local environmental protection units write most often about the unbearable noise.

The overall impression of Chinese urban environments is depressingly uniform, and therefore current write-ups in Chinese journals and newspapers differ only as far as the specific local figures are concerned. Typical is a recent review of Guangzhou's worsening environmental problems, lamenting "heavy" air pollution and "even greater" water pollution (besides the usual urban wastes caused by about 20,000 vessels, mostly small and hence difficult to control, discharging oil wastes and garbage into the city's harbors every day), hospitals and factories operating without any waste treatment (not surprisingly, the city's fishermen now take less than one-tenth of the catches of the 1950s), and noise exceeding 80 dB on main roads (He Shaoying 1980). Rather than gathering similar descriptions, I will take a closer look at the two largest cities of modern China, the capital, Beijing, and the country's foremost industrial center, Shanghai.

6.2.1 Beijing

In several Communist Chinese treatises on Beijing I have come across the same description of the pre-1949 city: there were very few industrial enterprises but a good many luxurious restaurants geared to sumptuous feasting by a monied clientele. One is tempted to add that the post-1949 decades could be, with simplification but far from unjustly, described as an all-out attempt to turn the former astounding imperial capital of the Jin, Yuan, Ming, and Qin dynasties into a large factory compound where there would be precious few good restaurants but plenty of dirty air, polluted water, stupefying noise, and hardly a trace of living nature.

The rapid growth of the city's population, and the even more rapid surge of its industries in a natural setting far from well suited to such an expansion, account for a large part of the environmental deterioration. Serious disproportions between investment in housing and its service infrastructure on the one hand and in industrial enterprises on the other, and between facilities geared to production and those needed to protect a livable environment explain the rest. The metropolitan area grew from 2.03 million people in 1950 to 8.7 million by the end of the 1970s. Part of this increase is accounted for by the addition of eight Hebei counties to Beijing Municipality in 1958. The capital is, together with Shanghai and Tianjin, one of the three urban areas with surrounding farms directly under central administration (its total area is 16,800 km^2; Figure 23).

Consequently, it is more meaningful to chart the growth of the city proper. In 1949 its built-up area occupied 109 km^2 and it housed 1.65 million people for an average density of 15,100 people per km^2; by 1979 the urban area had grown to 339 km^2 and 4.95 million people, giving a virtually unchanged mean density of 14,600 people per km^2. This is much less crowded living than in Shanghai (though denser than any Western metropolis), but it has to share the space with industries whose total output expanded by about 120 times between 1949 and 1980 and includes 2 million tons of steel and 10 billion kWh of coal-fueled

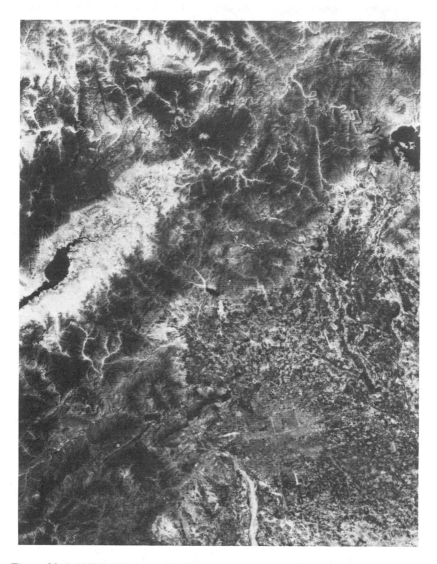

Figure 23. LANDSAT image of Beijing (May 24, 1975, band 5). The city itself appears as a fuzzy gray area near the lower right-hand corner: the broad perimeter road built in place of destroyed city walls delineates the rectangle of the city's old area. Suburbs are encroaching on the vegetable fields and wheat fields seen as a mosaic on three sides around the city; the Xi Shan (Western Hills) shelter the city from the west. The long reservoir near the left edge of the image is Guanting on the Yongding He, Beijing's main source of drinking water; the other large reservoir is Miyun near the top right corner.

electricity generation in an arid climate (in drought years it may not rain for many months) which exacerbates air pollution and is the main natural source of now chronic water shortages.

The total annual rainfall over Beijing municipality averages about 10.5 billion m³, of which about 75 percent is evaporated or otherwise lost; currently available water resources, that is, water contained in the reservoirs, underground aquifers, and the rivers flowing into the municipality, provide a sustainable withdrawal capacity of 4.487 billion m³ annually—yet the city's annual consumption in the late 1970s was 280 million m³ for households, 1.35 billion m³ for industries, and 3 billion m³ for suburban agriculture, a total of 4.63 billion m³, or some 140 million m³ above the sustainable level (Zhang Qin 1981). The difference, in other sources also estimated at slightly higher than 150-160 million m³, is accounted for by depletion of underground aquifers, an especially serious problem in the city's central ward where the water table has dropped by about 20 m, and in some suburbs where extensive funnels have formed (see also section 3.3).

The discrepancy between the sustainable supply and demand has been greatly aggravated during the dry years since 1979. While the long-term average annual rainfall is 626 mm, only 700 mm fell on the municipality during the two years between August 1979 and August 1981, creating "a crisis in water sources unprecedented since the founding of the nation" (BJRB, August 28, 1981, p. 1). In August 1981 only the city's two biggest reservoirs, Guanting and Miyun, had storages above the dead water level, while the other 84 large, medium, and small reservoirs could not release any water. From the two big storages, after subtracting their dead capacity, only 130 million m³ were releasable for the city's use, 620 million m³ less than in 1980 and an all-time low.

Two most troubling factors are the apparently rising frequency of droughts in the area and the huge increases in water needs envisaged for the city's future growth. Long-term analyses of weather records show that since the latter half of the nineteenth century until the 1980s, every seventh year was dry, but in the past two decades there has been a water shortage every fifth year (Zhang Qin 1981). Since 1949, Beijing's water consumption has risen 450 percent (Yuan and Zu 1981), and the need is expected to increase to 6-7 billion m³ by the year 2000, 50 percent above the current availability (NCNA, February 9, 1981, SWB 1123).

Improvements in living standards alone would triple the current per capita consumption by households to some one billion m³ by the year 2000 (no more is a television set the most prestigious item to own in a Beijing family—a small semiautomatic washing machine is the latest sign of affluence); new suburban housing in satellite towns and growing industries will add to the demand; and since in a country with China's meager transportation infrastructure and scarcity of fuels most of the vegetables will for the foreseeable future have to be grown right in the suburbs, there will inevitably be a rising demand for irrigation water. Despite all this, undisputably, it is clear from the capital's water balance that meeting future needs of more than 6 billion m³ would simply be impossible without large-scale water transfers—but from where? Not surprisingly, many experts call for strict consumption control and reuse as the only practicable partial solution and believe that the lack of water will be the chief determinant of Beijing's future growth.

Beijing's air pollution (so heavy that even visitors from what are considered "dirty" Western cities take note), water pollution (including the burning river), and precipitous losses of suburban farmland (and hence repeated shortages of even cabbage, the plainest of all China's vegetables) have all been detailed above (sections 4.1.1, 3.5.2, 2.5.1). As noted, the city is not, in general, as crowded as Shanghai, but this is merely a relative advantage, and hardly a cause for satisfaction. In the 1950s the ratio between the construction of factory buildings and housing projects was set at 1:1.13, but the standard was soon forgotten and, as has happened in all Communist industrializing countries, new industries kept coming up but housing lagged badly, with the ratio dropping to 1:0.7 in the 1970s (Zhou Jinghua 1979); the urban infrastructure fared even worse (Figure 24).

Not only are there too few shops or services in Beijing's new residential districts, a standard woe of Communist urban planning, but about 30 multistory buildings on Qiansanmen Street were actually completed without even essential engineering networks (gas, water, electricity) put into the ground first! Citywide statistics tell a depressing story of cramped living without privacy, long queues for basic daily necessities, and daily frustration. Average floor space is but 4.57 m² per person—although this is considerably more than the all-China urban average of 3.6m²—with about a quarter of a million households living in totally unsuitable conditions. Urban services are poorer than in 1949 when for every 100 residents there were 5.60 service workers; now only 3.64 are available.

Figure 24. Beijing's hutongs, compounds composed of traditional one-story houses with inner courtyards and separated by narrow alleys, still house most of the capital's residents, giving the old parts of the city their monotonous gray look, except where broken by rare greenery.

Getting around is also not easier. Although in 1979 Beijing had 41.5 times as many motor vehicles as in the early 1950s, and 17.5 times as many bikes and trolleys (increases not so impressive when one considers the near-total decrepitude of transportation in 1949), the number of riders shot up 70 times—and all this on roads that are only 10 times longer (and often hardly better) than in 1950. Contrasting these figures is enough to make one realize the city's traffic problems, leaving the unpredictable 3 million bicyclists aside. There are grand plans for a system of radial roads and five concentric rings of beltways, but these will not be completed soon; however, new subway lines are being added at an accelerated pace.

More enlightened attitudes of the central and municipal bureaucracies toward environmental management have started to bring some desirable changes. To begin with, the city's anomalous concentration of heavy industry (amounting to 44.5 percent of the local economy) is to be weakened to lower the excessive pollutant discharges. Here, indeed, lies much of the current predicament: for every ¥10,000 of output, light industries, which are labor-intensive and badly needed to employ the capital's bourgeoning population, use 0.2-2.7 tons of standard coal and 300 m³ of water, while for the same output value heavy industries (with low employment) need 20-50 tons of standard coal and 1,000 tons of water (Zhu Zuxi 1980).

Several scores of factories have already moved out or changed production, but this is still but a small dent in the city's steel and coal foundations. Faster results could be obtained in the new tree planting campaigns, providing the strict rules adopted in 1982 are enforced: if any production unit fails to fulfill its tree-planting quotas its leadership will be held responsible and penalized. The city needs to expand its vegetation very badly. Before the "Cultural Revolution" Beijing had 2,700 ha of parks, but since then about 430 ha have been ruined and the city now has less than 4 m² of greenery per person, about one-seventh of the usual urban standard (*GMRB*, March 2, 1977, p. 2), and less than at least a dozen other large Chinese cities.

Long overdue investments are finally beginning. A record 18 million m² of new floor space were planned for 1982, with priority given to projects upgrading living standards; interestingly, Beijing's deputy mayor put the building of a new 100,000-ton-a-year brewery and the renovation of a 50,000-ton-a-year older one in this category. The most encouraging signs, however, are commitments to dredge 5 rivers and lay 2 trunk sewers, widen 2 roads encircling the city, construct 14 new parks, and put in 5.5 million m² of new housing (*BR*, May 3, 1982, pp. 9-10). Two new sets of commendable regulations were also announced by the municipal government in June 1982. The first specifies that no less than 25 percent of any new road's total width should be a grass strip and that greenery should account for 25-30 percent of the total area in all new building projects, be they factories or residential housing (*BR*, June 14, 1982, p. 9).

The other document is interesting in the variety of activities it bans. The 15-article Regulations Concerning Urban Appearance and Environmental Sanitation, in force since July 1, 1982, forbids dumping of building materials, littering, graffiti, and putting up street sale stalls without permission; most notably, I think, anyone caught spitting in the street is to be fined half a yuan. Should this provision be enforced, the Beijing municipal government may be able to operate without state subsidies: the Chinese love to spit, and even a casual observer of China's reopening to the West in the 1970s will remember large ornamented spittoons strategically placed at the feet of the little tables separating the deep armchairs of Chinese guests and foreign dignitaries (the inevitable question: will there be a proscription of the leadership's spittoons as well?). Whatever the actual pace of Beijing's future environmental improvements, the city's prominence is perhaps the best guarantee of the eventual amelioration of many of its current most pressing space, water, air, noise, and vegetation problems.

6.2.2 Shanghai

Stereotypically to many Western minds, Shanghai's "very name still conjures romance and intrigue, the life of the Orient and faraway ports" (Dale 1980). To the citizens of China not living in the city but aware of its power and riches—creating one-eighth of the country's industrial production with one-hundredth of China's population and earning in the process four times more per capita than the national average—the place is a repository of dreams of affluence and opportunities. To most people living in the city, however, the still largely bichromatic crowds (green for the soldiers, blue for most others), dirt, smelly water, overflowing sewers, polluted air, street noise, and disintegrating houses do not conjure up anything romantic.

The city's development since 1949 is the principal cause of the truly appalling environment, but in this case one should make due allowances for the influence of past colonial blunders. Unlike Beijing, previously a rather placid city turned into a huge polluted factory settlement by the Communist regime, Shanghai's crowding and messy industrial locations were inherited in 1949 and just made worse since. The crowding is phenomenal: within the urban area of 158 km² there were 6.01 million people in 1980, or a staggering 38,000 inhabitants per km², 2.6 times Beijing's figure (Xia and Jian 1982). The total area of the centrally administered city and its peri-urban farming zone is 6,185 km, and 11.46 million people lived there in 1980 (Figure 25).

The whole municipality has over 7,100 factories, more than half of which are located within the city's built-up area where they occupy about 40 km², or nearly one-quarter of all the land. This high concentration might be a bit more bearable if the factories, or at least the major enterprises, were located in several industrial parks on the city's outskirts. However, this is not the case. In Shanghai one can find in almost any ward some heavy industry, plenty of small light industry enterprises, seemingly countless hole-in-the-wall workshops, crowded housing, and perhaps a little park. And it has been industry, led by metallurgy and heavy machinery, which has enjoyed the greatest attention since 1949, consuming 60 percent of all capital construction investment during the past three decades, while urban housing got only 9.6 percent (Xinhua, October 19, 1980, *SWB* 1106).

As in Beijing, virtually all housing investments went into building

Figure 25. LANDSAT image of Shanghai, China's largest city and one of the biggest metropolitan areas in the world (image acquired on July 4, 1978, in band 6). Huangpu Jiang, winding through the municipality on its way to the Chang Jiang, appears darker than the siltier large river. Multicropped wet fields can be seen everywhere; in coastal areas larger newly reclaimed fields are also visible. Most of the city lies on the Huangpu Jiang's western bank, with the eastern shore mostly occupied by port installations, storages, and factories.

new residential "villages" on the city's outskirts—depressing looking Soviet-style uniform assemblies of grayish blocks taking over previously fertile vegetable fields—and the old and older city housing has been left to sink into further and, so often it seems, unreconstructable disrepair. Only the years since 1979 have seen a shift in Shanghai's strategic planning. Some 340 new industrial projects have been canceled or postponed; production emphasis has shifted to light industry (which in 1981 accounted for 55.6 percent of the total, surpassing for the first time in decades heavy industry's share); and outlays for housing, public utilities, and environmental protection are up to 20.3 percent of new investments, still low but far higher than the average post-1949 share. Consequently, the new housing space of 3.04 million m² completed in 1980 was 41 percent above the previous year's level (Xia and Jian 1982; Figure 26).

Still, any fundamental improvements of Shanghai's environment will be long in coming even if the new policies are sustained and given all possible practical support rather than perfunctory bureaucratic nods. The news is, at best, mixed. On the one hand, since 1980, 60 percent of the city's large factory stacks have been equipped with electrostatic precipitators, appreciably cutting down fly-ash air pollution; new and quite strict regulations have been issued to control pollution of the Huangpu Jiang (Whangpoo River) by the busy port traffic; and major industrial enterprises working with mercury and cadmium have drastically reduced the releases of these heavy metals into the rivers. More good news concerning the very survival of the city has been the virtual control of its sinking. Between 1921 and 1965, the ground in some Shanghai wards sank by as much as 2.63 m, mainly owing to excessive withdrawals of ground water. Cutting down the pumping rates and replenishing the aquifers with used water slowed the sinking to one to 2 mm or more per year by the late 1970s (although the injection of used water increased ground-water pollution).

On the other hand, one comes across news items that make the recent official commitment to pollution control and environmental improvements very suspect. The Huangpu Jiang's serious pollution and lengthening periods of anaerobicity and smell in summer were described in section 3.5.1, and obviously water treatment specialists, which China is short of anyway, must be in a high demand in the city. Yet a local paper (*Wenhui bao*, July 2, 1980, p. 2) complains bitterly about an "eminent" pollution control specialist whose detailed proposals have been completely disregarded and who, although he is an assistant

Figure 26. Reconstructing Shanghai's core: new apartments are rising above old colonial houses, still home for most of Shanghai's residents.

chief engineer of the city's Environmental Protection Institute, could not even secure a desk for his office!

That Huangpu Jiang pollution cries out for massive and speedy improvement measures is all too clear. The already smelly and distasteful drinking water may become undrinkable as new factories add 150,000-200,000 tons of untreated water a year. And industrial pollution is spreading beyond the city boundaries, with many suburban villages eagerly developing parts subcontracting, including electroplating. In 1979, 96 percent of the surface water test points in Shanghai Municipality were found to be contaminated with heavy metals, and in 25 percent of the cases the water was no longer drinkable; naturally, all this pollution eventually ends up in the Huangpu Jiang (Gao and Jin 1980).

As in many similar instances around the world, heavily polluted water is believed to be a major contributor to rapidly rising cancer morbidity and mortality. The incidence of various cancers in Shanghai's population in 1979 was almost twice that of 1963, and the city now has unenviable primacy in China's cancer mortality. Heavy air pollution, of course, is another contributing factor. Gao and Jin (1980) cite an example of a 60-ha area bounded by West Baoxing Road, Zhongshan North Road, New Republic Road, and Liuying Road where more than 50 hazardous materials plants are interspersed with some 2,000 residences, where dust fallout surpasses the standard by three to eight times, where levels of sulfur dioxide (SO_2), hydrogen sulfide (H_2S), and hydrochloric acid (HC1) are tens or even hundreds of times above the standard, and where three-fifths of the local high school students have chronic rhinitis and one-third suffer from chronic pharyngitis.

Shanghai's major air pollution sources are now being gradually controlled, at least as far as the fly ash is concerned, but the city's solid and gaseous emissions are unusually large owing to the presence of heavy industries. In the late 1970s the municipality annually consumed 12 million tons of coal and 6 million tons of oil products, and nearly two-thirds of this total went to fuel, metallurgical (over one-third alone), chemical, and textile industries. In all cases, but especially in iron- and steel-making, combustion efficiencies are very low and even when one applies just the average particulate pollutant factors (i.e., 3.3 kg of fly ash and 20 kg of ash per 100 kg of coal burned) the annual releases amount to 400,000 tons of fly ash and 2.4 million tons of ash. As for SO_2 emissions, they total (with an average 2 percent of sulfur for all fossil fuels) at least some 360,000 tons (Figure 27).

To this huge pollution load released almost totally within an area of some 250 km² will be soon added a large, and unnecessary, source just north of the city, on the shores of the Chang Jiang near its point of confluence with the Huangpu Jiang. Baoshan steel mill—the largest in China, hastily conceived in the heady year of grand economic plans in 1978, carelessly planned (for example, Chinese ore will be impossible

Figure 27. Shanghai Iron and Steel Plant No. 1, here hidden behind the wharves of the city's huge port, releases huge quantities of uncontrolled emissions over the city.

to use and costly imports from Australia will be needed, yet the water depth at the location is inadequate to berth large ore carriers!), and most likely not needed at all in the first place—is just another costly blunder of the steel-loving Stalinists who still dominate China's strategic planning.

When the entire mill is in operation its uncontrolled SO_2 emissions will amount to about one-quarter of the total current SO_2 releases in Shanghai, and these large volumes, released from 200-m-tall stacks, will be carried during the winter half of the year by prevailing winds directly toward the city and, most incredibly, the anticipated area of the highest ground concentrations is Shanghai's downtown south of Hongkou. Indeed an exemplary case of new environmental awareness!

Knowing all this, it is hard to be optimistic about the environmental outlook for one of the world's largest cities. Polluted water is common elsewhere, but drinking, in terms of volume, water that is 50 percent sedimented and chlorinated sewage mixed with salty sea water during high tides in summer is far from usual. Other cities suffer from air pollution, but the production of about 1,600 tons of fly ash and 1,500 tons of SO_2 for each km² of urban area is, I believe, unique. Cramming more than 6 million people, 7,000 factories, 80,000 untuned ever-honking cars, and 1.8 million bikes and carts into about 150 km² is not common either. The gravity of the problem demands aggressive, determined, sustained, and, inevitably, costly remedies. I have deep doubts that they will be forthcoming soon.

These last two sentences could be applied just as well to many other environmental problems of today's China. The final chapter of this book will offer a closer look at the promising signs and the critical limitations, at policies changing as well as curiously regressive, and at several key strategic determinants of China's future that will be decisive in shaping the country's environment.

7
SOLUTIONS
AND LIMITATIONS

Heaven's favorable weather is less important than Earth's advantageous terrain, the
Earth's advantageous terrain is less important than human unity.

Meng Ke, Book II
(in D. C. Lau translation)

Heaven and Earth exist forever!
Mountains and rivers never change.
But herbs and trees in perpetual rotation
are renovated and withered by the dews
frosts: And the Man the wise, Man the
divine—Shall he alone escape the law?

Tao Qian, "Substance, Shadow and Spirit"
(in A. Waley translation)

Let me begin the last chapter of this book on an optimistic note: the very fact that all the preceding pages could be written on the basis of recent Chinese studies and reports is an encouraging sign. The country's environmental and other concerned scientists, as well as many newsmen and common citizens, have been using the period of new candor to publish an impressive array of revelations—and to gain, I think to a surprising degree, the attention of top policy-makers. The latter might have been expected, given their past performance and the current unsettled state of Chinese affairs, to notice little and act less.

That they noticed and comprehended enough to start China's bureaucracies moving in directions of caution, conservation, and control is an even more positive sign. But many fundamental limitations persist, of course, and several key problems related to the state of the Chinese environment not only have no easy and rapid solutions but appear to be growing more intractable. This book will close with a critical look at both the recent achievements and the continuing deficiencies and obstacles.

7.1 A new awareness

The current awareness of environmental degradation contrasts sharply with still very recent attitudes of complacency and self-praise, wherein the "actual situation . . . could not even be mentioned" unless one wanted to be labeled as "painting the socialist system black" (Gao and Jin 1980). Credit must go above all to those people in China who know something about the complexities of environmental affairs and the dangers of environmental degradation and who have been bringing information about the true and dismal state of China's environment to the public and policy-makers' attention. Obviously, this would have been impossible without the general change of many of the Party's public policies, but the risks assumed by individual scientists should not be underestimated.

For more than a decade, writing anything was impossible for most of these people, who were lucky to be weeding crops or feeding pigs or, less frequently, carrying on their research in much straitened or surreptitious ways. Only since 1978 have the senior researchers and their young associates finally been able to speak out, and some of them have carried their revelations and warnings into Party newspapers and journals, doing what they feel has to be done: warning the policy-makers that things *do* look bad and that extensive remedies are sorely needed. Such behavior carries no small personal risk, as they have exposed themselves to serious political accusations should a new reversal of Chinese policies come—and who, after the twists and turns of the past three decades, can be sure it will not?

Although these scientists now have both the forums and the audience to spread their message, a profound limitation to their efforts is their infinitesimal number. In the whole country of one billion there are less than 600 people educated in ecology, and until 1979 there have been no university curricula offering such expertise (Xiong and others 1979). Among the existing experts, largely aging men and women educated decades ago in the West, Japan, or the USSR, a perceptive Swedish observer (L. Lundegardh, leader of a Swedish delegation of environmentalists) found an impressive degree of theoretical knowledge— while he assessed practical measures in environmental control to be at the interwar level. I could not agree more with this accurate appraisal of affairs, which bespeaks a situation so common in Chinese science in general.

Even so, since 1979 the scholarly ferment has been surprisingly rich and sustained (as stressed earlier, this book could not have been written without it). The effort has taken several important forms. First, the researchers submit their papers to national, city, or provincial dailies to acquaint the largest possible numbers of the general public and, above all, Party and government bureaucrats, with their warnings and proposals. This is where *Guangming ribao* has assumed an importance difficult to overemphasize; its pages have been hospitably opened to literally scores of revelations whose publication would have been unthinkable just a few years ago, when they would have been a serious slander of Communist China's purity and achievements.

Then came waves of conferences convened, new learned societies established, and new professional journals founded. China's first national conference on ecology, sponsored by the Academy of Sciences, was held in Xining (Qinghai) in August 1978. About 120 people attended, 64 papers were presented (mostly on ecology of forests, farmlands, and pastures), and an eight-year research plan was drafted to promote cooperation among different disciplines (NCNA, September 3, 1978, *SWB* 998). The first national symposium on ecological equilibrium met in Zhuzhou (Hunan) in December 1980, and it focused especially on the appropriate resource use in the country's large subtropical and tropical region (NCNA, November 28, 1980, *SWB* 1115).

Among many other recent environment-related meetings have been several symposia on interbasin water transfer from the South to the North, river sedimentation, loess control, afforestation, desertification, fresh-water fisheries, and rural energetics. The Chinese Society of Environmental Sciences was established in March 1979, the Environmental Engineering Society was inaugurated in Jinan in March 1981, and in 1980 the State Scientific and Technological Commission approved the setting up of the Environmental and Physical Pollution Control and Research Center in Beijing.

Papers on environmental topics have appeared in a wide variety of publications, but the founding of several specialized journals devoted to interdisciplinary study of the environment has been of the key importance. They include *Huanjing* (Environment), published monthly in Guangdong; *Huanjing baohu* (Environmental Protection), a bimonthly from Beijing; *Huanjing kexue* (Environmental Science), another bimonthly published in the capital; and *Huanjing kexue xuebao* (Journal of Environmental Science), a quarterly from Liaoning.

Unlike so many specialized Chinese journals, these journals are commendably broad and truly interdisciplinary in their coverage, with papers ranging from air sampling and heavy metals in drinking water to economic planning and environmental medicine. The Chinese are now cooperating with all relevant branches of the UN (United Nations Environment Program, Man and the Biosphere Program, United Nations Industrial Development Organization, Food and Agriculture Organization) and with a host of other international organizations—although the choice of topics and people is often still politically guided to an uncomfortably high degree.

Public awareness has been heightened by the appearance of numerous shocking pieces written by prominent scientists and enterprising reporters. Since 1978 all the major dailies, above all *Renmin ribao* (People's Daily), *Guangming ribao* (Guangming Daily), *Gongren ribao* (Workers Daily), *Beijing ribao* (Beijing Daily), *Wenhui bao* (Wenhui News), and *Nanfang ribao* (Southern Daily), have been printing numerous letters of complaint sent by their readers, and they have often assigned their reporters to investigate or follow up the cases; water and air pollution, deforestation, sanitation, pesticide poisoning, overfishing, urban noise, and destruction of scenic and cultural sites are among the reported and investigated items. Governmental response has been also multifaceted. In late 1978 the State Planning Commission, the State Economic Commission, and the Environmental Protection Group under the State Council ordered 186 major metallurgical, chemical, oil, machine, textile, light industry, and construction enterprises to take necessary corrective steps to control their wastes by the year 1982—or face a shutdown. An even clearer sign of the serious awareness of pollution problems was the decision of the three high-level organizations requiring all major new or expanded industrial projects to install the necessary control equipment.

The culmination of the Center's effort to deal with environmental degradation was the promulgation of the "Law on Environmental Protection of the PRC (for Trial Use)" by the Eleventh Session of the Fifth National People's Congress Standing Committee in September 1979 (see the complete text in Appendix D). This is a general document dealing with nearly all aspects of environmental degradation, and individual provinces, regions, and municipalities have since been enacting specific rules and regulations based on the law. Finally, in May 1982, a new ministry was established to oversee environmental protection—but it appears to be an unfortunate bureaucratic hybrid. The Ministry of Urban and Rural Construction and Environmental Protection was organized by merging three state organizations dealing with capital construction with the National Bureau of Surveying and Mapping; how strong a say the environmentalists will have in this hybrid bureaucracy is far from clear.

From an individual viewpoint, the average Chinese city dweller is perfectly well aware of, and inconvenienced and annoyed by, various forms of environmental degradation: sleeping with closed windows during the sticky southern summers owing to the stench and noise outside, drinking smelly water or coughing incessantly, cannot be easily avoided by millions of China's urbanites. Still, with more to eat, with earnings up, with savings for a TV set ready and an electric fan humming on the table, the emerging Chinese urban "middle class" is not overly concerned with environmental quality, and if some inconveniences are the price of higher city earnings, so be it.

Kinzelbach (1981) illustrates the point with a telling episode from a fertilizer plant in Guangxi. "The workers at the plant's sulfuric acid workshop are paid a monthly allowance of ¥8 (compared to the average basic salary of ¥50) to compensate for health hazards caused by the acid mist prevailing around the workshop. The administrative cadres did not receive their bonus as their far-away office was not exposed to the acid. Therefore they moved their office into the immediate vicinity of the workshop. Now they inhale acid and obtain a monthly ¥4 bonus." Similarly, instances of casual rural attitudes and neglect have already been cited (see section 6.1.2). Clearly, a scientific popularization task of immense proportions will be needed to change the situation. New attitudes will be also required on all management levels to implement the newly proclaimed policies.

7.2 New policies: achievements and limitations

In a recent review of China's achievements in environmental protection, Guo Huanxuan (1981) gives a fairly extensive list of improvements, and these are worth recounting in abbreviated form. By 1980, heavy industries had introduced diverse controls and recycling processes resulting in a significant reduction of water and air pollutants: in China's oil fields waste water recycling was increased to 76.4 percent of total volume (from 40 percent in 1977) by building 78 new treatment stations; nonferrous smelters used waste gases to produce 800,000 tons of sulfuric acid (about a 60 percent increase in comparison with the early 1970s), cutting down sulfur oxide emissions. Other industrial improvements included the retrieval of alkali in many paper mills, the recovery of previously wasted acids in synthetic fats and detergents production, and the expansion of nonmercury batteries manufacture.

The renovations of boilers, the utilization of waste heat, and other energy conservation measures have somewhat improved the air quality of several large cities. Lanzhou is cited as the best example, with 1980 levels of winter sulfur dioxide below the state standard and dust content still high but 45 percent lower than in 1977. Water quality has improved in the Bo Hai and in the Huang Hai, and the Wuhan section of the Chang Jiang, the Jinan section of the Huang He, and the Gaoyao section of the Zhu Jiang, as well as Tai Hu, have been put under the world water quality monitoring system of the United Nations Environment Program and the World Health Organization; recent measurements indicate no serious pollution. Large-scale afforestation, especially the northern shelterbelt project, better protection of aquatic resources, establishment of new natural reserves, commencement of nationwide environmental monitoring in 290 locations, and new water quality monitoring stations along major rivers are the other listed achievements.

After reading through the litany of environmental *mals* gathered in this book it must be obvious that Guo's list of achievements is a mere prelude to a real reversal of China's multifaceted environmental degradation—and, quite realistically, the author and many of his informed colleagues are well aware of this fact. They recognize the enduring legacy of one-sidedly seeking quick economic results by thoughtlessly exploiting natural resources and neglecting their protection and regeneration; they acknowledge the widespread lack of know-how and experience regarding environmental management and also the continuing lag in economic management and production efficiency, especially the wasteful use of energy and raw inputs. Moreover, they are also well aware that the common "erroneous tendency to artifically separate environmental protection from production development, and even make them oppose each other," can be reversed only through "a drastic change in our perception" (Chen Xiping 1981). The need for such drastic changes becomes especially obvious when one discovers surveys showing 70 percent of all cases of industrial environmental pollution being caused by poor management, 20 percent by lack of comprehensive utilization, and only 10 percent by technical deficiencies or lack of control equipment (Liu Hongqi 1980). Even if somewhat exaggerated in the survey, the role of poor management is undeniable.

Many writers also lament a reality that is sure to persist: shortage of funds allocated for environmental control. Their approach must be, therefore, of necessity, gradual and concentrated on key industries and key cities (the capital, Shanghai, famous scenic attractions such as Hangzhou, Suzhou, and Guilin), and in the countryside, on the alleviation of the most pressing intertwining problems of deforestation, erosion, and household fuel shortages. While considerable environmental improvements in rural areas can be achieved by such simple measures as allocating private woodlots and encouraging crop diversification, eliminating and controlling the discharges of pollutants by industries is more problematic.

Currently fees are by far the most popular tool for forcing negligent factories to reduce or eliminate their effluents. To encourage cleanup, the penalties are set a little higher than the cost of proper disposal. During 1980, 1,500 factories were fined, but the approach can hardly be effective with all of China's some 400,000 enterprises, which release each year 28.7 billion tons of waste water, 3.8 trillion m^3 of waste gases, and 450 million tons of solid residues (NCNA, August 18, 1980, *JPRS* 76374). Problems with the emission fee system, copied from the Western practice, in a centrally planned Communist economy are obvious. To begin with, unlike under depraved capitalism, enterprise interests and society's interests are supposed to be essentially identical; moreover, "the state can use planning of the national economy to make economic development and environmental protection proceed in harmony with each other" (Zhou Fuxiang 1980).

By fining the enterprises, the state is, literally, fining itself, as it is its heavy hand that runs everything. How do the adherents of the most progressive idea of all explain the slight contradiction? Easily: "In practice, because their positions are different, enterprises generally lay particular emphasis on product output rather than on pollution control, and some, for the particular economic interests of the enterprise, purposely discharge pollutants and harm society's interests" (Zhou Fuxiang 1980). Perfectly clear! Pollution fees are thus levied so the enterprise will take economic responsibility for the damages—and many Chinese writers have found the effects "outstanding."

But "as long as the director of a plant has to obtain the consent and the capital for a treatment facility from his respective ministry, it is hard to imagine how the detour via fees—which in the end are used to build such facilities—should be more successful than the direct order of the past" (Kinzelbach 1981). Precisely, and fines can be effective only if the enterprises are granted near independence and broad decision-making powers. One thus cannot escape the impression that the fee system is pushed so enthusiastically largely to finance a new growing bureaucratic apparatus, the environmental protection bureaus whose budgets can only be boosted by such fees (Kinzelbach 1981). Not surprisingly, then, the collection of fees had started even before the preparation of environmental standards was completed.

Even if the mechanism were to work better than one has a right to expect—after all, the equally tough older forestry law did little to stop the wave of deforestation; investment capital and technology shortages will change only slowly: and in a country with already high urban unemployment, closing the factories or reducing their operation could hardly be a popular political decision—there would still be a problem of timely and accurate emission monitoring to assess compliance and set fees. Even in rich Western nations, reliable pollution monitoring networks were put into regular operation only since the late 1960s and, as in all such similar cases, besides financial and equipment shortages, it is the acute inadequacy of trained manpower that limits Chinese capabilities: in all of China only 4,000 persons were available for environmental research and monitoring in early 1980.

Of the financial limitations little need be said: during the past two decades Western countries have learned that the cost of controlling environmental pollution is far from trivial, and that for certain processes it can boost production costs by several tens of percent. Chinese estimates are that air and water pollution each causes annual damage worth about ¥5billion, while Kinzelbach (1981) estimates that ¥10 billion is needed to treat all industrial waste water in China, and he also states that cleaning urban air will be even more expensive. Still, even if the total cost of industrial pollution cleanup were ¥30 billion, elimination of the annual loss of ¥10 billion would repay such an investment in just three years.

However, all this appears in a very different light when one realizes that the government's total expenditures in 1980 came to ¥121 billion (including a deficit of nearly ¥13 billion). Clearly, any multibillion yuan investments in pollution control in a country that must import millions of tons of cereals and has potentially nearly unlimited technological and infrastructural needs will be impossible for a very long time. Moreover, as illustrated previously with various examples of foot-dragging water pollution control (section 3.5.3), in the Chinese economy the availability of finances and orders even from the highest levels do not guarantee that the work will be done promptly, or at all.

Again, the descriptions of Guilin's failure to control environmental degradation are most illustrative. The municipal Party committee, the bureaucrats in real command, took only a perfunctory interest in the matter (issuing decrees about pollution control without specifying any deadlines or penalties), let the closed portions of factories resume operation, ignored the State Council's injunction against new construction or expansion of existing enterprises, tolerated "bandit projects" and "frightful" pollution in the heart of the city (Rongshan Lake), and disregarded the pleas of some factories that wanted to move away voluntarily (Wang and Gui 1980). And all that the Environmental Protection Group of the State Council has been able to do is demand "sufficient recognition" of the importance of preserving Guilin's unique scenery, particularly by the municipal Party committee, the very people who have with impunity disregarded all previous orders to act.

The most candid Chinese appraisal of the difficulties lying ahead in environmental protection work is an honest, and in places almost bitterly cynical, brief article by Liu Pei'en published in March 1980 in *Guangming ribao*; it is an unusually telling accomplishment even for that year of greatest publishing freedom on environmental topics. The following extensive quotes from those four short paragraphs are an excellent evaluation of China's environmental control prospects.

"Although an environmental protection code has already been promulgated, there is no way to implement it, and in actuality it can only function as propaganda. At present, even criticism is subject to permission, so why bother even to discuss the rest? . . . At present, capital for control of the 'three wastes' [solid, liquid, gaseous] is distributed by environmental protection organs, while the other concerned departments are only uninvolved observers. When they need funds they are very enthusiastic and vocal, but once they have their money they lose their enthusiasm for controls. . . .

"Our present environmental protection system is weak and powerless. . . . When other systems were established, the concerned departments of the Party Central Committee immediately informed the lower levels of their organizational system; environmental protection has been the only exception. None of the responsible bureaus or large and medium-sized plants and mines have environmental protection organs. How can a limited number of environmental protection cadres tackle this huge task all alone? There are also no special capital construction funds for scientific research in environmental protection or for a network of monitors, so how is such work supposed to be developed?'' (Liu Pei'en 1980).

One of the most appealing approaches to effective and economic environmental control is extensive recycling of raw materials and wastes, and China's potential in this respect is very great indeed. This may come as a surprise to many an admirer of Oriental frugality, clinging to an image of China where there is nothing that would not be reused, a paragon of recycling that some naïve Westerners have misrepresented in misplaced admiration (Kapp 1975, with his wide-eyed praise, is a fine example).

To be sure, the list of things collected and recycled in China is long: paper and rags (in the late 1970s Beijing recovered about 60 percent of its raw materials input for local papermaking), bones (for glue and glycerol), chicken and duck feathers (for stuffing), broken glass (to melt and for filler), cigarette butts (many smoke them, some make an insecticide out of them), broken mirrors (to extract the mercury), bottle caps (for the metal as well as the thin cork layer), bits of hair (brushes or dolls with real hair), scrap metals, rubber, and plastics (one ton of plastic waste is recycled into 2,000 pairs of sandals). And, of course, there is the traditional recycling of human and animal wastes.

The most bizarre method of recycling I came across in the Chinese sources was a report from Shanghai, where ''one chemical works sends out people every day to collect discarded oils and fats from dishwashing from the sewerage system of hotels and restaurants''; this thriftiness was repaid by more than 600 tons of fat between 1971 and 1973, enough for 3 million bars of soap (NCNA, September 18, 1974, *SPRCP* 74 40).

Kinzelbach (1981), however, correctly remarks that no matter how admirable all these recycling practices are ''they originate from necessity owing to general shortages rather than from environmental consciousness; whether they will prevail once those shortages vanish is difficult to say.'' Plain poverty rather than a purposeful preservation of nature's purity is the cause of extensive recycling of odd household wastes and bits and organic materials; but in reusing their now voluminous industrial waste (discharged ''collectively''), the Chinese have not shown any similarly extensive enthusiasm.

Not only have they let go of the wastes whose recovery is expensive and requires complex technologies and high capital investment (a poor country would have a legitimate excuse here), but they have dumped easily recoverable wastes that even in the richest countries are turned into good products. One such example is coal ash resulting from combustion in power plants and industrial boilers: of some 30 million tons of ash so generated each year only 10 percent is used, and about 15 million tons is dumped into rivers (Kinzelbach 1981). In contrast, West Germany, another heavy user of steam coal, recycles about two-thirds of its ash (utilization choices include, above all, building materials, ingredients for paving compounds, and fertilizers).

Even more surprisingly, until very recently the Chinese have been extremely negligent in utilizing the two inputs which are the irreplaceable core of human survival and whose mismanagement has serious environmental impacts: water and energy. Consequently, even in Beijing Municipality, whose serious water shortages were described in section 6.2.1, no more than 40 percent of industrial water is recycled; in suburban vegetable irrigation 45 percent of the water is wasted; and in some residential districts water is not metered and households pay a flat monthly fee and hence do not care how much they use—some of these families use up to 610 liters of water per person a day (Zhang Qin 1981). For comparison, in rich Western countries typical household consumption is 70-250 liters per capita a day, and Beijing's families with a metered supply use around 50 liters! Energy, of course, cannot be recycled, but before it degrades into unusable low temperature heat it should be made to work with greatest efficiency and, as already detailed, the Chinese record in this respect is dismal.

If recycling and conservation have not been very successful and if, as Liu Pei'en (1980) complains, "there are only slight results in controlling the sources of pollution that have long been with us," what will happen with the coming sources, the new pollutants, the new developments leading toward environmental degradation? As in the past, several underlying causes will determine the nature and extent of these changes: the growth of the country's population, the necessity to provide at the minimum at least as much food and energy in per capita terms as is available today or, much more preferably, to increase the living standards substantially through large-scale economic modernization.

7.3 Population growth

The absolute numbers are overwhelming. China's first modern census in 1953 counted 601.938 million people, and the third, taken in July

Figure 28. Even with birthrates sharply lowered during the 1970s, every year China is adding 15 million people to its one billion total. When the children in this picture reach marriageable age in the late 1990s the country will have to practice even stricter population control to avoid irreversible ecosystemic damage and to raise living standards.

1982, counted 1,008,175,288: about 450 million people were added during the 33 years between 1949 and 1982, an average natural increase of 1.8 percent a year. Every year now more than 14 million people are being added to the total; yet the rate of this increase must be seen as a success, as the outcome of a recent intensive population control campaign that brought the natural increase down from 2.3 percent in 1957 (birthrates 3.4 and death rates 1.1 percent) to the census-established 1.455 percent by 1981, with natality at 2.091 and mortality at 0.636 percent (Appendix A.10; Figure 28).

The Chinese claim that this latest census was extremely accurate, with a net overcount of a mere 0.15/1,000; but, interestingly, births are estimated to be undercounted at a rate of 1.83/1,000. When taken at face value, therefore, the recent natality figures would appear to be a bit too low. Whatever the precise values, in international comparison the most recent Chinese vital statistics look admirable. All other poor populous nations are growing much faster: India at about 2 percent, Indonesia at nearly 2.5 percent, Brazil at almost 3 percent, a rate similar to those of Bangladesh, Pakistan, and Nigeria. Chinese rates now are quite close to the Japanese ones and rapidly approaching the North American and European values; several European countries now have, in fact, higher natalities than China but also higher mortalities with aging populations; so Europe's natural growth is below 0.6 percent.

Disaggregated figures deepen the impression of successful population control, showing the natural increase falling to even more impressive levels in nearly all large cities—8.41/1,000 in Tianjin in 1980, 7.71/1,000 in Beijing in 1979, and only 5.31/1,000 in Shanghai in 1980—and in several populous provinces. In 1980 Shandong had the lowest rate with 7.03/1,000; Zhejiang was a close second with 7.07/1,000; Shaanxi was not far back with 7.19/1,000; while Jiangxi had 9.11, Fujian 9.33, and Henan 9.53 children added for every 1,000 inhabitants (NCNA, March 9, 1981, *SWB* 1126).

And yet the Chinese find surprisingly little comfort in these figures. Why the halving of natural increase in 25 years is not occasion for self-satisfaction is easily explained by what Jay Forrester (1971) calls a "counterintuitive behavior of complex systems." To begin with, the halving has not been a gradual process: in 1970 the country's population growth was 2.6 percent, higher than in 1957 and not much different from the rest of poor Asia. After 1957, population control was denounced as a Malthusian ploy, with Maoist slogans about the desirability of a large population replacing any sensible discussion of the problem, and the subsequent loss of social order during the Cultural Revolution helped to raise birthrates to the record highs of the 1960s and early 1970s.

China's family planning campaign started only in 1971, and during the past decade the natural increase has dropped from 2.34 percent in 1971 to 1.2 percent in 1980. This means that the children born during the population booms of the 1960s and the early 1970s (50 percent of the Chinese population is now under twenty years old!) are now entering marriageable age: the 1980s and the early 1990s will see, on the average, some 20 million young people passing into that category every year; a continued natural growth rate of just 1.2 percent would push China's population to about 1.3 billion by the year 2000. This is a staggering increase of 300 million— more than the USSR has today, two-fifths of India's total—in a single generation.

Not surprisingly, then, the official Chinese policy now is "one couple, one child," and lowering population growth is considered to be a "strategic task and a matter of top priority," and interesting research is done regarding the optimum supportable population total (Hu et al.

1981 is perhaps the best example). The goals set during the Fifth National People's Congress in the summer of 1979 called for increases of one percent in 1980, half a percent by 1985, and zero growth by the year 2000. Such drastic reductions are to be achieved not only through the strengthening of measures long used for population control—delayed marriages, free distribution of contraceptives, sterilization on demand—but above all by a combination of rewards and penalties.

Details vary from province to province, but the essential points of the policy are as follows. Children of one-child families will have priority in school enrollment, medical treatment, and hospitalization (in some provinces, all education and health care for them will be free). Urban families with one child will receive a monthly bonus payment of 5 yuan, the same floor space in new housing as for a couple with two children, priority in day-care center enrollments and job selection, and exemption from manual labor in the countryside. Rural parents will receive work-point bonuses, more housing space, and retirement benefits, while the child will get an adult food ration and an extra share of private plot area. Penalties for more than two children include 5 percent income or work-point reductions (raised by one percent for each additional child after three), withdrawal of health care subsidies, no paid maternity leave, and reduced rations for subsidiary foodstuffs and commodities.

The measures will certainly be more successful in the cities than in the countryside, where the inertia of traditions combined with a relatively greater prosperity spreading since the abolition of command farming in the late 1970s will keep favoring larger families. Not surprisingly, one can already find in the Chinese professional literature statements about rural population growth getting out of control, admissions that there is no long-term effective method to control it, and assertions that the target of 1.2 billion people by the year 2000 will certainly be exceeded—while already there are 500 million poverty-stricken peasants (Weng et al. 1981). And even urban growth rates may not be that easy to control because many more people are getting married and many others immigrating. In Beijing, for example, 59,000 couples married in 1977, 130,000 in 1979, and since 1980, 900,000 people have been reaching marriageable age annually, and on top of all this the freer movement of people brought 120,000 new residents in 1979 alone (NCNA, September 27, 1980, *SWB* 1103). And the latest available nationwide growth rate shows an increase to 1.4 in 1981 from 1.2 percent in 1980 (State Statistical Bureau 1982).

182 THE BAD EARTH

Naturally, opinions on the eventual outcome of China's population program range from the guardedly optimistic to the outright denial of the possibility of coming near a zero growth rate in 20 years' time. This is not the place to go into such arguments. What is important to realize is that even a very favorable outcome would result in a huge population increase during the next two decades. The most likely range is defined on the upper end by the already noted total of nearly 1.3 billion (1,280 million is the precise figure based on the 1982 census total) resulting from a continuation of the recent growth rate, and on the lower end by a complete success of the control policies (a gradual decline of the growth rate to 0.5 percent in 1980, zero in 2000), which would hold the total to just 1.054 billion at the end of the century.

Such a low figure is highly improbable, as is any return to substantially higher growth rates than today's. Within the range of 1.050-1.280 billion, most informed observers would certainly opt for totals closer to the upper end. The total increment will almost certainly be at least 100 million, more likely 150-200 million, and a quarter of a billion total is not out of the question. The social and economic implications of such increments are obviously wide-ranging. According to Li Shiyi (1982), about half of the annual net increase in national income will be required just to bring up the annual net addition of up to 20 million babies to be born at the peak of the coming birth boom, and to provide this growing population with a higher standard of living—which it expects and which it has also been repeatedly promised by the government—will tax the country's environment enormously. Nowhere will the pressures be as acute and as irreconcilable with the preservation of acceptable ecosystemic balances as in getting more food and more energy, especially when the per capita consumption levels are to rise substantially in an unprecedented modernization effort.

7.4 Agricultural strategies

Major changes in China's agricultural strategies would be needed even if the country's population growth were to remain stationary. As discussed in Chapter 6, food supply remained very precarious until the late 1970s, and only the most recent changes have brought it a bit above bare subsistence levels, although in qualitative and variety terms it remains rather inferior, with a very high share of cereals, very small quantities of meat, fish, and fruit, and with often inadequate amounts of vegetables.

The recent partial retreat from the "grain-first" policy has brought back some of the traditional crop specialization and brought as well some notable improvements in meat and fish output; not surprisingly, crop diversification, large-scale extension of animal husbandry, and fresh-water and marine aquaculture have been among the key proposals of long-term agricultural strategies vigorously discussed in the Chinese popular and scientific press since 1978. Obviously, these are far-ranging and intriguing problems of critical importance for China's future, and Shi Shan (1980) summarizes the basic dilemma of the recent past perfectly.

"At present, our nation's agriculture is in a vicious circle from which it cannot immediately free itself. On the one hand, everyone admits that in agriculture the five sectors (i.e., crops, livestock, aquatic production, forestry, and sidelines) must be developed in an overall manner, and that measures should be suited to local circumstances. On the other hand, because of the shortage of food grains, many ways must be found to engage in food grain production. Thus, economic crops are being pushed out, and improper reclamation of wasteland, expansion of planting, and irrational increases in multiple cropping have occurred everywhere. Mountains, forests, grasslands, lakes, and ponds are destroyed and soil fertility is massively depleted. As farmland fertility drops and water and soil are lost from the slopes, grasslands become deserts, the environment is destroyed, . . . increases in food grains slow, then stagnate. We are forced to expand plantings further. . . . This situation has affected us all."

Indeed it has, and the country looks for an escape from the vicious circle, for breakthroughs. Not *breakthrough*: there is no single way out; rather there must be a combination of changes and the pursuance of several essential strategies. The overriding concern that must bind these developmental approaches is the ecosystemic sanity of all long-range moves. Consequently, I will appraise several of the key ingredients of China's badly needed food production breakthroughs largely from this ecosystemic point of view alone.

In spite of some residual counterarguments, crop diversification appears to be perhaps the least controversial stratagem, and the last few years have seen some very impressive increases in areas sown to previously neglected but traditionally highly prized oil crops such as rapeseed, peanuts, sesame seed, and sunflowers. As a result, the 1981 output of oil-bearing crops was 32.7 percent above the 1980 level which, in turn, was 19.5 percent higher than the 1979 harvest (State Statistical Bureau 1981; 1982). Areas devoted to soybeans, sugarcane, jute, and tea have been also substantially enlarged (as were, unfortunately, areas devoted to tobacco growing). After two decades of neglect and outright destruction, more attention is also being paid to orchards, mulberry trees, tung oil, and tea oil, as well as to other minor tree crops.

Yet sharply expanding the areas of noncereal crops has not brought a reduction in grain harvests, just the opposite, in fact, because staple grain crops are again predominantly being cultivated on soils and in locations most suitable for their growth rather than indiscriminately planted over large areas but often bringing pitiful yields. That some of the spirit of command farming and grain-first policies still remains is obvious but, in general, the diversification argument has been translated into a widespread reality and formally incorporated into the central economic planning. A much more intractable problem still remaining is that of suitable varieties: high-yielding varieties with high fertilizer and moisture requirements are often sown on dry, infertile land, resulting in reduced, rather than improved, yields. Such a mismatch of crop varieties and local soils is estimated to add up annually to losses of over 600,000 tons of grain in Shandong Province alone (Mao Zhicun 1980).

The universal use of diversified cropping with proper rotations is perhaps the most beneficial step toward a sustainable agroecosystem, especially in the southern half of China with its extensive multicropping. Under the Maoist grain-first commands, triple-cropping, the most intensive form of the practice, consisted most often of two crops of wheat and one crop of rice, or three crops of paddy rice. This nonrotation system brought high costs, small gains, and rapid soil deterioration—and many locations later discovered that more grain could be harvested and at less cost, with just two grain crops.

Many rotations are possible for both wetland and dry crops. The rotation of paddy rice with peanuts, hemp, vegetables, potatoes, tobacco, or sugarcane will improve soil structure, raise the soil's organic content, prevent or eliminate pest and disease outbreaks, and raise unit yields; of course, the same results can be achieved with the regular cultivation of green fertilizer crops, mostly various leguminous species (among many others see, for example, Huang Chaowu 1980 and Liang Guangshang 1980, for details on Guangdong, where the multicropping index averages 229 percent, the highest in China). Recent experiments in Guangxi saw outstanding improvements in yields and soil qualities achieved with the regular winter planting of vetch as green manure (see section 2.5 for details).

Figure 29. How precious every piece of land is can be seen in this picture from Sichuan: even the dividing ridges between the small fields are planted to vegetables, a sight common throughout this province with 100 million people and a mere 650 m² of cultivated land per capita.

Another essential ingredient of any sustainable agricultural strategy that cannot be challenged is the preservation to the utmost of the country's dwindling arable land (Figure 29; see section 2.5). New comprehensive regulations, finally issued by the State Council in the summer of 1982, were directed against unlawful purchases and rentals of land by governmental organizations, enterprises, schools, communes, and production brigades (*DR*, July 19, 1982, pp. 5-6). However, as in many similar circumstances, opportunities for a quick gain too often have proved irresistible, and the new agency planned by the Ministry of Agriculture to oversee "unified land management" will almost certainly keep on reporting additional farmland losses in the years ahead.

In the past it was easy to argue that the reclamation of new land could remedy this situation to a large extent, and even today one can come across an occasional piece that extols the rich potential for reclaimable farmland. In general, however, I believe this approach has ceased to be an automatic part of China's agricultural strategy mainly for two reasons. First, of course, has been the negative environmental consequences of past reclamation efforts, effects ranging from deforestation and heavy soil erosion to desertification, soil fertility declines, local climatic changes, and meager crop yields. Second is the heavy financial, energy, and labor costs of such enterprises, investments that would have brought greater benefits elsewhere—and without comparable environmental disruptions. And the overall reclamation potential is not, after all, so impressive. China has some 33 million ha of wasteland suitable for agriculture, of which some 10 million ha, mainly in Heilongjiang, Xinjiang, and hilly areas of the South, have either good or relatively good soils (He and Sun 1980), but even if expensive reclamation were to open up all of this better land, the country's cultivated area would expand by only one-tenth, replacing only one-third of the losses of the past quarter century.

A sustainable and sensible strategy would be to combine the conservation of existing farmland with a maximum effort in agroforestry practices, afforestation of nonagricultural wasteland, and continuation of traditional organic recycling, which has been in decline for two reasons. First is the dangerously precipitous qualitative decline of urban wastes traditionally taken out of the cities to fertilize the surrounding land. These wastes now contain ever higher shares of untreated toxic industrial substances whose field application would make the crops inedible or hazardous to eat. Similarly, the composition of household garbage is also changing in the large cities: while formerly it contained almost exclusively coal or wood ashes and organic waste from food preparation, lately the share of paper and solid inorganic trash has been growing and the farmers are no longer eager to use it (Kinzelbach 1981). And with the recycling of crop residues and feces in the countryside, persistent pesticides will also be increasingly recycled. The second reason is economic: the gathering, composting, and application of organic wastes is, naturally, much more time-consuming than the use of inorganic fertilizers, and it leads to higher production costs and seasonal labor shortages.

The benefits of organic farming, now recognized even in the most advanced Western nations, are undeniable (see section 2.5), but more and more Chinese peasants are abandoning the practices that have made China the paragon of recycle farming. In some regions the retreat is truly massive, as illustrated by Zhen Xiazheng's (1982) description of the recent situation in Zhejiang: "This year, complaints of fertilizer shortage were heard in many localities; however, some people have noticed that no commune members are coming to the cities to collect garbage from street and lane residents. Very few peasants still blend soil with ash from straw. No peasants fight to collect feces and urine in the cities . . . at present people yearn only for chemical fertilizer. Urea and ammonium sulfate are needed, the more the better. It seems that organic manure is out of fashion.'' The restoration of extensive organic waste recycling, composting, and green manuring will thus be among the top strategic tasks for China's farming (Figure 30).

Besides afforestation, agroforestry, conservation of farmland, crop diversification, and organic recycling, the expansion of aquaculture is yet another desirable ingredient of China's agricultural strategy that will yield considerable environmental benefits. Fresh-water breeding opportunities are extensive (see section 2.4), and the recent reversal of lake reclamation policies and the encouragement of both private and communal acquaculture have opened new possibilities for this traditional part of Chinese food production. In addition to concentration on intensive pond breeding, the most rewarding form of aquaculture, with possible average annual yields of around 2,000 kg per ha, two uniquely Chinese aquacultural approaches are ecosystemically outstanding and worth the greatest possible extension.

First is the ancient method of rearing fish in rice fields, practiced in Sichuan, Guangdong, and Hunan since the Three Kingdoms period (AD 220-280). In Sichuan in 1980 fish were kept in 107,000 ha of ricefields, a 60 percent increase compared with 1979 (Xiao Peng 1981). Second is the integration of mulberries, silkworms, and fish in a closed nutrient cycle, a practice in use for some four centuries in parts of Guangdong's Zhu Jiang (Pearl River) delta. Mulberries are planted around fish ponds, and their leaves and silkworm chrysalises and droppings feed the fish, while the pond sediment is periodically used to fertilize the trees. Pond silt can also be used to fertilize sugarcane, whose residues can be fermented to produce good fish food. Shunde County, where these practices are most widespread, has nearly 17,000 ha of fish ponds and over 5,000 ha of mulberry trees, and its silkworm cocoon yields are three times as high as those in the Tai Hu area of Jiangsu, China's other prime silkworm center, while pond fish output accounts for one-quarter of the province's total (yet Shunde has only 600,000 people, or some 1.6 percent of Guangdong's population).

A suitable legal framework for the protection of aquatic species was established by the State Council regulations of February 10, 1977, which list nearly 50 kinds of fish, 7 species of shrimp and crab, over 10 shellfish, half a dozen algae, as well as lotus root, water chestnuts, sea turtles, and sea cucumbers to be protected as especially important and valuable (Xinhua, March 27, 1979, *SWB* 1027). Detailed size and

Figure 30. For centuries the very high productivity of China's traditional farming has been sustained by heavy organic waste recycling. In Chengdu, Sichuan's capital, thousands of urban waste collectors still mingle with modern traffic during their everyday routine—but in many other places organic recycling is down, and changes in soil properties follow.

weight standards are set for individual species eligible to be caught; adequate numbers of mature fish must be preserved; and edible aquatic plants can be harvested only when fully grown. Spawning grounds are to be protected, and no catching will be permitted on the approaches to such areas.

Only approved fishing equipment is to be used, and strict penalties are prescribed for blasting, poisoning, and the use of electric shock in fishing. The regulations also proscribe construction of dams without necessary fish passages, industrial and urban pollution of breeding waters, and caution against careless lake- or beach-land reclamation. Yet, as described elsewhere (sections 3.2.1, 3.5, and 5.1), China's largest hydrostation, straddling the country's largest river, is being completed without appropriate fish passages.

The opportunities for mariculture are also considerable. Along China's more than 18,000-km-long coastline there are 1.5 million km² for continental shelf fishing waters (within 200 m depth) of which half a million ha are suitable for marine breeding (Cong 1979). More than 700 species of fish, crustaceans, and other marine products, ranging from sea cucumbers (*Holothuroidea*) and mussels (*Mytilus edulis*) to kelp (*Macrocystis pyrifera*) and sea turtles (*Dermochyles, Chelonia, Caretta* spp.), have a traditionally important place in the largely plant-based Chinese diet. Indeed, for tens of millions of Chinese along the coast, fish and crustaceans are the only source of high quality animal protein, and during the 1950s marine catches rose rapidly, from 448,000 tons in 1949 to 3.116 million tons by 1957.

But these rapid gains led first to a localized and then to a more general overfishing that even involved catching young fish and shrimp for fertilizer (Tu 1979). The output peaked at 4.66 million in 1977 and has been declining ever since as new policies restricting allowable catches in order to replenish the disappearing resources take hold. Breeding zones were put off limits for specific periods of time, and quotas were set for the most endangered species. Also, the indiscriminate reclamation of beaches was forbidden, and mariculture is now being much encouraged.

The last major strategic shift in China's agriculture that I will discuss here is a much greater stress on animal husbandry, a proposal which has met, not surprisingly, with a mixed reception. In virtually all presentations of this proposal the authors cite the country's large northern grasslands as an underutilized resource waiting to be exploited in a bold fashion. For example, Zheng Boquan (1980) notes that the animals in northern pastures totaled only 83.9 million in 1978, while 180 million heads of cattle, sheep, and goats were raised in farming regions, either penned or grazing on hilly land and odd patches of land—despite the fact that pasture areas in the northern grasslands are three times as extensive as the grassed areas in the crop farming regions. Based on this comparison alone, it would seem that the northern pastures could easily accommodate another 100 or 200 million head and that the prospects for Chinese pastoralism are bright indeed. Furthermore, it would be impossible to argue against the need for increased meat and dairy production in the country. Currently the Chinese eat in per capita terms only half of the world's average meat consumption (that is, only one-seventh to one-tenth of rich countries' supply) and drink milk equivalent to a mere one-hundredth of the global mean.

The debates on a shift to a much more livestock-oriented agriculture have been lively. A special readers' column, "Discussions on Guidelines for Agriculture," was started in July 1979 in *Renmin ribao*, China's largest daily, and about 1,000 contributions were received by the end of that year. Tong Dalin, vice-minister in charge of the State Science and Technology Commission (the man who also revealed the truth about the pitiful living conditions on the Loess Plateau), and Liu Zhenbang of the Chinese Institute of World Economics have emerged as the top proponents of an "animal husbandry first" strategy, and Shi Shan (1980) also states unequivocally that the eagerly sought breakthrough for China's farming lies in livestock production.

But it is very doubtful that expansion of meat and dairy production could be achieved by more extensive utilization of the northern grasslands. Besides the previously mentioned desertification (section 2.3) and degeneration (when fields reclaimed from grasslands are abandoned and overgrown with weeds providing only inferior feed for cattle and sheep), there has already been considerable overgrazing, recurrent shortages of winter feed, and extensive damage by rats (see section 5.1).

The extent of environmental damage done to the grasslands and the effects of overgrazing are best illustrated by the fact that the amount of available grass in 1980 had declined to about half of the amount available in the early 1950s; while in 1949 an average of 6.7 ha (100 *mu*) of grazing land was available for each sheep unit, the area had shrunk to only 2.7 ha (40 *mu*) by 1980 (Weng et al. 1981). In Qinghai Province the grassland available for each sheep decreased to 40 percent of the 1949 value, and the saturation point has been reached in many localities

(Xinhua, December 12, 1979, *SWB* 1061). And even where summer grazing conditions are reasonably good, during the long (six to eight months) winter-spring season the herds are often hungry (weight loss is usually about one-third of body weight) and mortality is high. Yu Guoyao (1980b) estimates that these losses amount annually to about five times the state's purchases of meat from the northern grasslands.

Shi Shan (1980) advocates another approach consisting of large-scale planting of grazing grasses on 66.7 million ha (one billion *mu*) in over 100 counties, stretching from Da Hinggan Ling to the eastern edges of the Xizang plateau, which lie in the transitory zone between eastern farmlands and northern and western pastures. He believes that this expansion could be accomplished in a decade, clearly a wildly optimistic estimate, and that if one ha of these artificial pastures could be taken as an equivalent of 10 ha of natural grassland, again an overly liberal assumption, it would be possible to harvest annually 300 kg of meat per ha. I have to agree with Zhang Heqing (1980), who has remarked that theoretical calculations of this kind are "unscientific" and "frequently far removed from realities." Nor would it be easy to expand Chinese animal husbandry through modern intensification. Again, the potentials are great as the feeding periods for China's livestock are long while slaughter rates are low (Yu Guoyao 1980). Nothing illustrates this better than a comparison of Chinese and American pig farming. The Chinese now have around 300 million pigs, but their average take-off rate is only 65 percent and meat yield is only about 55 kg, so that the annual meat production is around 11 million tons. In contrast, less than 60 million American pigs are slaughtered at a 150 percent take-off rate (that is, at only eight months of age) to yield some 75 kg of meat per pig, thus yielding a total of nearly 7 million tons of meat.

In other words, with less than one-fifth the number of China's pigs, American farmers produce nearly two-thirds the amount of China's pork. Or, in global terms, the Chinese, with 40 percent of all pigs produce only 15 percent of the pork. Similarly poor performances can be seen for other domestic animals: cattle fattening requires three years, and the yield is only 70 kg of meat; sheep fattening takes more than a year, for a mere 10 kg of meat.

However, a substantial shortening of the fattening period and major increases in carcass weight could be achieved only through widespread feeding of concentrates—grains, legumes or, as in rich countries, combined, balanced meals. In a country where food grains are strictly rationed and only sufficient to cover essential human needs when consumed directly, this remains a dubious proposition for large-scale application. Undoubtedly, further expansion of new suburban feedlots producing pork, poultry, and eggs will continue to improve the supply to large cities, but to advocate the remolding of Chinese animal husbandry along the intensive North American or Western European model is nothing but wishful thinking.

Western feeding rates vary with grain availabilities and local practices, but usually 4 to 8 kg of grain are fed for each kg of pork produced and 1.5-5 kg of concentrate feed go for each kg of beef produced. To double their pork output by intensive feeding, that is, to produce an extra 10 million tons of meat, the Chinese would have to feed the animals at least 40 and as much as 80 million tons of grain annually. Clearly, this massive amount could not be taken from the current output, so the future grain harvest would have to increase substantially to provide for China's animals. This could not be accomplished easily.

In 1949 the average unprocessed grain output (including tubers converted at one-fifth of cereal value) was just 209 kg per capita, an extraordinary low value caused by long years of war and economic disorder. After the return to normal, more or less, the average per capita grain output rose rapidly to 307 kg in 1956—yet two decades later it was still at the very same level, with output increases just sufficient to keep up with population growth. Improvements of the late 1970s and the early 1980s raised the mean to the vicinity of 330 kg a year, still barely above the subsistence level.

The Chinese consider 400 kg per capita adequate; therefore if the population were to reach 1.2 billion people by the year 2000, 480 million tons of grain would be needed, almost 50 percent above the most recent harvests and a very difficult task indeed. Keeping the population to 1.1 billion by the year 2000 would require a 35 percent rise in grain output. But if past growth trends were to continue, leading to a population of 1.28 billion by the year 2000, a 58 percent grain boost would be needed. If the area sown to grain crops were kept at the late-1970s level of 120 million ha (that is, about four-fifths of all sown area with a multicropping index of 150 percent) yield increases of 35-58 percent over a period of two decades certainly do not appear impossible for corn, wheat, and minor grains, but pushing the current rice yield up by nearly 60 percent, that is, to some 6.7 tons per ha on the average, may not be possible: it would be a performance that would top today's record holders (Japan, South Korea, Taiwan).

On the one hand, to effect balanced improvements in China's still insufficient diet, the area sown to grain crops should be reduced and the plantings of leguminous, oil, sugar, and other crops should be greatly expanded, a long-overdue change that has finally begun in recent years and that would bring even higher future yield gains in grain fields. On the other hand, if consumption of animal foods, still well below 10 percent of the total energy intake, were to increase on a large scale, requirements for food grains would decrease. For example, an annual per capita reduction of 50 kg in grain consumption would, by the year 2000, obviate the production of 60 million tons of food grains—but it would also necessitate a massive increase of feed grains. To substitute meat for 60 million tons of grains would require, even assuming that all meat was highly caloric pork, some 40 million tons of pig carcasses, of which today China produces only 12 million tons; in protein equivalents about the same mass would be needed when just the quantity is taken into account, but, of course, pork protein is qualitatively much superior to grain proteins.

To produce 40 million tons of pork, however, would require at least 160-200 million tons of feed grains, raising the total needed grain harvest to 640-680 million tons by the year 2000—a doubling of the current performance. Assuming, certainly realistically, no major farmland gains, this would necessitate doubling the current grain yield in less than two decades, an extremely unlikely achievement. There seems to be no doubt, therefore, that the bold per capita goals for the year 2000—600 kg of grain (of which 200 kg would go for feed) and 40-50 kg of meat (Xinhua, April 11, 1979, *SWB* 1026; Shi Shan 1980)—will not be reached, and that the search for agricultural strategies able to sustain good nutrition for the still expanding population of at least 1.2 billion on the shrinking land will continue.

7.5 Energy use and modernization

Like the success or failure of population control programs and long-term agricultural strategies, the decisions about developments of China's energy industries will have far-reaching effects on the nation's environment in the decades ahead. Instead of dwelling on the details of resource and technology options (the interested reader can consult Smil 1978; 1980d; 1981a for these) here I will only outline the probabilities of future consumption levels.

Obviously, the more widespread the conservation efforts, the higher the conversion efficiencies and the lower the future consumption increments, and the lesser the impact on China's environment. No pollution control or subsequent environmental conservation can be as effective as not releasing the dusts, gases, and contaminated water or destroying farmlands and forests with coal mines, hydrocarbon fields, or power plants in the first place. Keeping primary energy use to the lowest possible level commensurable with a desired economic advance is thus the key environmental protection measure.

Long-range forecasts of energy needs have never been very accurate, and the complex links between energy consumption and economic growth especially have been misinterpreted in simplistic ways. There is no generally preordained amount of fuel and electricity a nation must consume in order to achieve a certain level of economic development. Undoubtedly, stronger economies and rising affluence will require higher energy use, but the energy/GNP elasticities differ widely even among nations with very similar economic performance and standards of living. Consequently, one nation may double its energy use while doubling its economic output while another may triple its fuel consumption to achieve the same doubling of economic advance.

The economic energy intensity of each nation stems from a complex that embraces developmental history and industrial orientation, structure and quality of fuel consumption, climate, living standards and habits, and governmental policies. Unfortunately for China, hers is the worst performance of all large populous nations, be they developing or developed. Per capita commercial energy use of 607 kg of coal equivalent and the officially quoted GNP of US$235 in 1979 translate into a required 2.4 kg of coal equivalent for each GNP dollar. International comparisons show that even energy-wasting North America stands at about 1.3, while West Germany gets by with 0.7 and Japan with 0.6 kg of coal equivalent; only India comes close to China with about 1.9.

The fourfold difference of energy intensities between China and Japan, or the twofold difference between China and the United States (or China and Mexico or Pakistan), is perhaps the most persuasive indicator of China's energy waste, inefficiency, and mismanagement, but it tells us little about what the future Chinese course will be. Comparing energy intensities of the country's industrial and agricultural (including sidelines) production makes this very clear. Using the State Statistical Bureau's (1980) official 1979 output values and Wu Zhonghua's (1980) sectoral energy breakdowns, it is easy to calculate that each yuan in heavy industry needs 1.25 kg of coal equivalent, while in light industry each yuan needs just 0.27 kg and in farming only 0.17 kg of coal equivalent.

Thus, incontrovertibly, China's runaway energy intensity and its associated heavy environmental pollution are the inheritance of her Stalinist past, a past that is still uncomfortably with her today. A disproportionate stress on heavy industry, and especially the obsession with steel output, not only distinguished the country's First Five-Year Plan (1953-57), when heavy industry received eight times more investment than light industry, and the tragic Great Leap Forward (with Mao fantasizing about a world being shaken by 60 million tons of Chinese steel by the year 1962)—but it continued to be a major theme throughout the 1960s and into the 1970s (the light to heavy industry investment ratio in 1971-75 was 1:10.2, higher than in 1953-57).

And, unfortunately, the Four Modernizations campaign was launched in 1978 with the totally unrealistic target of 60 million tons of steel by 1985, and it continues to burden the country today (these days perhaps one should call it the Baoshan syndrome). Moreover, as Feng Baoxing (1979) candidly wrote in *Hongqi*, China's heavy industry is "to a great extent still a kind of self-service industry," contributing more to the perpetuation of its own inefficiency than to the advancement of the rest of the economy. What is obviously needed is a substantial shift to light industry and to diversified farming, and since 1978 there have been some encouraging signs of such moves, but any critical outside observer cannot fail to ask: is it for real this time? Many insiders share this doubt. To quote Feng Baoxing (1979) once more: "Some comrades raise this question: Is your desire to develop agriculture and light industry genuine or feigned?"

Should China not only sustain a push toward light industries and diversified, modernized farming but also expand and improve the myriad of badly inadequate services, her very unfavorable energy intensity would gradually improve. And should this be coupled with several critical consumption shifts—such as no unrefined crude oil to be used for power generation, maximum displacement of fuel oil by coal in the same industry, greater mine-mouth generation based on poorer coals, extended use of gases for urban household and commercial use and electrification of railways—China's energy intensities could be greatly reduced, laying the ground for a modernization effort surely more sustainable than many designs of the past five years, which still bear a recognizable Stalinist imprint. What could Chinese energy use then be by the end of the century?

Energy/GNP elasticities have been used more often than any other forecasting tool to answer such questions by deriving future energy consumption needs from planned or desirable GNP levels. Some years ago I undertook to dismantle some of the myths associated with these measures: that advanced industrialized countries have elasticities equal to about one; that coefficients for developing nations are considerably higher than one; that over time the coefficients tend asymptotically to one (Smil and Kuz 1976; also Slesser 1978). The reality is more complex, or more confusing, than such unwarranted simplifications would imply, and so I am amused that some Chinese experts are still taking the traditional elasticity business rather seriously.

The authors (economists I assume) of one of the most detailed analyses of China's energy situation (Chen, Huang, and Xu 1979) flatly state that as the GNP/energy growth rate for developing countries is about 1:1, and given China's average annual industrial growth of 13.5 percent, "the current rate of development of the national economy calls for an appropriate annual increase of 80 million tons of coal." Indeed, 13.5 percent of 586 million tons of coal equivalent comes to almost exactly 80 million tons, and it is an awesomely huge mass of fuel to add in one year!

Similarly, Gong Guangyu (1980) writes that "elasticity value follows a common pattern" and assumes an elasticity of 1.2 for the 1980s. When based on his average annual GNP growth rate of 6 percent, this ratio implies annual additions of about 60 million tons of standard fuel in the coming years, and the doubling of total energy use during the 1980s.

Yet, fortunately for the Chinese, that much is not needed. The first three authors overlooked the crucial fact that GNP is not comprised of industrial output alone, not even in China; thus all statements about a "common pattern" for energy-GNP links are erroneous. Rational management and conservation efforts can make a profound difference: for example, between 1973 and 1979 the U.S. GNP grew by the exponential rate of 2.5 percent a year, but energy use was climbing by only 1.29 percent annually; and corresponding figures for Japan are even more stunning—3.58 and 0.69 percent! This is a sharp departure from pre-1973 trends and shows how much below 1.0 the elasticities can sink.

And, after all, there is China's own example: since 1977 national income has been increasing by over 7 percent annually (in constant prices) while commercial energy consumption has been rising by less than 3 percent. Naturally, in this case much of the energy consumption slowdown can be accounted for by one-time savings resulting from the return to normal management and rational operation after years of chaos. Even so, however, the conservation reserves in China's economy are staggering: just recall the country's extremely high energy intensity ratio and its average conversion efficiency of a mere 30 percent!

To achieve Deng Xiaoping's favorite target of US$1,000 per capita GNP by the year 2000, the economy would have to grow, starting from the 1979 value of US$253 per capita and assuming just a modest one percent population growth and hence 1.2 billion people by the end of the century, by an exponential rate of 7.5 percent per year. The choices are for the Chinese to make: the continuation of a kind of Stalinist "ferrofilia" (if the Oxford dictionary listed this word it would mean, of course, the love of iron) would require at least a matching energy consumption growth, or some 45 million tons of coal equivalent annually in the next few years.

Diversification of the economy and the development of China's greatest asset by far—a genetic pool comprising nearly a quarter of mankind with a correspondingly large number of outstanding brains—through education and scientific and research opportunities would be the opposite and, I am hardly alone in believing so, the best route to take. Following this path, the Chinese could manage, even when considering their clearly large unfinished infrastructural requirements, with no more than a 5 percent energy consumption growth. Assuming that they first turn about and gradually decrease their high energy intensities, if only by a certainly achievable 30 percent, the nationwide average conversion efficiency would reach 40 percent, and the current consumption of some 590 million tons of coal equivalent could be managed with only about 440 million tons of coal equivalent. A 5 percent annual exponential increase on top of this total starts with some 20 million tons of equivalent fuel: still a respectably large mass of fuel but one undoubtedly within China's current capabilities.

This would mean that instead of requiring 1.9 billion tons of standard fuel by the year 2000, a total considered to be "minimal" by Gong Guangyu (1980), or even as much as 2.75 billion tons, the Chinese could do with something between 1.3 and 1.5 billion tons (depending on how well and fast they are able to accomplish their conservation efforts). Current primary energy consumption would thus go up only two to two-and-half times over the next two decades, rather than three or four times, a great difference indeed in terms of ensuing environmental impacts.

7.6 The outlook

The magnitude of China's accumulated environmental problems owing to the legacy of ancient neglect and recent destruction is depressing. The dimensions of the future tasks in population control, food and energy supply, and overall societal modernization are overwhelming, and the potential for further accelerated environmental degradation is quite considerable. Alleviating or eradicating past blunders and preventing future destruction would be a daunting challenge in the best of circumstances. Yet in China the reverse is true more often than not. The state has little money to allocate to environmental affairs in an economy where everything clamors for urgent attention, and even the small budgeted sums frequently get spent improperly or not at all; skilled manpower shortages are even more acute as there is virtually a missing generation of well-educated people, a reality affecting not only the current management, monitoring, and enforcement but also, above all, the needed long-range research.

Social factors are no less important. The existence of a "parallel economy" (black market, embezzlement, falsification of production documents, graft)—in the West often used to describe the Soviet or Italian arrangements—is very pronounced in China, and it will clearly counteract many an effort to deal with the problems of the common good. In general, the attitudes of people who have just emerged from long years of privation onto the threshold of a life promising a bit more freedom and a little more prosperity are not conducive to conservation, savings, and the eschewing of immediate consumption; just the opposite is likely to be true, putting further accelerated pressure on the environment. Indeed, here is a perfect illustration of a key ecological concept well known as the tragedy of the commons, or killing the goose that lays the golden egg.

And, as always, in a country where to pass a qualifying examination for the imperial civil service was the dream of millions for millenia, there are the complex and uncoordinated bureaucracies always good at promulgating new laws and regulations and holding grand conferences (disguised banqueting mostly) but much less adept at getting things done. Nor are provincial interests unimportant, or the considerations of the still heavily militarized (though less so than a decade ago) economy. The absence of many essential infrastructures, the profound economic mismanagement and inefficiencies, and the political implications of foreign technology acquisition hang over every major decision in China like a huge cloud.

And, finally, there is the pervasive state ideology, that political worship, that unpredictable ever-twisting Party line that one day makes a capitalist criminal out of a man planting a handful of trees in his backyard while rewarding a county secretary who ordered a massive destruction of trees, lakes, garlic patches, and pond ducks—only to turn around the next day to instruct the self-same secretary that he should gain the enthusiasm of the masses for backyard garlic growing, tree planting, and duck feeding; the Party line that encourages a "hundred flowers to bloom" so that the "poisonous weeds" of intellectual independence, courage, and honesty can be more easily identified; the Party line that, as in any other Communist country, by removing all political freedoms has turned everything into politics and left only the single arbiter to determine merit. The occasional murmurs of critics can be tolerated, and this book owes its existence to one such short-lived aberration of relatively open criticism.

Only a naïve mind could not be overwhelmed by this state of affairs. The best outlook is for some gradual localized improvements and for the prevention of further major degradation in key sectors and areas. That, I maintain, would be a grand success. On the implications of the failure to do so I will not speculate: that they are grim is all too clear and, unfortunately, this outcome is at least as likely as the other.

To believe otherwise would be to perpetuate the fatuous naïveté of Western admirers of the Central Kingdom in Communist clothes, at a time when some responsible Chinese are themselves all too acutely aware that many of the developmental policies of the past three decades have led to unprecedented destruction and degradation of the country's environment, and that this poses a real threat to the nation's physical well-being, and hence to its social stability. And all of these informed Chinese who have exposed the country's environmental debacle are also aware of but don't write about another critical thing—the cloud of political uncertainty that hangs over the future.

In a recent paper, the Policy Research Office of the Ministry of Forestry (1980) concluded starkly but forthrightly: "If we do not take firm and decisive action now . . . the dire consequences are unimaginable." Such is the state of the Chinese environment as viewed by knowledgeable Chinese, and it provokes an unorthodox conclusion: it is not the large population *per se*, not the relative poverty of the nation, not its notorious modern political instability, but rather its staggering mistreatment of the environment that may well be the most fundamental check on China's reach toward prosperity, a hindrance also the most intractable and difficult to deal with.

REFERENCES

American Institute of Physics. 1975. *Efficient Use of Energy*. New York: American Institute of Physics.

Anonymous. 1979a. "Strengthening Research on Forestry Economics." *GMRB*, March 17, p. 4.

Anonymous. 1979b. "Sandstorms Threaten Beijing." *GMRB*, March 2, p. 1.

Anonymous. 1980a. "Damage to Fujian Forests." *RMRB*, March 23, p. 3.

Anonymous. 1980b. "Eastern Route Considered Unsuitable for Northward Diversion of Water from South. *GMRB*, March 18, p. 2.

Anonymous. 1980c. "Industrial Waste Water Spells Disaster for River Fish." *GMRB*, June 6, p. 2.

Anonymous. 1980d. "Shangyou Factories Dump Large Amount of Oil Containing Waste in the Ba He." *BJRB*, March 18, p. 1.

Anonymous. 1980e. "Let Us Keep Lu Shan Looking Like It Always Has." *GMRB*, September 22, p. 1.

Anonymous. 1981a. "Sichuan after the Flood." *BR*, no. 39, September 28, pp. 19-22.

Anonymous. 1981b. "Strictly Control Use of Land for Capital Construction." *RMRB*, November 28, p. 2.

Anonymous. 1981c. "Yangtze Gorges Scheme Could Yield 110 TWh/year." *Water and Dam Construction*, Vol. 33, No. 4, pp. 21-23.

Anonymous. 1981d. "Everyone Is Responsible for Conserving Water." *BJRB*, August 2, p. 1.

Arnold, J.E.M. 1979. "Wood Energy and Rural Communities." *Natural Resources Forum*, vol. 3, pp. 229-252.

Berezina, Y. I. 1959. *Fuel and Energy Base of the PRC*. Moscow: IVL.

Budowski, G. 1978. "Food from the Forest." Paper presented at the 8th World Forestry Congress, Jakarta.

Cao Hongfa. 1980. "Should Sewage Irrigation Be Developed?" *GMBR*, March 26, p. 3.

Central Committee of the Chinese Communist Party. 1979. *Zhongfa* No. 4. Translated in *Issues & Studies*, vol. 15, pp. 105-106.

Central Intelligence Agency. 1976. *People's Republic of China's Timber Production and End Uses*. Washington, D.C: CIA.

Chen Ruchen, Xiao Zhiping, and Li Nianguo. 1979. *Digesters for Developing Countries*. Guangzhou: Guangzhou Institute of Energy Conversion, Chinese Academy of Sciences.

Chen Shangkui. 1978. "A Survey on the Project to Transfer Southern Water Northward." *DLZS*, no. 11, November, pp. 1-3.

Chen Xi, Huang Zhijie, and Xu Junzhang. 1979. "Effective Use of Energy Sources Is Very Important in Developing Our National Economy. *JJYJ*, no. 5, May, pp. 20-24.

Chen Xiping. 1981. "Environmental Protection Work Should Be Stepped Up During the Period of Readjustment." *HJ*, no. 4, pp. 2-3.

Chen Yongzong. 1976. "Development of Erosion on the Slopes of the Hilly Loess Region Along the Middle Reaches of the Huang He. *DLJK*, no. 10, December, pp. 35-51.

Chen Zhikai. 1981. "Our Nation's Water Resources." *GMRB*, October 9, p. 3.

Chen Zhiqiang and Zhou Chuan'an. 1980. "Eagerly Meet the Needs of the Masses." *WHB*, February 14, p. 1.

Cong Ziming. 1979. "Produce More Aquatic Products for the People" *GRRB*, September 27, p. 2.

Cong Ziming. 1981. "Vigorous Development of the Fresh-water Fish Industry." *NCKX*, no. 11, November, pp. 1-2.

Dale, B. 1980. "Shanghai Portfolio." *National Geographic*, vol. 158, no. 1, July, p. 2.

Deng Keyun. 1981. "Investigation into the Ways and Methods of Resolving the Problem of Energy Sources in Rural Areas." *XNY*, vol. 3, no. 3, June, pp. 25-29.

Department of Desert Research, Lanzhou Institute of Glaciology, Chinese Academy of Sciences. 1978. "Desert Transformation in China." *Scientia Sinica 21*, 251-277.

Du Xinyuan. 1981. "What Has Been Shown by Sichuan's Victory in Antiflood and Relief Work?" *HQ*, no. 21, November 1, pp. 31-34.

Eckholm, E. P. 1976. *Losing Ground*. New York: W. W. Norton.

Ensminger, M. E., and A. Ensminger. 1973. *China—The Impossible Dream*. Clovis, California: Agriservices.

Environmental Hydrology Group, Ministry of Geology. 1980. "The Environmental and Geological Problem of Municipal Water Supplies in China." *HJBH*, no. 1, pp. 4-5, 35.

Fan Defang. 1980. "Prevention and Control of Farm Production by Agricultural Chemicals." *ZWBH*, no. 1, February, pp. 22-25.

FAO. 1962. *Forest Influences*. Rome: FAO.

FAO. 1977a. *Freshwater Fisheries and Aquaculture in China*. Rome: FAO.

FAO. 1977b. *China: Recycling of Organic Wastes in Agriculture*. Rome: FAO.

FAO. 1978. *China: Forestry Support for Agriculture*. Rome: FAO.

FAO. 1979. *Aquaculture Development in China*. Rome: FAO.

FAO. 1980. *Production Yearbook*. Rome: FAO.

FAO. 1981. *Fertilizer Yearbook*. Rome: FAO.

Feng Baoxing. 1979. "Bear in Mind Historical Lessons in the Lopsided Development of Heavy Industry." *HQ*, no. 12, December, pp. 14-17.

Feng Shouxian and Li Mingfu. 1980. "Build Houses without Taking Away Too Much Farmland." *RMRB*, June 22, p. 2.

Forrester, J. W. 1971. *World Dynamics*. Cambridge, Mass.

Galbraith, John K. 1973. *China Passage*. Boston: Houghton Mifflin.

Gao Weisheng and Jin Dingxin. 1980. "Finding the Subjective Causes and the Objective Solutions for the Pollution and Environmental Problems in Shanghai." *HDSFDXXB*, no. 6, pp. 9-14.

Ge Xianjun. "Panda Preserve." *CR*, December, pp. 56-57.

Gong Guangyu. 1980. "China's Energy Needs in the Year 2000." *XDH*, no. 9, September, pp. 1, 9.

Greer, Charles. 1979. *Water Management in the Yellow River Basin of China*. Austin: University of Texas Press.

Gu Sandu. 1975. "Fish Biology in China." *Copeia*, vol. 2, pp. 401-412.

Guo Huanxuan. 1981. "Environmental Protection in China." *BR*, no. 26, June 29, pp. 12-15.

Guo Tingfu. 1980. "Soil and Water Conservation Workers Appeal for the Adoption of Effective Measures to Improve Ecology of Some Areas of the Chang Jiang Valley." *GMRB*, November 10, p. 2.

Guo Yongwen. 1980. "The Prospect for Controlling Salinity in the Plains of the Huang He, the Huai He, and the Hai He Is Good." *RMRB*, May 27, p. 2.

Guo Zuyuan. 1980. "Eliminate Waste, Protect the Environment." *BJRB*, April 21, p. 2.

Han Xishan and Wang Jingqian. 1980. "Effects of Airborne Particulates on Solar Radiation in the Shenyang Area." *HJKX*, vol. 1, no. 6, December, pp. 9-13.

Hao Yushan. 1981. "Survey of Afforestation of the Jiangsu-Shanghai-Shandong-Henan Plain." *ZGLY*, no. 9, September, pp. 6-8.

He Kang and Sun Xiang. 1980. "Agricultural Production and Population Growth." *RMRB*, July 8, p. 5.

He Shaoying. 1980. "Guangzhou's Daily Worsening Environmental Pollution Demands Attention." *NFRB*, June 2, p. 2.

He Xibao. 1979. "Serious Environmental Pollution by Zhanjiang Paper Mill Is Threat to Public Health." *NFRB*, December 10, p. 3.

Heinsdijk, D. 1975. *Forest Assessment*. Wageningen: Centre for Agricultural Publishing and Documentation.

Ho Chin. 1975. *Harm into Benefit. Taming the Haiho River*. Beijing: Foreign Languages Press.

Hsiung Wenyue and F. D. Johnson. 1981. "Forests and Forestry in China." *Journal of Forestry*, vol. 79, no. 2, February, pp. 76-79.

Hu Baosheng, Wang Huanchen, Zhu Chuzhu, and Li Weiye. 1981. "Research and Study of the Total Population Target in China." *XAJTDXXB*, no. 2, April, pp. 115-125.

Hu Huanyong. 1981. "China's Population and Food Grains." *DLZS*, no. 3, March, pp. 1-2.

Hu Liebin and Tian Zhuang. 1981. "Water Surfaces Should Be Used in the Same Way as Cultivated Land." *RMRB*, February 19, p. 2.

Huang Chaowu. 1981. "Balanced Increase in Agricultural Yield in Guangdong Based on Crop Structure and Distribution of Varieties." *GDNYKX*, no. 6, November, pp. 4-6.

Huang Yongshi. 1981. "Expand Forestry and Maintain Ecological Balance." *JJYJ*, no. 3, March, pp. 41-45, 58.

Huang Zhijie and Zhang Zhengmin. 1980. "Development of Methane Is an Important Task in Solving the Rural Energy Problem." *HQ*, no. 21, November 1, pp. 39-41.

Husar, R. B., J. P. Lodge, Jr., and D. J. Moore, eds. 1978. "Sulfur in the Atmosphere." *Atmospheric Environment*. vol. 12, pp. 1-796.

Jing Shaogao. 1979. "Why Ban a Good Thing Helpful to Peasants?" *RMRB*, November 13, p. 2.

Jing Hua. 1981. "Small Hydropower Stations." *BR*, no. 32, August 10, pp. 22-27.

Kapp, K. William. 1975. " 'Recycling' in Contemporary China." *World Development*, vol. 3, nos. 7-8, July-August, pp. 565-573.

Ke Huan. 1980. "Great Strides in Environmental Research." *HJBH*, no. 2, pp. 1-2.

King, F. H. 1927. *Farmers of Forty Centuries*. New York: Harcourt, Brace & Co.

Kinzelbach, Wolfgang K. H. 1981. "Environmental Problems in the People's Republic of China." Paper presented at the Third International Conference on Energy Use Management, West Berlin, October 26-30.

Kinzelbach, Wolfgang K. H. 1983. "China: Energy and Environment." *Environmental Management*, vol. 7. pp. 303-310.

Kittredge, J. 1948. *Forest Influences*. New York: McGraw Hill.

Li Changzhe. 1980. "Plant Numerous Conservation Forests in Places with Soil Erosion." *GMRB*, March 10, p. 2.

Li Chaobo. 1980. "Speech at the Workshop on Popularization of Environmental Science." Chinese Society of Environmental Sciences, January.

Li Shaozhong. 1979. "Developing Utilization of Organic Energy Resources to Contribute to Agricultural Modernization." *RMRB*, June 13, p. 2.

Li Shiyi. 1982. "Developmental Trends in Chinese Population Growth." *BR*, no. 2, January 11, pp. 23-25.

Li Tongbo and Huang Jianchuan. 1979. "Haikou's Environmental Sanitation Needs Overhaul: The Voice of the People Cannot Be Ignored." *NFRB*, December 8, p. 2.

Li Wei. 1981. "Silting of a Hydropower Dam." *GMRB*, October 23, p. 1.

Li Weiya. 1981. "Broad Prospects for Development of China's Ground Water." *RMRB*, November 28, p. 3.

Li Xianfa. 1980. "Saving Beijing's Underground Water Resources Is an Urgent Matter." *BJRB*, April 21, p. 2.

Li Xinghuai. 1980. "Pollution of Wuhan's Dong Hu." *GMRB*, July 9, p. 2.

Li Yin. 1980. "Vigorously Promote Sanitation Work in Farm Byproduct Markets." *JFRB*, March 3, p. 2.

Liang Deyin, Lin Bao, and Li Jiakang. 1980. "Proposal to Solve the Problem of Unbalanced Supply of Nitrogen, Phosphate, and Potassium for Crops." *RMRB*, March 31, p. 4.

Liang Guangshang. 1980. "Direction of Development in Reforming the Planting System in Guangdong." *GDNYKX*, no. 3, May, pp. 8-10.

Lin Xi. 1979. "Protection of National Forests Brooks Not a Moment's Delay." *NFRB*, May 28, p. 1.

Lin Yin. 1980. "The Secrets of Green Manuring." *NFRB*, January, 24, p. 3.

Lin Zi. 1980. "Forests." In: *Zhongguo baike nianjian 1980* (China Yearbook 1980). Beijing: State Statistical Bureau.

Liu Haifeng. 1980. "Information about Soil Erosion in Sichuan." *GMRB*, August 11, p. 2.

Liu Heng. 1980. "Peasants Hard Hit by Pollution on Upper Yaerh Hu." *RMRB*, August 18, p. 2.

Liu Hongqi. 1980. "Protecting the Environment and Developing Production." *HJBH*, no. 5, pp. 12-14.

Liu Pei'en. 1980. "Some Suggestions on Environmental Protection Work." *GMRB*, March 6, p. 2.

Luo Yongquan. 1981. "Development of Edible Oil Economic Crops." *RMRB*, November 5, p. 3.

Ma Dayou. 1980. "Greater Control over Urban Noise Essential." *BJRB*, April 21, p. 2.

Ma Junfeng. 1981. "Protection against Pollution in the Spring Planting Season." *HJ*, no. 3, March 30, p. 7.

Ma Shijun and Chang Shuzhong. 1980. "It Is of Immediate Urgency to Protect Our Environment and Natural Resources." *JJGL*, no. 10, October, pp. 28-29, 39.

Ma Wenyuan. 1980. "Measures to Prevent Desertification." *HJBH*, no. 6, pp. 20, 36.

Ma Zhenbo and Yang Yuxin. 1980. "First Use of Oxygenation Ponds to Purify Liquid Waste Is Successful in Treating Yaerh Hu." *GMRB*, December 11, p. 2.

MacLaine, Shirley. 1975. *You Can Get There from Here*. New York: Norton.

Mao Zhicun. 1980. "Getting Output from Rational Distribution of Crop Varieties." *RMRB*, June 23, p. 2.

Marcus, Leonard. 1979. "China Chronicles." *High Fidelity*, vol. 29, no. 8, p. 64.

Ministry of Forestry. 1958. "Forest Regeneration Must Catch Up." *JHJJ*, no. 4, pp. 13-15.

Myers, Norman. 1980. "The Present Status and Future Prospects of Tropical Moist Forests." *Environmental Conservation*, vol. 7, pp. 101-114.

Needham, Joseph (in collaboration with Wang Ling). 1965. *Science and Civilization in China*. Vol. 4, part II. Mechanical Engineering. Cambridge: Cambridge University Press.

Needham, Joseph (in collaboration with Wang Ling and Lu Guei-Djun). 1971. *Science and Civilization in China*. Vol. 4, part III. Engineering and Nautics, Cambridge: Cambridge University Press.

Nickum, James E. 1981. *Water Management Organization in the People's Republic of China*. Armonk, N.Y.: M. E. Sharpe.

Policy Research Office, Ministry of Forestry. 1981. "Run Forestry Work According to Law." *HQ*, no. 5, March 1, pp. 27-31.

Pritchard, G. I. 1980. *Fisheries and Aquaculture in the People's Republic of China*. Ottawa: International Development Research Center, 32 pp.

Qian Ning et al. 1980. "The Problems of River Sedimentation and the Present Status of Its Research in China." Presented at the International Symposium on River Sedimentation, Beijing, March.

Qin Ling. 1980. "A Discussion of China's Environmental Protection Technology." *RMRB*, August 4, p. 4.

Qing Jianhua and Huang Zhulan. 1980. "Natural Preserves." In *Zhongguo baike nianjian 1980* (China Yearbook 1980). Beijing: State Statistical Bureau.

Qiu Hongquan. 1979. "The Ox's Nose and Soil Power." *NFRB*, January 22, p. 2.

Qiu Yuan. 1981. "Vegetable Plots in Large Cities Must Be Stabilized." *RMRB*, February 11, p. 2.

Qu Geping. 1980. "Major Impending International Environmental Questions—Poisonous Chemical Products in the Environment." *HJBH*, no. 5, pp. 1-4.

Richardson, S. D. 1966. *Forestry in Communist China*. Baltimore: The Johns Hopkins University Press.

Rou Hengxiang. 1980. "Haihe Water for Tianjin." *TJRB*, July 10, p. 1.

Ryther, J. H. 1979. "Aquaculture in China." *Oceanus*, vol. 22, no. 1., pp. 21-28.

Schaller, George B. 1981. "Pandas in the Wild." *National Geographic*, vol. 160, no. 6, December, pp. 734-749.

Shangguan Changjin. 1980. "Ways Must Be Found to Solve Energy Problems in Rural Areas." *NYJJWT*, no. 4, section 4, pp. 56-58.

Shen Gangqin. 1981. "Brief Discussion of the Environmental Conservancy Problem." *HJBH*, no. 2, pp. 13-15.

Shi Shan. 1980. "Where Is the Breakthrough in Our Nation's High Speed Development in Agriculture?" *NYJJWT*, no. 2, pp. 33-36.

Shi Wen. 1982. "Use of New and Renewable Energy Resources in China." *BR*, no. 16, April 19, pp. 18-20.

Slesser, Malcolm. 1978. *Energy in the Economy*. London: The Macmillan Press.

Smil, Vaclav. 1976. *China's Energy*. New York: Praeger Publishers.

Smil, Vaclav. 1977. "Intermediate Energy Technology in China." *The Bulletin of the Atomic Scientists*, vol. 33, no. 2, p. 25-31.

Smil, Vaclav. 1978. "China's Energetics: A System Analysis." In: *Chinese Economy Post-Mao*, pp. 323-369. Washington, D.C.: USGPO.

Smil, Vaclav. 1979a. "Controlling the Yellow River." *The Geographical Review*, vol. 69, no. 3, pp. 253-272.

Smil, Vaclav. 1979b. "China's Water Resources." *Current History*, vol. 77, no. 449, pp. 57-61, 86.

Smil, Vaclav. 1980a. "Environmental Degradation in China." *Asian Survey*, vol. 20, no. 6, August, pp. 777-788.

Smil, Vaclav. 1980b. "China's Environment." *Current History*, vol. 79, no. 458, September, pp. 14-18, 42.

Smil, Vaclav. 1980c. "Deep Structural Differences." *The China Business Review*, vol. 7, no. 1, pp. 64-65.

Smil, Vaclav. 1980d. "Energy." In: *Science in Contemporary China*, L. A. Orleans, ed., pp. 407-434. Stanford, California: Stanford University Press.

Smil, Vaclav. 1981a. "Energy Development in China." *Energy Policy*, vol. 9, no. 2, June, pp. 113-126.

Smil, V. 1981b. "China's Food. Availability, Requirements, Composition, Prospects." *Food Policy*, vol. 6, no. 2, May, pp. 67-77.

Smil, Vaclav. 1981c. "China's Agroecosystem." *Agro-ecosystems*, vol. 7, pp. 27-46.

Smil, Vaclav. 1981d. "Land Use and Land Management in the People's Republic of China."*Environmental Management*, vol. 5, no. 2, pp. 301-311.

Smil, Vaclav. 1982. "Chinese Biogas Program Sputters." *Soft Energy Notes*, vol. 5, no. 3, July/August, pp. 88-90.

Smil, Vaclav, and T. Kuz. 1976. "Energy and the Economy—Global and National Analysis." *Long Range Planning*, vol. 9, no. 3, June, pp. 65-74.

Smil, Vaclav, Robert Goodland, and G. Toh. 1982. *The People's Republic of China: Environmental Aspects of Economic Development*. Washington, D.C.: Office of Environmental Affairs, The World Bank.

Soil and Fertilizer Institute, Chinese Academy of Sciences. 1979. "Rational Use of Land Resources." *GMRB*, August 17, p. 2.

Sommer, A. 1976. "Attempt at an Assessment of the World's Tropical Moist Forests."

Unasylva, vol. 28, nos. 112-113, pp. 5-24.

State Statistical Bureau. 1960. *Ten Great Years*. Beijing: Foreign Languages Press.

State Statistical Bureau. 1980. "Communique on Fulfillment of China's 1979 National Economic Plan." *BR*, no. 19, May 12, pp. 12-15.

State Statistical Bureau. 1981. "Communique on Fulfillment of China's 1980 National Economic Plan." *BR*, no. 19, May 11, pp. 23-27.

State Statistical Bureau. 1982. "Communique on Fulfillment of China's 1981 National Economic Plan." *BR*, no. 20, May 17, pp. 15-24.

State Statistical Bureau. 1983. "Population and Natural Resources." *BR*, no. 2, January 10, pp. 26-27.

Sun Huiqing. 1980. "Industrial Pollution in Scenic Spots of Guilin Still Increasing." *GRRB*, April 11, p. 1.

Sze, Mai-mai. 1959. *The Way of Chinese Painting*. New York: Random House.

Tai Qisheng. 1980. "Atmospheric Pollution in Beijing." *HJBH*, 1980, no. 6, pp. 5-6.

Teng, Tse-hin. 1955. "Report on the Multipurpose Plan for Permanently Controlling the Yellow River and Exploiting Its Water Resources." *People's China*, no. 9, September, pp. 7-15.

Tian Congming and Liu Yushan. 1979. "Fish Return to Ulansuhai Hu. *RMRB*, March 20, p. 2

Tong Dalin and Bao Tong. 1978. "On the Policy for the Construction of the Northwest Plateau." *RMRB*, November 26, p. 2.

Tong Dalin. 1980. "A Talk on the Outlook for Modernized Construction of the Loess Plateau and the Northwest Region." *RMRB*, April 21, p. 4.

Tu Yali. 1979. "Adopt Effective Measures to Protect Fishing Resources." *GMRB*, March 20, p. 2.

Tuan Yi-fu. 1968. "Discrepancies Between Environmental Attitude and Behaviour: Examples from Europe and China." *Canadian Geographer*, vol. 12, no. 3, pp. 176-191.

United Nations. 1977. *Desertification: Its Causes and Consequences*. New York: Pergamon Press.

van der Leeden, Frits. 1975. *Water Resources of the World*. Port Washington, New York: Water Information Center.

Wang Dengsan and Gui Tingqiong. 1980. "Another Appeal: 'Save Guilin.' " *GMRB*, March 28, p. 2.

Wang Ganmei. 1981. "The Significance of the Forest Ecological System to Agriculture in Mountainous Areas." *JJYJ*, no. 4, April, pp. 71-73.

Wang Guichen. 1979. "Quickly Save the Offshore Fishery Resources." *JFRB*, no. 3. pp. 27-28.

Wang Huanxiao and Zhou Hong. 1981. "Why Are Drought and Flooding on the Increase in Yunnan?" *HJ*, no. 1, pp. 20-21.

Wang Jingcai. 1978. "On Scientific Afforestation." *GMRB*, July 12, p. 4.

Wang Lichao. 1981. "China Achieves Unique Developments in Desertification Research." *GMRB*, February 19, p. 1.

Wang Mengkui. 1980. "Pay Attention to Solving Rural Energy Problems." *GMRB*, July 19, p. 4.

Wang Renjie, Yang Yubin, and Zheng Tianlu. 1980. "Cultural Sites Well Known at Home and Abroad, the Yin Tombs, Are under Serious Threat." *GMRB*, October 28, p. 1.

Wang Weizhang. 1980. "Care Should Be Given to Conservation of Farmland When Building Houses in Villages." *ZJRB*, July 23, p. 2.

Wang Yongyan and Zhang Zonghu, eds., 1980. *Loess in China*. Xi'an: Shaanxi People's Art Publishing House.

Wang Zhan and Chen Chuanguo. 1981. "Do Not Let the Chang Jiang Become Another Huang He." *GMRB*, December 25, p. 3.

Wang Zhongren. 1981. "Protection of the Chang Jiang Fish Resources Cannot Be Delayed." *RMRB*, February 18, p. 2.

Watts, I. E. M. 1969. "Climates of China and Korea." In: *Climates of Northern and Eastern Asia*, H. Arakawa, ed., Amsterdam: Elsevier.

Weaver, P. 1979. "Agrisilviculture in Tropical America." *Unasylva*, vol. 31, no. 126, pp. 2-12.

Wen Zixiang and Liu Zhongqing. 1981. "Survey and Zoning of China's Desertified Area Resources." *GMRB*, June 15, p. 1.

Weng Yongxi, Wang Zhishan, Huang Jiangnan, and Zhu Jianing. 1981. "Views on Strategic Problems in China's Agricultural Development." *JJYJ*, no. 11, November 20, pp. 13-22.

Westoby, Jack C. 1979. " 'Making Green the Motherland': Forestry in China." In: *China's Road to Development*, N. Maxwell, ed., pp. 231-245. Oxford: Pergamon Press.

Wittfogel, Karl A. 1957. *Oriental Despotism*. New Haven, Connecticut: Yale University Press.

Wu Baolang. 1980. "Results Obvious in Energy Conservation Competition among Fuel Corporations in 72 Cities." *GRRB*, March 29, p. 1.

Wu Guoguang. 1980. "Serious Environmental Pollution in Yantai." *GMRB*, March 6, p. 2.

Wu Zhonghua. 1980. "Solving the Energy Crisis from the Viewpoint of Energy Science and Technology." *HQ*, no. 17, September 1, pp. 32-43.

Xi Chengfan. 1979. "Environmental Scholar Studies Soil." *JFRB*, January 18, p. 2.

Xia Zhen and Jian Chuan. 1982. "Shanghai Leads in Modernization March." *BR*, January 4, pp. 19-27.

Xiao Peng. 1981. "Develop Fresh-water Breeding and Bring about a Prosperous Rural Economy." *HQ*, no. 22, November 16, pp. 24-25.

Xiao Shuxian. 1980. "The Effect of Increasing Production by Different Methods of Multiple Cropping." *ZGNYKX*, no. 2, May, pp. 59-66.

Xie Zijun. 1980. "Make the Most of Special Natural Advantages, Strive to Develop Economic Forests." *SCRB*, July 14, p. 2.

Xing Guangqian. 1979. "Who Is Helped by the 'Helping Field'?" *RMRB*, January 5, p. 2.

Xiong Yi et al. 1978. "Earnestly Strengthen Scientific Study of Ecosystems." *GMRB*, November 28, p. 2.

Xu Dixin. 1981. "The Position and Role of Forests in the National Economy." *HQ*, no. 23, December 1, pp. 40-45.

Xu Senzhong and Qi Bingkun. 1981. "Relationship of Forestry to Economic Readjustment." *RMRB*, February 26, p. 5.

Xu Shangwu. 1980. "Initial Results in Control of Pollution in Bo Hai and Huang Hai." *GMRB*, February 29, p. 2.

Xu Zuiwei, Qian Wenheng, Sun Hanzhong, and Zhao Jiahua. 1980. "Chloral Pollution and Its Degradation in Soil." *TRXB*, vol. 17, no. 3, August, pp. 217-226.

Yan Ruizhen. 1981. "A Tentative Discussion of the Interaction Between Grain Production and Diversified Economy." *JJYJ*, no. 7, July 20, pp. 40-45.

Yang Dechun. 1980. "Use and Economic Benefits of Fertilizer." *NYJJWT*, no. 6, p. VI-51.

Yang Haiqun. 1979. "Reclamation from the Sea for Building Fields Cannot Displace Sea Breeding." *RMRB*, October 18, p. 1.

Yang Wuyang and Dong Liming. 1980. "Wind Regime in Urban Planning and Industrial Distribution." *Scientia Sinica*, 23; 766-773.

Yang Yuguang. 1980. "Protecting Wildlife Resources of Xishuangbanna." *GMRB*, January 18, p. 2.

Yi Zhi. 1980. "Protecting the Environment, Bringing Benefit to the People." *RMRB*, November 10, p. 5.

Yi Zhi. 1981. "We Should Control the Use of Cultivated Land as Strictly as We Do Population Growth." *HQ*, no. 20, October 16, pp. 43-46.

Yu Futong. 1980. "Pay Attention to Solving the Production and Utilization Problems of Chemical Fertilizers." *RMRB*, April 23, p. 2.

Yu Guangyuan. 1981. "Study of National Land Economics." *ZRBZFTX*, no. 6, pp. 16-20.

Yu Guoyao. 1980a. "Some Understanding of China's Agricultural Production Policies." *HQ*, no. 5, March, pp. 28-30.

Yu Guoyao. 1980b. "Livestock Industry Should Concentrate on Amount of Meat Produced." *RMRB*, June 7, p. 4.

Yuan Zigong and Zu Yuting. 1981. "The Problem of Rational Utilization of Water Resources." *RMRB*, September 21, p. 5.

Yue Ping. 1980 "Afforestation and Protection of Forests Is a Great Cause That Brings Benefits to the People." *HQ*, no. 3, February 1, pp. 11-16.

Zhai Ziheng, Li Zhaoyin, Cui Yuduo, and Zhao Guangong. 1980. "Masses in Pingying, Tengxian, Ningyang, Dongping, and Other Areas Complain That Rat Packs Destroy Crops in Daytime." *DZRB*, August 23, p. 1.

Zhang Anghe, Lin Longzhuo, Zhan Zhaoning, Zhao Rong, and Li Haiwen. 1981. "Better Protection and Management of Forests Needed." *RMRB*, February 23, p. 2.

Zhang Dachang. 1981. "Underground Reservoirs." *XDH*, no. 9, September 16, p. 17.

Zhang Guanzhong. 1981. "Where Have the Fish Gone?" *HJBH*, no. 1, pp. 11-13.

Zhang Heqing. 1980. "This Account Has Been Done Erroneously." *NFRB*, August 21, p. 2.

Zhang Junjie. 1981. "Strictly Prevent Poisoning by Farm Chemicals." *DZRB*, August 6, p. 1.

Zhang Mingqing, Xiao Huijin, and Xu Yiming. 1980. "Save Fujian's Forest Resources." *RMRB*, December 8, p. 2.

Zhang Pinghua. 1981. "Conscientiously Implement Private Woodlots and Energetically Raise Firewood and Charcoal Forests." *ZGLY*, no. 3, March 5, pp. 4-5.

Zhang Qin. 1981. "Conserving the Use of Water Should Be the Long-term Policy of Beijing Area." *BJRB*, August 18, p. 2.

Zhang Qinghai. 1981. "Practical Solutions to Rural Energy Problems in Arid Areas of Northwest China," *NYJJWT*, no. 10, pp. 57-58.

Zhang Qinwen. 1981. "Tentative Discussion of a Strategy for Organic Dry Crop Agriculture in North China." *NCGZTX*, no. 10, October, pp. 18-19, 27.

Zhang Songlin. 1980. "Study of Eradication of Leeches to Eliminate Suffering of the Peasantry." *RMRB*, May 25, p. 3.

Zhang Tianxiong. 1980. "Vigorously Protect Hainan Island's Forest Resources." *GMRB*, July 2, p. 2.

Zhang Zhenming. 1980. "Shout Loudly for Conservation in the Use of Land." *RMRB*, April 29, p. 5.

Zhang Zhoulai. 1981. "Some Opinions on Strengthening Agricultural Planning Work." *JJYJ*, no. 3, March 20, pp. 36-40.

Zhao Dianwu, Mou Shifen, Chen Lenan, and Liu Kena. 1981. "Acid Rain Investigations in Beijing." *HJKX*, vol. 2, no. 2, April, pp. 50-54.

Zhao Zongyu. 1981. "Altering the Composition of Urban and Rural Energy Resources to Control Environmental Pollution." *HJBH*, no. 3, pp. 1-5.

Zhen Xiazheng. 1982. "Present Composition of Fertilizers Hampers Increase in Agricultural Output Since Organic Fertilizers Should Be Stressed to Achieve Bumper Harvests." *ZJRB*, February 9, p. 1.

Zheng Boquan. 1980. "Several Opinions on Strengthening Construction of Grasslands." *NYJJWT*, no. 3, pp. 34-35.

Zheng Jingshan. 1981. "Do Not Wait Until There Is a Crisis in Water Sources." *RMRB*, June 9, p. 3.

Zheng Yijun. 1980. "Vigorously Develop Coal Gas to Solve Beijing's Air Pollution Problem." *GMRB*, July 3, p. 2.

Zheng Zhouje. 1981. "The Need for Serious Attention to Research and Production of Edible Beans." *RMRB*, November 5, p. 3.

Zhou Fuxiang. 1980. "The Theory of Pollutant Discharge Fees and an Investigation of Problems Arising in Its Implementation." *HJBH*, no. 5, pp. 23-26.

Zhou Jinghua. 1979. "Beijing for Three Decades." *BR*, August 10, pp. 9-23.

Zhou Zheng. 1981. "China's Largest Hydropower Project." *BR*, no. 35, August 31, pp. 20-27.

Zhou Zongliu. 1981. "Readjust the Economy and Protect the Environment." *JJYJ*, no. 5, May 20, pp. 67-73.

Zhu Zuxi. 1980. "A Discussion of the Development of Beijing's Industry in Terms of the Current State of Environmental Pollution." *HJBH*, no. 5, pp. 5-7, 11.

APPENDICES

Appendix A.1

Chinese provinces

214

Appendix A.2

Major Chinese cities

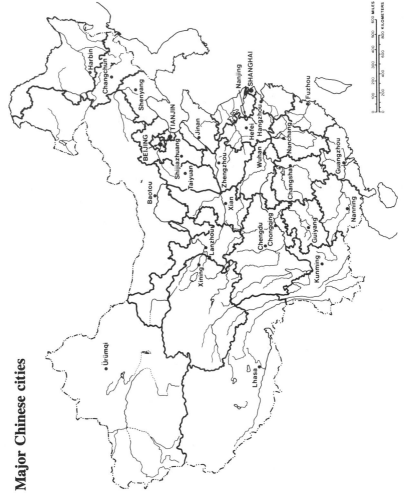

Appendix A.3

Relief map of China

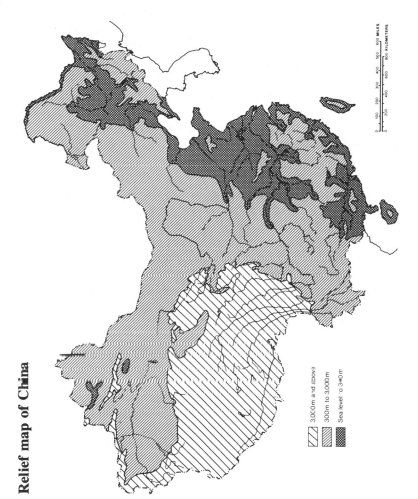

3,000m and above

300m to 3,000m

Sea level to 300m

0 100 200 300 400 500 600 MILES

0 200 400 600 800 KILOMETERS

APPENDIX A.4

China's mountains—selected LANDSAT images (facing page)

Clockwise from the top left: A.4 a . The Qomolangma Feng (Mount Everest) area of Xizang (Tibet). The world's highest mountain (8,848 m) is the large tetrahedron-like mass near the lower right corner of the image (LANDSAT November 14, 1976). The valley of the East Rongbuk Glacier leads to the mountain from the north, the famous Khumbu Glacier from Nepal in the south. The treeless, windswept Tibetan Plateau extends north of the glaciers, and permanently snow-covered ranges are in the southern parts of the image. A.4.b. River valleys and heavily forested slopes of Da Hinggan Ling in northernmost Nei Monggol. The peaks here reach just over 1,000 m, and the area remains China's richest boreal forest with often huge but slowly maturing trees. Summer clouds (image scanned on September 1, 1976) dot the picture. A.4.c. The Tian Shan fills the upper part of this LANDSAT image from November 15, 1972. The peaks are nearly 7,000 m high in this part of the range near the Soviet boundary, and glacier meltwaters rush onto the desert plains on the fringes of Tarim Basin and make possible some surprisingly intensive irrigated farming, famous especially for its melons, raisins, and fruits. A.4.d. Most of South China is filled with mountains and hills: in this image (LANDSAT December 24, 1975) they enclose the lowland and delta of the Zhu Jiang (Pearl River) in Guangdong. These irregular massifs used to be covered by dense forests, but deforestation has left undamaged growth only on the higher slopes.

APPENDIX A.5

China's fields—selected LANDSAT images (facing page)

Clockwise from the top left: A.5.a. A band of irrigated fields above the Qingtongxia reservoir on the Huang He in Ningxia and a large area irrigated by the reservoir's waters below the dam in the upper part of the image (LANDSAT June 11, 1976, band 7). Spring wheat and corn fields appear as light patches, while paddies show as dark tones (this is a unique area with high-yield rice cultivation in the midst of deserts). Irrigation canals fan out from the main river channel just below the dam. A.5.b. Mosaic of rice fields around Dongting Hu in northern Hunan. Countless paddy fields, ranging from tiny ones to large plots on the newly reclaimed land from the lakes, fill the area between the lake's irregular northern shore, its extensive shallow flats on the western shore (white color), and the Chang Jiang (the river channel is just cutting into the image, acquired on April 29, 1978, at the top right). A.5.c. The northern shore of Xingkai Hu (Lake Khanka for the Russians) in Heilongjiang Province very near the Soviet boundary is shown in this LANDSAT image from July 18, 1978. Here, as elsewhere in the province, fields are very large, and the two most important crops, wheat and soybeans, are cultivated in a relatively mechanized manner. A.5.d. Once more a mosaic of tiny irrigated fields in the coastal part of central Jiangsu between Gaoyou Hu and the Dong Hai. This whole landscape is only a few meters above sea level, and numerous canals had to be dug to drain the waters away; still, as seen in the lower left corner, waterlogging in parts of the region is severe. Wheat, cotton, rice, and oil seeds are the main crops, and huge salt pans can be seen along the coast where new fields are also being reclaimed by the building of dikes (see the top of the image).

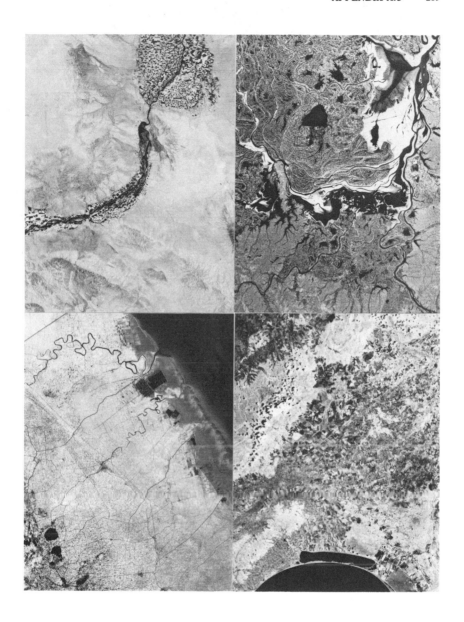

Appendix A.6

Land use-land cover in China (1978-1980)

Land use-Land cover	Area (10⁶ ha)	Share of Chinese surface (percent)
Total area	960.0	100.0
Arable land	99.3	10.3
Irrigated land	46.7	4.9
Sown area	146.7	—
Grain fields	80.0	8.3
Paddy fields	33.3	3.5
Cotton fields	4.8	0.5
Oil crops	14.0	1.5
Stable high yields fields	23.3	2.4
Tree crops	6.4	0.7
Fruit trees	3.0	0.3
Oil-bearing trees	3.1	0.3
Rubber trees	0.3	0.0
Grasslands	319.1	33.2
Pastures	224.3	23.4
Tall grass pastures	38.7	4.0
Medium quality pastures	101.6	10.6
Desert pastures	79.7	8.3
Degenerated pastures	46.0	4.8
Grassy hills and slopes	66.0	6.9
Forest lands	174.5	18.2
Fully stocked forests	122.0	12.7
Lightly stocked forests	15.5	1.6
Shrub lands	31.0	3.2
New tree plantings	5.2	0.5
Nurseries	0.8	0.1
Barren land suitable for afforestation	83.5	8.7
Land reclaimable for farming	33.0	3.4
Inland waters	16.6	1.7
Lakes	6.3	0.7
Reservoirs	2.0	0.2
Waters suitable for fish breeding	5.0	0.5
Deserts	109.0	11.4
Dune deserts	64.3	6.7
Gravel and other deserts	44.7	4.7
Swamps	10.0	1.0
Coastal mud land	1.3	0.1
Barren hills and stony soils	86.0	9.0
Mountains and plateaus above 2000 m	315.8	32.9
Glaciers, snowcapped mountains	4.7	0.5
Cities, towns, industrial areas	66.7	6.9

Sources: Smil (1981); State Statistical Bureau (1983).

Appendix A.7 Climatological data for China's major monitoring stations

	Temperature				Precipitation		Sunshine	Wind	
	Daily mean	Daily mean range (°C)	Highest	Lowest	Annual mean (mm)	Number of days	Mean duration (hrs)	Most frequent direction	Mean wind speed (m/sec)
Northeast									
Harbin	3.3	11.9	39.1	-41.4	577.4	108.2	2715.1	S	4.8
Changchun	4.7	12.2	39.5	-36.0	631.9	106.7	2745.0	WSW	3.6
Shenyang	7.3	11.9	39.3	-33.1	710.7	93.3	2660.4	S	2.7
North									
Baotou	6.4	14.5	38.4	-32.8	204.2	60.0	2986.8	ESE	2.5
Beijing	11.8	12.1	42.6	-22.8	623.1	63.7	2704.6	E	2.4
Taiyuan	10.0	14.5	41.4	-29.7	395.0	55.8	2382.3	SSE	1.5
Jinan	14.8	10.9	42.7	-19.2	631.3	71.0	2168.4	SW	2.9
Northwest									
Xian	14.0	11.4	45.2	-19.1	575.9	90.8	1733.7	NE	1.8
Lanzhou	9.5	13.8	38.0	-23.1	337.6	71.7	2146.6	E	1.5
Xining	6.9	13.8	32.4	-23.1	377.2	76.9	2618.9	E	1.3
Ürümqi	5.3	11.6	38.1	-41.5	276.3	93.7	2606.9	NW	2.0
East									
Hefei	15.5	8.1	37.9	-20.7	830.1	88.7	2261.6	S	3.1
Nanjing	15.7	8.7	43.0	-13.8	911.3	124.8	2057.6	NE, ESE	4.7
Shanghai	15.3	9.2	40.2	-12.1	1143.0	128.8	1871.7	SE	4.5
Hangzhou	16.3	8.9	42.1	-10.5	1489.7	152.6	1782.7	E	1.7
Central-South									
Wuhan	16.8	8.1	41.3	-13.0	1202.0	114.0	1967.0	NNE	1.9
Nanchang	17.4	8.7	39.4	-5.9	1769.9	136.6	1939.2	N	2.9
Changsa	17.2	7.7	43.0	-8.1	1529.3	157.8	1559.4	NW	2.5
Fuzhou	19.8	7.2	39.8	-2.5	1450.4	120.1	1857.9	SSE	1.8
Guangzhou	21.9	8.1	37.7	-0.3	1720.1	152.7	1867.3	N	1.8
Southwest									
Chengdu	17.0	7.8	40.1	-4.0	1146.1	146.4	1152.2	NE	1.4
Chongqing	18.6	7.2	44.0	-2.5	1038.7	132.2	1280.8	N	1.1
Guiyang	15.6	9.0	39.5	-9.5	1214.0	182.3	1323.8	N	1.8
Nanning	22.2	6.6	38.8	1.7	1321.8	130.3	1727.6	E	1.7
Kunming	15.7	10.8	33.0	-5.4	1094.6	121.4	2169.5	SW	2.4

Source: Watts (1969).

Appendix A.8

Simplified regionalization of Chinese climates

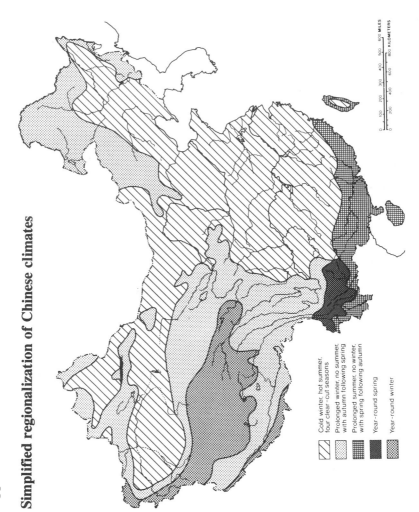

Cold winter, hot summer,
four clear-cut seasons

Prolonged winter, no summer,
with autumn following spring

Prolonged summer, no winter,
with spring following autumn

Year-round spring

Year-round winter

Appendix A.9

China's potential vegetation regions

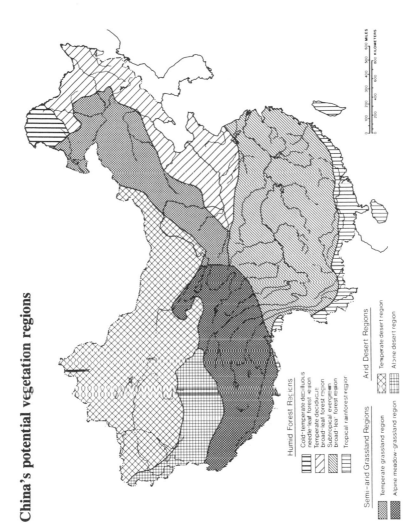

Humid Forest Regions

▤ Cold-temperate deciduous needle-leaf forest region
▨ Temperate deciduous broad-leaf forest region
▩ Subtropical evergreen broad-leaf forest region
▤ Tropical rainforest region

Semi-arid Grassland Regions

▤ Temperate grassland region
▤ Alpine meadow-grassland region

Arid Desert Regions

▨ Temperate desert region
▦ Alpine desert region

Appendix A.10

Basic population statistics from the national census of July 1-10, 1982 (unless otherwise indicated all figures are in millions)

Nationwide total (29 provinces, municipalities
and regions)   1,008.175
    Males (51.5 percent)   519.433
    Females (48.5 percent)   488.741
    Han nationality (93.3 percent)   936.703
    Minorities (6.7 percent)   67.233

Provincial totals

Hebei	53.005	Hubei	47.804
Shanxi	25.291	Hunan	54.008
Nei Monggol	19.274	Guangdong	59.299
Liaoning	35.721	Guangxi Zhuang	36.420
Jilin	22.560	Sichuan	99.713
Heilongjiang	32.665	Guizhou	28.552
Jiangsu	60.521	Yunnan	32.553
Zhejiang	38.884	Xizang (Tibet)	1.892
Anhui	49.665	Shaanxi	28.904
Fujian	25.931	Gansu	19.569
Jiangxi	33.184	Qinghai	3.895
Shandong	74.419	Ningxia Hui	3.895
Henan	74.422	Xinjiang	13.081

Municipalities under central administration
    Beijing   9.230   Tianjin   7.764   Shanghai   11.859

Vital statistics for 1981
    Birthrate   20.91/1000   Death rate   6.36/1000
    Natural increase   14.55/1000

Population in cities and towns
    236 cities   144.679   2,664 towns   61.909   total   206.588

Source: State Statistical Bureau (1982b).

Appendix A.11

Basic agricultural statistics (all output figures are in million tons; animal counts are million heads at year-end)

	1949	1952	1957	1978	1981
Grain	113.20	163.90	185.5	304.75	325.02
Rice	48.65	68.45	86.8	137.00	143.21
Wheat	13.80	18.10	23.65	54.00	58.49
Tubers	9.85	16.35	17.57	34.60	24.99
Soybeans	5.09	9.52	10.05		9.25
Oil Crops					10.21
Peanuts	1.27	2.32	2.57	2.38	3.83
Rapeseed	0.73	0.93	0.89	1.87	4.07
Sesame	0.33	0.48	0.31	0.32	0.51
Sugar crops					
Sugarcane	2.64	7.12	10.39	21.11	29.67
Sugarbeets	0.19	0.48	1.50	2.70	6.36
Cotton	0.45	1.30	1.64	2.17	2.97
Jute and hemp	0.04	0.31	0.30	1.08	1.26
Silkworm cocoons	0.03	0.06	0.11	0.17	0.31
Tea	0.04	0.08	0.11	0.27	0.34
Large animals	60.02	76.46	83.46	93.89	97.64
Sheep and goats	42.35	61.78	98.58	169.94	187.73
Pigs	57.75	89.77	145.90	301.29	293.70
Meat	2.38	3.39	3.99	8.16	12.61
Aquatic products	0.45	1.67	3.12	4.66	4.61

Sources: State Statistical Bureau (1960; 1979; 1982b).

Appendix A.12

Basic industrial statistics (all figures are in million tons unless otherwise noted)

	1949	1952	1957	1978	1981
Primary energy (million tons of coal equivalent)	22.85	47.48	96.45	580.00	580.00
Fossil fuels					
Coal	32.43	66.49	130.00	618.00	620.00
Crude oil	0.12	0.44	1.46	104.05	101.22
Natural gas	–	0.08	0.60	–	12.74
Electricity (10^9 kWh)	4.31	7.26	19.34	256.55	309.30
Hydroelectricity	0.25	1.93	5.94	34.79	34.17
Pig iron	0.25	1.93	5.94	34.79	34.17
Rolled steel	0.16	1.35	5.35	31.78	35.60
Cement	0.66	2.86	6.86	65.24	84.00
Chemical fertilizers	0.00	0.18	0.63	8.69	12.39
Nitrogenous	0.00	0.18	0.62	7.64	9.86
Phosphates	–	–	0.01	1.03	2.51
Potash	–	–	–	0.02	0.02
Timber (million m^3)	5.67	11.20	27.87	51.62	49.42

Sources: State Statistical Bureau (1960; 1979; 1982b); Smil (1976).

State Council Forestry Circular

Text of an emergency circular on banning the reckless felling of trees, issued by the State Council on December 5, 1980, to all provincial, municipal, and autonomous regional governments, and all departments, commissions, and organizations directly under the State Council.

In many localities today, trees are being logged arbitrarily, and timber is being resold for profit. Our forest resources are being seriously sabotaged. It is necessary to take effective measures to curb this immediately. Therefore the following emergency circular is issued:

(1) The people's government at all levels must immediately check on the implementation of timber and bamboo production plans transmitted to lower levels by provincial and regional authorities. It is imperative to immediately stop the felling of trees not covered by the plan. In places where trees have been recklessly felled and forests seriously sabotaged, it is necessary to impound any timber, bamboo, and semifinished products felled and procured, pending investigation. Before the completion of clearances, nobody is allowed to continue felling trees. Violators should be punished as forest saboteurs.

(2) The state monopoly on the purchase and marketing of timber and bamboo must be strictly practiced. Timber produced by state-run forestry units and communes and brigades in forest areas should be purchased and marketed by the Ministry of Forestry; bamboo should be purchased and marketed by departments designated by the provincial and regional people's governments. No other departments, organizations, bodies, plants, mines, schools, People's Liberation Army (PLA) units, or individual persons are allowed to enter forest areas to fell, purchase, or process timber and bamboo; those who have entered must leave immediately. All timber and bamboo free markets in forest areas must be closed. It is necessary to seriously reorganize all commune- and brigade-run timber processing pants in forest areas.

(3) If the jurisdiction over a mountain forest is not clear or is controversial, the local people's government should make great efforts to solve the issue by acting according to the principle of benefiting production and unity. Pending the settlement of the issue, no party is allowed to fell trees. Those who deliberately concoct disputes involving the jurisdiction over forests, or who sabotage forests, must be punished.

(4) It is necessary to strengthen timber logging and the management of timber transport in forest areas. State-run forestry units must fell trees in accordance with the timber-production plan relayed by the state. With regard to logging in collective-owned forests, the county forestry administrative

departments must first examine and approve it according to the plan relayed by the state and to the related stipulations of the "Forest Act (draft)" and issue logging certificates. No timber or its semifinished products in timber-producing areas can be transported out of a county without transport certificates issued by the county forestry administrative departments; nor can they be transported out of a province or an autonomous region without transport certificates issued by the provincial or regional forestry administrative departments. No railway, communications, or other transport departments are allowed to transport timber without seeing the certificates issued by the forestry administrative departments. Violators must be sternly dealt with, and forestry departments violating these stipulations must be severely punished.

(5) People's governments at all levels must examine and handle cases of seizing, plundering, chopping, and stealthily felling trees, profiteering on timber and bamboo, and beating up forest-protection personnel. It is necessary to punish severely the archcriminals who sabotage forests and who kill or wound forest-protection personnel. It is necessary to investigate and affix the responsibility of the leading personnel who connive at, or support, the sabotage of forests, and deal harshly with them.

It is hoped that the above circular will be seriously carried out by all provinces, municipalities, and autonomous regions. It is also hoped that the results of carrying out the circular will be reported to the State Council.

Source: *RMRB*, December 6, 1980, p. 1.

APPENDIX C

The State Council on the voluntary tree-planting campaign

The following implementation measures are formulated for effectively carrying out the "Resolution on a Nationwide Voluntary Tree-planting Campaign" adopted by the Fourth Session of the Fifth National People's Congress.

1. People's governments at and above the county level should all set up an afforestation committee to provide unified leadership for each area's voluntary tree-planting campaign and afforestation work as a whole.

A few places, where a tree-planting campaign is really difficult to develop owing to climatic and land condition restrictions, may be exempt from the nationwide voluntary tree-planting campaign and need not set up an afforestation committee, provided it is approved by the afforestation committee of the province, autonomous region, or municipality directly under the central government.

2. Afforestation committees at all levels should organize and push the various departments and units in each area to give various forms of wide and in-depth publicity to the "Resolution on a Nationwide Voluntary Tree-planting Campaign" and these implementation measures, publicize the great significance of nationwide afforestation aimed at covering the motherland with trees, conscientiously do a good job of ideological mobilization, increase understanding, build up momentum, and make it known to every household and every person.

3. All citizens of the People's Republic of China, males ages eleven to sixty and females ages eleven to fifty-five, with the exception of the disabled, should undertake voluntary tree-planting tasks.

4. This voluntary labor is limited to the planting of state and collectively owned forests within the jurisdiction of each county or city.

5. The forestry rights to trees planted by voluntary labor on state-owned lands belong to the units currently managing these lands; where there are no definite managing units, the forestry rights belong to departments or units designated by the local governments. The forestry rights to trees planted by voluntary labor on collectively owned lands belong to the collective units.

6. To guarantee nursery stocks required for voluntary tree-planting, all localities should strive to do a good job in running the existing state-operated and collectively owned nurseries and arrange needed lands and specialized personnel for the expansion of nurseries and the building of new ones to grow superior stocks and healthy saplings.

7. Vigorous efforts must be made to strengthen cultivation, management, and protection of trees planted by voluntary labor as well as existing wooded areas, ensuring that they will survive and grow into forests without being destroyed.

8. In tree planting and afforestation, it is necessary to pay attention to science and put the stress on practical results.

9. Every unit must, each year, conduct an inspection of the trees planted by voluntary labor and make a truthful report on fulfillment of tasks to the higher authorities.

10. Under the leadership of the afforestation committees, the forestry and parks departments at various levels together with other departments concerned should strive to do a good job in planning, in growing nursery stock, and in other specific tasks. Weak grass-roots organizations should be strengthened and improved.

11. Nursery stock costs and management and maintenance expenses required for voluntary tree-planting are generally paid by the units holding forestry rights according to the principle of self-reliance, thrift, and hard work.

12. The nationwide voluntary tree-planting campaign is a major measure to promote afforestation as a whole. In launching the campaign, the localities must combine it with accelerating overall afforestation work and make overall arrangements for the use of nursery stocks, funds and technical manpower, the management and protection of forests, and so forth, in order to do a good job in voluntary tree-planting and fulfill the annual afforestation plan at the same time.

13. In accordance with the stipulations of the "Resolution on a Nationwide Voluntary Tree-planting Campaign" and these implementation measures, the people's governments of the provinces, autonomous regions, and municipalities directly under the central government may formulate detailed rules for implementation in the light of actual conditions.

Source: NCNA release, March 12, 1981.

Law on Environmental Protection of the People's Republic of China (for Trial Use), as adopted in principle by the Eleventh Session of the Standing Committee of the Fifth National People's Congress

Chapter I. General Principles

Article 1

This law is formulated pursuant to Article 11 of the Constitution of the People's Republic of China, which stipulates that "the state protects the environment and natural resources and prevents and eliminates pollution and other hazards to the public."

Article 2

The Law on Environmental Protection of the People's Republic of China undertakes to rationally utilize the natural environment and control and prevent pollution and damage to the ecology so as to create a clean and salubrious environment for people's life and work, protect people's health, and promote economic growth in the interest of socialist modernization.

Article 3

The term environment used in this law encompasses the air, water, land, mineral resources, forests, grasslands, wild plants and animals, aquatic life, places of historical interest, scenic spots, hot springs, resorts, and natural areas under special protection as well as inhabited parts of the country.

Article 4

The work concerning environmental protection shall be done in accordance with the principles of overall planning, rational arrangement, multipurpose utilization, changing harmful things into beneficial ones, relying on the masses, and engaging everybody in protecting the environment and benefiting the people.

Article 5

The State Council and its subordinate departments as well as local people's governments at all levels must effectively protect the environment. While formulating national economic development plans, overall arrangements for environmental protection and improvement shall be made, and such protection and improvement shall be carried out conscientiously and in an organized manner. Necessary plans must be worked out to cope with any existing environmental pollution and other hazards to the public so as to eliminate them in a planned and gradual way.

Article 6

In selecting construction sites, making designs, carrying out construction projects, and embarking on production, all enterprises and other undertakings shall pay adequate attention to preventing environmental pollution and damage. While carrying out new construction or renovation projects, a report on matters that may affect the environment shall be submitted first, and design work can be started only after such a report has been reviewed and approved by the department concerned. Facilities for preventing pollution and other hazards to the public must be designed, built, and put into operation simultaneously with the principal project. The discharge of all harmful materials shall be carried out in accordance with the standards prescribed by the state.

Those units that have already caused environmental pollution or other hazards to the public shall work out plans and bring them under effective control in accordance with the principle that whoever has caused the pollution must bring it under control, or they shall obtain necessary approval from the competent authorities for a change in the type of operation or seek relocation.

Article 7

In renovating old urban areas and building new towns, an appraisal of the possible impact on the environment of the industrial zone, residential area, public utilities, and green area shall be made on the basis of meteorological, geographical, hydrological, and ecological conditions. Overall plans shall be made to prevent pollution and other hazards to the public so as to build modern and clean cities.

Article 8

All citizens have the right to supervise, inform against, and accuse any departments or individuals of causing environmental pollution and damage; the said departments and individuals shall not resort to any retaliation.

Article 9

All foreign nationals and foreign aircraft, vessels, vehicles, materials, and living beings entering or transiting the territorial land, waters, and airspace of China must observe this law as well as other regulations and rules for environmental protection.

Chapter II. Protection of the Natural Environment

Article 10

Land must be used rationally according to local conditions, soil improved and conserved, vegetation increased, soil erosion prevented, and land kept from hardening, salinizing, and becoming sandy waste.

To reclaim wasteland, to reclaim land from lakes or seas by building dikes, or to build large or medium-sized water conservancy projects, comprehensive scientific research must be conducted in advance, and effective measures of environmental protection and improvement must be taken to prevent damage to the ecosystem.

Article 11

The waters of rivers, lakes, seas, and reservoirs must be protected and a good quality of water maintained.

Aquatic life must be protected, developed, and rationally utilized, and destructive fishing and damage must be prohibited.

Water for industrial, agricultural, and daily use must be strictly controlled and economized, ground water rationally exploited, and the drying up of water sources and surface subsidence prevented.

Article 12

In exploring mineral resources, comprehensive prospecting, evaluation, and utilization must be carried out, indiscriminate mining strictly prohibited, tailings and slag properly disposed of, and damage to resources and deterioration of the natural environment prevented.

Article 13

The state forest law must be strictly observed, forest reserves protected and developed, forests rationally opened to use and properly tended and reforested; reclamation of wasteland by destroying forests as well as denudation must be strictly prohibited and forest fires prevented.

Afforestation must be vigorously promoted, with waste hills, wasteland, deserts, villages, towns, cities, and mining and industrial areas afforested.

Wherever possible, trees and grass must be planted on odd lots near plants, mining areas, schools, government offices, villages, roads, homes, and waters so as to turn the land into gardenlike fields.

Article 14

Forage resources must be protected and developed. Grassland building must be actively planned and carried out, grazing rationally carried out, the regenerative capacity of grasslands maintained and improved, the degeneration of grasslands prevented, the indiscriminate reclamation of land from grasslands strictly prohibited, and prairie fires prevented.

Article 15

Wild plants and animals must be protected, developed, and rationally utilized. Hunting and catching of valuable and rare wild animals as well as picking of valuable and rare wild plants must be strictly prohibited in accordance with the state regulations.

Chapter III. Prevention and Control of Pollution and Other Hazards to the Public

Article 16

Effective measures must be taken to control and prevent pollution and damage to the environment caused by waste gas, waste water, slag, dust, sewage, radioactive material, and other harmful matter, as well as pollution from noise, vibration, and toxic odors emitted from mining and industrial enterprises and found in urban life.

Article 17

No enterprise or institution that may pollute the environment may be built near living quarters in cities and towns or beside protected areas of water, places of historical interest, scenic spots, hot springs, resorts, or natural areas under protection. As for those already existing, measures should be taken to control their pollution, to readjust them, or to remove them to other sites in a given period.

Article 18

New technology and methods of processing as well as new products that will cause no or less pollution should be actively tested and adopted.

Enterprise management must be strengthened, civilized production carried out, and multipurpose utilization of waste gas, waste water, and slag that may pollute the environment carried out so as to turn harm into benefit. Those enterprises that must discard waste gas, waste water, and slag must reduce the waste materials to standards fixed by the state; those enterprises that do not meet state standards in this regard must take measures to control the pollution within a given period; and those that fail to reduce their pollution to state standards within the given period must limit the scope of their production.

Fines should be levied in accordance with the amount and density of pollutants as stipulated by regulations on enterprises that discard more pollutants than the state standards permit.

Article 19

Effective measures must be taken to eliminate smoke and dust from all smoke-emitting equipment, industrial kilns and furnaces, motor-driven vehicles, and boats and ships. Harmful gas should be reduced to standards fixed by the state.

Energy sources with no or little pollution such as coal gas, liquified petroleum gas, natural gas, marsh gas, solar energy, and geothermal heat should be vigorously developed and utilized. A regional heat supply system in cities should be actively promoted.

Article 20

No rubbish or slag should be discarded in rivers, lakes, or seas. Draining of waste water should meet the standards fixed by the state.

Boats and ships must be prohibited from draining materials containing oil or poison as well as other harmful wastes into waters protected by state regulations.

Draining of harmful or poisonous waste water through seepage pits or crevices as well as by solving or diluting should be strictly prohibited. Seepage of industrial waste water should be prevented so as to ensure that ground water is not polluted.

The source of drinking water should be rigorously protected, and sewage as well as water-purifying facilities in cities should be improved step by step.

Article 21

Insecticides having high efficiency with low poisonous effect and residual toxity should be actively developed. Multipurpose and biological control should be promoted, sewage irrigation rationally utilized, and pollution of soil and crops prevented.

Article 22

Control of industrial noise and vibration in cities should be strengthened. All machines, motor-driven vehicles, and airplanes that cause enormous noise and vibration should be equipped with silencers and vibration-proof devices.

Article 23

Airtight production equipment and methods of processing should be actively adopted at all units that cause harmful gas and dust to spread, and devices for ventilation, dust collection, air purification, and reclamation should also be installed. The amount of harmful gas and dust in working areas should meet standards fixed by state regulations concerning industrial sanitation.

Article 24

Registration and control of poisonous materials should be kept sealed. Leakage in the course of storage and transport should be prevented.

Radioactive materials as well as electromagnetic radiation should be strictly protected and controlled in accordance with relevant regulations of the state.

Article 25

Pollution of foods in the course of production, processing, packing, transporting, storing, and selling should be strictly prevented. Examination should be strengthened, and those foods that do not meet the sanitary standards of the state should be strictly prohibited from being sold, exported, or imported.

Chapter IV. Environmental Protection Organizations and Their Responsibilities

Article 26

The State Council shall set up an environmental protection organization, and its main responsibilities are as follows:

A. Implement the principles, policies, laws, and decrees of the state governing environmental protection and supervise their enforcement;

B. Draft rules, regulations, standards, and economic and technical policies on environmental protection in coordination with the departments concerned;

C. Formulate long-term and annual plans for environmental protection in coordination with the departments concerned and supervise their implementation;

D. Organize unified monitoring and surveying of the environment, have a good grasp of environmental conditions and their developing trends throughout the country, and set forth measures for their improvement;

E. Organize and coordinate scientific research on the environment and the conduct of education in this regard in coordination with the departments concerned and actively popularize advanced experience and technology acquired at home and abroad in environmental protection;

F. Direct the environmental protection work of various departments under the State Council and of all provinces, autonomous regions, and municipalities directly under the central government; and

G. Organize and coordinate international cooperation and exchanges in environmental protection.

Article 27

The people's governments of all provinces, autonomous regions, and municipalities directly under the central government shall set up environmental protection bureaus. The people's governments of [other] municipalities, autonomous prefectures, counties, and autonomous counties shall set up environmental protection organizations according to their needs.

The main responsibilities of local environmental protection organizations are to check and supervise the implementation by various departments and units in the areas under their jurisdiction of the state principles, policies, laws, and decrees governing environmental protection; draft standards and rules for local environmental protection; organize monitoring and surveying of the environment; have a good understanding of environmental conditions and their developing trends in their areas; formulate long-term and annual plans for environmental protection in coordination with the departments concerned in their areas and supervise their implementation; organize scientific research on the environment and the conduct of education in this regard; and actively popularize advanced experience and technology acquired at home and abroad.

Article 28

The departments concerned of the State Council and of various local people's governments, big and medium-sized enterprises, and the institutions concerned shall set up environmental protection organizations according to their needs and shall be respectively responsible for environmental protection in their own systems, departments, or units.

Chapter V. Scientific Research, Propaganda, and Education

Article 29

The Chinese Institute of Environmental Science, the scientific research organizations concerned, and institutions of higher learning should vigorously engage in research on the basic theories of environmental science, environmental management, environmental economy, comprehensive technology for environmental control, assessment of environmental quality, environmental pollution and man's health, rational use and protection of the natural environment, and other questions.

Article 30

Culture and propaganda departments should actively disseminate and conduct education in the knowledge of environmental science in order to raise the understanding and scientific and technological level of the broad masses in environmental protection.

Specialized personnel in environmental protection should be trained in a planned way. Education departments should open required courses or special studies on environmental protection in institutions of higher learning and write adequate information on environmental protection into textbooks for primary and middle schools.

Chapter VI. Reward and Punishment

Article 31

The state shall commend and reward units and individuals who have made noticeable achievements and contributions in environmental protection.

The state shall reduce taxes for products of enterprises that use waste gas, water, and residue as their main raw materials and exempt them from taxation or give policy consideration to their prices; and the profits of these enterprises shall not be turned over to higher authorities and shall be used for pollution control and environmental improvement.

Article 32

As for units that pollute and harm the environment and endanger people's health in violation of this law and other rules and regulations governing environmental protection, environmental protection organizations at various levels, with the approval of the corresponding people's governments, shall criticize, give warnings to, or levy fines on those units or order them to compensate for losses or stop production to bring pollution under control according to their individual cases.

The leaders of units, those directly responsible, or other citizens who pollute and harm the environment so seriously as to cause people's deaths and injuries or heavy losses in agriculture, forestry, animal husbandry, sideline production, or fishery should be investigated for their administrative, economic, or even criminal responsibility.

Chapter VII. Supplementary Article

Article 33

The State Council may formulate rules and regulations governing environmental protection in accordance with this law.

Source: Xinhua, September 16, 1979, *JPRS* 74353.

APPENDIX E

A selective list of rare, endangered, and protected animals in China

Mammals

Asian elephant	*Elephas maximus*
Chinese river dolphin	*Lipotes vexillifer*
Chinese tiger	*Panthera tigris amoyensis*
Chinese water deer	*Hydropotes inermis*
Ermine	*Mustela erminea*
Gaur	*Bos frontalis*
Giant panda	*Ailuropoda melanoleuca*
Golden monkey	*Pygathrix roxellana*
North Chinese sikka	*Cervus nippon mandarinus*
Phayre's langur	*Presbytis phayrei*
Pilcated gibbon	*Hylobates concolor*
Sable	*Martus zibellina*
Serow	*Capricornus sumatraensis*
Siberian tiger	*Panthera tigris altaica*
Sichuan takin	*Budorcas taxicolor tibetana*
South Chinese sikka	*Cervus nippon kopschi*
Tibetan macaque	*Macaca thibetana*
Wild Dactrian camel	*Camelus bactrianus ferus*
Zibet	*Viverra zibetha*

Birds

Brown-eared pheasant	*Crossoptilon mantchurticum*
Chinese monal	*Lophophorus lhuysii*
Crested ibis	*Nipponia nippon*
Green peafowl	*Pavo muticus*
Oriental white stork	*Ciconia ciconia boyciana*
Peregrine falcon	*Falco peregrinus*
Sclater's monal	*Lophophorus sclateri*
Siberian white crane	*Grus leucogeranus*
Silver pheasant	*Lophura nycthemerus*

Source: Smil, Goodland, and Toh (1982)

APPENDIX F

Foodstuffs sold in markets must
undergo sanitation inspections

In order to conscientiously implement the "People's Republic of China Food-stuff Sanitation Administration Regulations," the Shanghai Municipality Industrial and Commercial Administrative Bureau, Municipal Sanitation Bureau, and Municipal Public Security Bureau have gone a step further in strengthening the administration of foodstuff sanitation at the agricultural by-products markets in this city. They recently jointly issued a "Public Notice Concerning Strengthening of Administration of Foodstuff Sanitation at Agricultural By-products Markets." This public notice stipulates the following:

1. All types of foodstuffs sold in markets must undergo sanitation inspection to guarantee quality, achieve safe conditions and sanitation, and comply with regulations and stipulations promulgated by the state and the municipality.

2. It is forbidden to sell the following types of foodstuffs: (a) globefish, wild mushrooms, and other toxic animals or plants; (b) salted mud (flat) snails, salted amphibious crabs, salted swimming crabs, crab paste, shrimp sauce, and other fresh edible marine products; (c) all types of cooked meat products and cut or peeled melons and other ready-to-eat foodstuffs; (d) any fowl or livestock with a serious disease, or which died of disease or from being poisoned (including game), or meat products from same; (e) dead rice-field eels, soft-shelled turtles, tortoises, river crabs, amphibious crabs, and all kinds of shellfish; and (f) any foodstuffs which have petrified, become seriously moldy, or which are harmful to the people's health.

3. All violators of this public notice will be dealt with, according to the seriousness of the offense, by critical reeducation, rectification of the situation within a fixed length of time, or the levy of a fine. All types of foodstuffs prohibited hereby will be confiscated. Serious cases that result in mishaps will be dealt with according to the law.

At present, 63 agricultural by-products markets throughout the city have provided specialized foodstuff sanitation inspectors and have gone a step further in strengthening the administration of foodstuff sanitation in markets.

Source: *Wenhui bao*, June 26, 1980, p. 1.

INDEX

ABOUT
THE AUTHOR

Vaclav Smil is currently Professor of Geography at the University of Manitoba. Educated in Czechoslovakia and the United States, he received his Ph.D. from the Pennsylvania State University.

Professor Smil's main research interests are interdisciplinary studies of energy and the environment. He has published over 100 papers on these topics as well as the following books: *Energy and the Environment* (1974), *China's Energy* (1976), *Energy in the Developing World* (1980; co-editor with W. E. Knowland), *Energy Analysis and Agriculture* (1982; principal author with P. Nachman and T. V. Long II), and *Biomass Energies* (1983).